Doing
Media
Research

Doing Media Research

An Introduction

Susanna Hornig Priest

Illustrations by Scott McCullar

SAGE Publications
International Educational and Professional Publisher
Thousand Oaks London New Delhi

For information address:

SAGE Publications, Inc.
2455 Teller Road
Thousand Oaks, California 91320
E-mail: order@sagepub.com

SAGE Publications Ltd.
6 Bonhill Street
London EC2A 4PU
United Kingdom

SAGE Publications India Pvt. Ltd.
M-32 Market
Greater Kailash I
New Delhi 110 048 India

Printed in the United States of America

Library of Congress Cataloging-in-Publication Data

Priest, Susanna Hornig.
    Doing media research: An introduction / Susanna Hornig Priest.
      p. cm.
    Includes bibliographical references and index.
    ISBN 0-8039-7292-X (cloth : alk. paper). — ISBN 0-8039-7293-8
(pbk. : alk. paper)
      1. Mass media—Research—Methodology.   2. Social sciences—
Methodology.   I. Title.
P91.3.P75   1995
302.23'072—dc20   95-36401

This book is printed on acid-free paper.

96 97 98 99 10 9 8 7 6 5 4 3 2 1

Sage Production Editor: Astrid Virding
Sage Copy Editor: Joyce Kuhn
Typesetter: Christina M. Hill

Dedicated to my sons

Andy and Wes Hornig

Brief Contents

Detailed Contents

Part III. Toolbox: Quantitative Analytical Techniques

Part IV. Cookbook: Analyzing Qualitative Data

About This Book
Information for Instructors

This is a book about social science research methods written for mass communication students. Its goal is to help beginning research students understand methodological options and get started doing meaningful small-scale studies. While studying research methods can be a lifetime occupation, everyone needs to begin with a grounding in what research is about, why it is important, and how it is done. This book will help mass communication students do just that—get started, whether as undergraduates or beginning graduate students. It is also designed to encourage them to learn by doing rather than studying methods only in the abstract.

Just as journalism and media studies are most often classified as social sciences, our methods are most often drawn from anthropology, sociology, and psychology. Methods for empirical research, both qualitative and quantitative, that originated in these three disciplines are therefore the core of this book, just as they are the original core of our field. In recent years, methods from other disciplines, such as literary and rhetorical criticism, history, and economics, as well as the blend of theory and method sometimes referred to as the "critical cultural" approach, have increasingly enriched our studies. So, although the traditional empirical methods of social science are emphasized in this book and its scope does not include an exhaustive survey of the many alternatives to these methods, I've also tried to make regular mention of the existence of a broader range of choices. In discussing those that are drawn from these core social sciences, I have been careful not to privilege quantitative techniques over qualitative ones.

In relying on the historical separation between the social sciences and the humanities as one guideline to determine what should go into this book, I recognize that the line between the two is getting less and less distinct, especially in communication studies. Further, new media technologies, new perspectives such as feminist scholarship, and new insights and issues continually challenge the methods of traditional social science as applied to mass media issues. At the same time, however, I don't think we have exhausted the usefulness of empirical social science for exploring such problems as the social implications of technological change or questions of gender and ethnicity. I have tried to balance a strong statement that these and other contemporary issues present compelling new challenges with an equally strong invitation to draw from the best that our traditional methods have to offer in rising to meet these challenges.

The emphasis on the scholarly origins of our traditional methods results from years of teaching students who sometimes have not only no statistics or methods background but in many cases only the most minimal grounding in the social sciences. Part I of this book is devoted to discussing these outside origins—most methods texts available to media research students pay relatively little attention to them. The mass communication research community has been trying hard to establish its own independence; this has sometimes made us reluctant to emphasize how we've borrowed our methods from fields with different histories and objectives. But contemporary sociology of knowledge tells us that scientific method and social purpose are inseparable. To understand research methods *and their limits* and to fully understand the contemporary critiques of our traditional methods, we need to understand their historical origins, not just how they work.

This book attempts to introduce complex issues as simply as possible, using simple language and straightforward examples, and to encourage student researchers to go right to work on problems they find interesting. Although oversimplification is necessarily a risk of this approach, students in those social sciences from which we've borrowed all begin to learn research methods at the undergraduate level, and each of these fields has found ways to let students participate in the research process from the start. It's time we did the same in mass communication studies.

If this book contains errors (as I am sure it does, despite my care to avoid them), I hope they will inspire my colleagues to join in the attempt to communicate what we're about ever more clearly and simply. As *communication* researchers, we have a special obligation to do this even better than our colleagues in the other social sciences!

—Susanna Hornig Priest

Introduction

This book is for beginning research students in mass communication or journalism at either the undergraduate or graduate level who do not necessarily have a background in either media theory or statistics. It is designed to teach you to think creatively about the relationship between the mass media and our society, to ask interesting and important questions that social science research can help answer, and to choose the right method or technique to answer them.

APPROACHING THE RESEARCH FIELD

To make wise decisions about methods requires an understanding of the types of problems that inspired their original development, so Part I of this book is devoted to a brief discussion of the historical development of those fields from which media researchers have borrowed most heavily.

There are really only two prerequisites for making good use of this book: an interest in how mass communication works in its social context and a willingness to believe that research just might be a lot of fun. Designing a meaningful research project that will work out well in practice requires some skill, a little luck, and a lot of effort and thought. Further, if you ask for the cooperation of others in your research effort (whether through filling out survey forms, letting you observe a bit of their lives, or giving you access to materials), you create a special obligation to make sure that you are making good use of their time or resources.

Despite the amount of work and care required, however, research is often exciting. The thrill of discovering the answer to a question that you think is important, one that no one else has ever asked or answered in just the same form before, is unique.

Everything taught in this book is designed to be practiced not years in the future but right now. Each chapter has examples of research done by others and exercises to help you learn how to apply your research skills.

This book should provide a good foundation for every student in a mass media research class, whether or not any of you choose to study advanced research methods later on. Those of you headed for the professional world will be better prepared to interpret and apply research done by others. Those of you who are just curious about how the media and society interact will learn new ways to unravel this complicated question. And those of you choosing to become researchers yourselves will be off to a running start.

Nothing in this book assumes that you have studied advanced algebra. Instead, the emphasis is on learning how to think like a researcher. Important and interesting discoveries about media processes and other kinds of social phenomena can often be made using simple methods. The basic ideas behind statistical tests are presented using simple examples with a minimum of algebra.

Those of you who choose to learn more—either now or later on—about more advanced techniques used in special situations will find that the same kind of thinking applies. Even if you never take another methods course, you will still learn from this book what kinds of questions more complex research techniques can answer, as well as something about how to evaluate research evidence that others have gathered.

Today's social science researchers rely heavily on computer software packages, such as SPSS/PC+™ (Statistical Package for the Social Sciences, personal computer version), for all but the most routine calculations—and you will too.

Professionally trained researchers often study and use highly sophisticated methods that can require an advanced knowledge of statistics. But you can ask and answer important questions and can understand the principles of good social scientific research without this specialized training. Some of you who first study research methods from this book will go on to study more complex techniques, but understanding the important foundations of good research—asking questions carefully and answering them systematically—does not require this kind of background.

The best social scientific research, including research about the mass media, uses social scientific theory to help identify and clarify the questions to be asked. This book will help you understand more about how this works. You don't have to have taken a course in media theory or in social science to understand this material. Important theories and concepts from social science generally, as well as those more specific to media research, appear throughout the book.

WHY DO MEDIA RESEARCH?

When you do research about mass communication, you are engaged in something that is quite different from actual journalistic work, although there are also some important connections between these two activities. You are trying to understand how the media actually work—what influences they have, and what in turn influences them. This works best if you can put yourself in the mood to step back from your everyday life and look at it as though you never saw it before.

This is the frame of mind that anthropologists once adopted in studying cultures very different from their own, where even the simple activities of daily life could be difficult to understand for an outsider. But you can adopt the same approach in your own culture and learn things you might never have noticed otherwise.

WHAT IF . . . ? AN EXAMPLE

If you were an alien from outer space arriving here for the first time, much human activity would not make sense to you. You would have to find explanations for things that earthlings take for granted in the course of a normal day. What on earth is that cold white stuff that comes in jugs or cartons, and how is it made? Why do people drink it out of glasses sometimes, and sometimes pour it into bowls with chunky stuff and white powder? And when they eat it from their bowls, why do they sometimes sit near those big flat things with the black and white designs that they keep folding in different ways?

If you could communicate with an earthling, that being might explain to you that you are observing milk, cereal, and newspapers, but you'd be a long way from really understanding what life is like for a human being. You'd have to ask a lot of questions about what these things are, where they come from, how they're used, and what they mean to begin to understand. You'd learn some things you didn't know, and you might even learn some things that the earthlings don't know—or at least have never thought about!

Journalism Versus Social Science

Often, student researchers find it hard at first to conceptualize the difference between doing journalistic work and doing social science. This isn't surprising because there are many important similarities between the two. Ideally, both rely on the careful and systematic collection and analysis of data, whether in words or in numbers. Both strive for objectivity, although experienced professionals in either field recognize that personal interpretation inevitably has an important place as well. Sometimes, the two even use the same methods for data gathering and analysis (e.g., when the media sponsor public opinion surveys).

What's different is the purpose. Journalists are interested in keeping the public informed about events they believe are important. (In this book, the word "journalist" means broadcast as well as print journalists, public relations and public information practitioners as well as those employed by media organizations directly.) Social scientists, however, are interested in understanding and explaining human social behavior. They want to know how social institutions, including mass media institutions, work. Some social scientists are more concerned with practical problems, such as how to make educational campaigns more effective. Others are more focused on developing abstract theoretical understanding. Their primary goal in each case, however, is *generating* knowledge, whereas the primary goal of journalism is *communicating* it.

Finding out more about how the mass media work can help you understand modern societies. The results can help resolve controversies about violence in the media, unravel questions about the effect of news on public opinion and politics, and understand the ways in which the media can meet audiences' needs. The answers to these questions can help us:

- Manage media organizations more effectively from a business point of view,
- Become more socially responsible as communication professionals and more aware as media consumers, and
- Make better decisions as a society about how to manage and regulate the media.

Social science can never answer most of these questions "once and for all," but it almost always provides important insights.

Finally, understanding how to do this type of research about the media will help you understand how social science works more generally because you will be using social scientific approaches. That knowledge can also make you better journalists and better citizens.

The media both reflect and help shape our perceptions of the appropriate roles of men and women and our stereotypes (both positive and negative) of ethnic groups, professional groups, and public figures. They teach us what public issues are important and provide us with much of the information we use to form opinions. They also serve social as well as informational needs and contribute to our entertainment as well as our education. In fact, in today's world of talk shows and docudramas, the line between news and entertainment is harder and harder to draw.

The media's influence on modern societies can be powerful, although this is not a one-way street. Media content and media organizations are also powerfully influenced by the types of government, the social values, and the cultural legacies of the societies in which they arise. Mass media exist in all developed societies, but the exact form that they take and their content vary a great deal. The media's influences on our thinking, their role in our everyday life, and the variations in media institutions from one society to another are all important and meaningful areas of research.

WHAT THIS BOOK PRESENTS

The methods that researchers use to help unravel the complex relationship between media and society are most often borrowed from sociology, psychology, and anthropology. The empirical methods originally developed and used in these three disciplines have yielded the major portion of the social scientific knowledge that we have about how the media actually interact with society and culture. So methods from these three fields are emphasized in this book, even though methods from other areas such as history, economics, philosophy, and literary criticism (not covered here) have also contributed. Part I of the book provides some sense of the history of these three disciplines, set in the context of background material on the important philosophical issues involved in making methodological choices.

Next, in Part II, you'll learn how to choose and explore a focused research question and something about the range of specific methodological choices available to you, both qualitative and quantitative. Media research, like other social science, sometimes uses qualitative or interpretive methods that summarize results in words and sometimes uses quantitative or statistical methods that summarize results in numbers. Often, those trained in one type of method have little knowledge of the other type. This book tries to give equal weight to both, although the amount of *space* devoted to quantitative approaches is somewhat greater.

Because this text is intended to make sense to those who haven't taken a statistics course, a limited amount of technical background could not be avoided, and this expanded the amount of space in Part III that had to be devoted to methods based on counting and measuring. However, the principles of producing a clear descriptive account of the results of a qualitative research project will be a little less foreign to the majority of mass communication students, so it was possible to make these discussions (in Part IV) a bit more concise.

The frontiers of communication research in such areas as feminist scholarship, research on the new electronic media, and problems in international and intercultural communication (including that between subcultures in modern multiethnic societies) represent challenges to traditional social science research methods. In the next to last chapter of this book (Chapter 14), you'll consider briefly the nature of some of these challenges and the ways that social scientific research can and can't adequately be applied to these problems. If you choose to take up these challenges, you'll find that the discussions provided here serve only as a starting point for further study and research.

Media technology is constantly changing. The computer is increasingly used for communication—to produce "desktop published" materials, as a new commercial mass medium ("videotex"), and as a direct link between individuals (electronic mail). The forces that create this change and the effects it will have on future generations are not fully understood. How is our society changing now that electronic networks are creating "communities" that are physically dispersed across the country or around the world? What will social life be like once computer-generated "virtual realities" make new kinds of experiences, such as "traveling" to distant locations, commonplace? These developments have created an important research "frontier" that a growing number of today's media researchers are exploring.

Other important contemporary research frontiers involve the relationship between gender and ethnic stereotypes and the portrayals of these groups in the mass media along with the impacts of media across national and cultural boundaries. Increasing the diversity of the people working in media professions is one way to increase the diversity and representativeness of media content; without this, democracy itself could fail. One goal of social science research on the media is to identify and overcome barriers to achieving this goal.

As the relationship between media and society evolves along with the new technologies, will the diversity of ideas and viewpoints communicated multiply, or will a few powerful voices dominate? What does it mean to do research from a woman's (or a man's) point of view? Can existing social science research methods at least contribute to answering these less traditional questions?

Finally, in Chapter 15, you receive specific guidance on how to construct a research report. This chapter covers the basic conventions of research report organization and writing. Whether your study is a statistical test of a hypothesis or a descriptive analysis of a social setting, your goal is to produce a clear and compelling description of what you did, why, and what you discovered.

PART I

ROOTS
Social Science Foundations

Quantitative and qualitative researchers have a hard time finding common ground.

A Philosophy of Social "Science"

Some controversy exists about whether social science is actually "science" at all. One of the earliest sociologists was the 19th-century scholar Auguste Comte, who first thought of society as being like a biological organism—divided into parts that function together. This was an analogy derived directly from a branch of science. Strict reliance on an **empirical** (or data-based) **research method** in social science continues to be associated with Comte's **positivist** philosophy, which held that it was both possible and desirable to develop a "science" of society.

As sociology developed, the argument that society could best be understood by applying the methods of science, based on direct observation, continued to be made. Science had come to be thought of as being objective (free from opinion, prejudice, and outside influence)—at least ideally. Social science has often aspired to copy this by concentrating on collecting objective data about observable phenomena. Historically, the emphasis in science on using evidence from direct observations to settle issues of truth had arisen in part as a reaction against reliance on traditional beliefs, intuition, or personal opinion. Surely, social science could develop most fruitfully by relying on the same approach, or so many social scientists have believed.

However, others later began to question the usefulness of this version of the scientific model for social science. A few began to see the positivist position as a weak point or limiting factor rather than a strength of social scientific inquiry. How is it possible, scholars began to ask, to study important social phenomena "objectively" when "subjective" individual thought and interpretation are so characteristically human? Another issue was whether the possibility of having positivist social science wasn't at least partly an illusion in the first place. Can social science researchers ever really claim to be doing anything other than personal interpretation? How can they be sure they are actually measuring abstractions like attitudes and beliefs in the same sense that a physicist might measure the strength of an electric field, or a chemist might assess the acidity of a compound?

The assertion that it is possible and desirable to measure or assess, in an accurate way, everything that is of interest to a social scientist simply cannot be supported. Some **quantitative** research—that is, research that uses numerical measures to investigate social phenomena—has been criticized for being overly positivistic in this sense. By choosing to limit investigations to factors that can be measured accurately, some quantitative research has been forced to ignore important aspects of human communication, such as meaning itself.

Mass communication researchers have recently begun to question the assumptions of positivism and their own past overreliance on quantitative methods. These methods are excellent choices for some types of problems, less useful for others. Today, researchers are more likely to also recognize the value of **interpretive** methods—that is, methods that make use of (rather than try to eliminate entirely) the thoughts, feelings, and reactions of the researcher. Interpretive methods are generally **qualitative** ones; the results are expressed in language rather than in numbers. But both qualitative and quantitative social science can still be empirical in the sense that they rely on systematic observations. It is the reliance on observational data that most clearly distinguishes social science (whether qualitative or quantitative) from the humanities.

It's been seen over and over again that what's accepted as scientific truth today may be thought of as illusion or prejudice tomorrow. For example, people gave up thinking that the sun revolves around the earth when a simpler explanation for astronomical observations was offered. It is no less likely that in the next century researchers will give up some currently held theories as other explanations of the same data are developed. Will our grandchildren believe in the "big bang theory" of the universe's origins, for example? Scientific thinking actually changes in revolutionary leaps and bounds, not just evolutionary increments, as Thomas Kuhn (1970) was the first to point out. The instruments and techniques that scientists have available to them affect the kinds of experiments they can do and therefore have powerful effects on what kind of new knowledge is created. So do politics, history, and culture.

Scientists must often choose what problems to work on based on what kind of grant funding they can obtain, for example, as well as what sorts of things they have learned to think of as worth studying. For example, nuclear weapons were created by a society desperate to win a war, while the new science of ecology has emerged in an era of concern over environmental problems. In communication research, World War II concern with propaganda set the research agenda for much of our early work; concern in the 1960s and later with the effects of television violence became more important as society's interests and priorities shifted away from winning a war and toward understanding domestic unrest.

Regardless of how social and political factors influence the choice of research problems and of what methodological approach is used to study these problems, the underlying strategies that have made science so useful in modern societies have not changed. *Good science uses theory well, gathers evidence systematically, and contributes to the accumulation of knowledge.* This continues to be the basis of good science—and of good social science. Good social scientists, whether positivists or interpretive researchers, whether using qualitative or quantitative methods, follow these same principles.

It's been said that the best social science sounds like common sense when it's finished. If it doesn't ring true, it's likely there's a false assumption somewhere. However, this doesn't mean that we can jump to good social scientific conclusions based solely on our intuition. Even interpretive researchers gather empirical evidence carefully, evaluate it systematically, and present it cautiously.

QUALITATIVE VERSUS QUANTITATIVE METHODS

The distinction between qualitative and quantitative methods is important, although it is often overemphasized.

Qualitative

Qualitative methods are designed to explore and assess things that cannot easily be summarized numerically. Descriptive observations of another culture's rituals, interviews that use open-ended questions, and verbal analysis of the tone of the arguments in a set of newspaper editorials are all examples of qualitative research. Many of the most important methods discussed in this book are qualitative—that is, they rely on the interpretation and analysis of what people do and say without making heavy use of measurement or numerical analysis as quantitative methods do. (A **method** is a general approach to a research problem; a **technique** is a more specific procedure that is part of a particular method.)

Qualitative researchers often reject the positivist assumption that everything of interest can be accurately measured. Their training and experience have taught them the value of looking at subtle aspects of human social life that we only know how to describe with words; furthermore, there is not necessarily a single, accurate description that we'd all agree on. The use of language and symbols is a key characteristic of human beings. How can people and their communication be studied in a meaningful way if we limit ourselves to looking at only those aspects that can be reduced, or simplified, to numerical representations? Qualitative social science researchers may believe that quantitative research is flawed by this tendency toward **reductionism.**

Instead of seeing investigators' insights and responses to what's going on around them as something unfortunate that interferes with accurate observation, qualitative researchers doing interpretive research make use of those insights and responses in a systematic way. They argue that quantitative researchers tend toward **reification** of the objects of their study—that is, they trick themselves into thinking that abstractions like attitudes, values, and content themes are objectively real when they are actually just convenient categories invented by the researcher. Qualitative researchers look for conclusions in the form of consistent descriptions of how something works, not mathematical equations. Interpretive, qualitative research is sometimes called "naturalistic."

Quantitative

Quantitative methods, simply put, use numbers. Most survey research, many kinds of personality testing, and studies that count the different themes in newspaper stories or the proportion of entertainment versus educational programming on television are all examples of quantitative research.

You've already learned that quantitative methods are associated with the positivist assumption that the things scientists (or, in our case, social scientists) are interested in can and should be measured as accurately as possible. From this viewpoint, the accuracy and adequacy of scientific measurement instruments (e.g., survey questionnaires or laboratory equipment) is a central focus of concern. An important underlying assumption here is that if only those instruments could be made powerful enough, we could determine an exact value for anything we might want to measure—*a number we could all agree on.* This is the sense in which quantitative methods are sometimes argued to be more objective than qualitative ones. Quantitative researchers who have been influenced by positivist philosophy argue that qualitative research results are of less value because they are too subjective.

Blurring the Difference

Every individual researcher might come up with a different analysis or interpretation of a particular social situation. How, then, can a body of scientific knowledge ever be built up when each new study produces different results?

Indeed, this has happened many times; different researchers produce different answers to questions like whether the globe is really growing warmer or what actually causes crime. In part, this is simply the way that scientific consensus is achieved and scientific knowledge is built up. Yet subjectivity is not confined to researchers who use qualitative methods, as numbers can be gathered and interpreted in many different ways as well. Our measurement instruments are *not* perfect, so we make judgments that are partially subjective about which ones to believe. We also make judgments about the significance of our research results.

The line between these two "camps" is blurred in many other ways. Qualitative researchers may use numbers, which can be a great help when summarizing the results of a complex qualitative investigation, for example. And the advanced statistical techniques of quantitative analysis can be used interpretively, recognizing that they are only one of many possible ways of looking at the object of the research.

For our purposes, the important thing to remember is that social scientists often have major disagreements about the relative merits of using words or numbers to represent what they are studying. Anthropologists tend to use qualitative methods, but some of them use advanced statistical techniques. Psychologists tend to use quantitative methods, but some of them (especially those trained in clinical therapy or counseling work) are more comfortable with the qualitative approach. Sociologists are more evenly divided on this issue—and seem to fight among themselves more than other social scientists!

BOX 1.1
AN EXAMPLE OF MIXING METHODS

Say you are interested in how the images of gender roles suggested in children's television might influence young minds. In a quantitative approach, kids' attitudes and beliefs might be measured and related to the type and amount of television they watch. As you'll see later on, establishing causation for this kind of problem is extraordinarily difficult. Nevertheless, this type of quantitative study could certainly yield important insights. Alternatively, you might prefer to just talk to kids about what they watch, who their heroes are, and why. This qualitative approach affords a rich understanding of their world that numerical measures would be unlikely to capture—but at some loss of precision. For this problem, the best solution may be to combine quantitative and qualitative methods.

Economists generally use quantitative methods because they are concerned with the flow of money and goods around the world, and these things are relatively easy to count. After all, numbers were probably invented in large part to keep track of things like livestock and property—although even economists argue about the correct interpretation of particular sets of numbers and the best definitions of things like unemployment or productivity. Literary scholars generally use qualitative methods because they are most concerned about the meaning of symbolic communication. The beauty of a piece of great writing (and the social significance of a contemporary text) lies in subtle connotations that are very hard to capture. Yet even Shakespeare has been studied using quantitative analysis.

You can avoid the trap of assuming that only one type of method is valid or useful by simply recognizing that some things about human existence are most easily expressed in numbers and some most easily expressed in words. Both can be valid; neither is perfect. Much depends on the nature of the question being asked (see an example in Box 1.1). *It is clear thinking—not the choice of method—that will help you avoid reductionism and reification.*

DEDUCTIVE VERSUS INDUCTIVE LOGIC

Another distinction useful in understanding the forms that social science research can take is the distinction between **deductive** and **inductive** logic, or reasoning.

Deductive

The traditional model of scientific research is primarily a deductive one in which the researcher reasons from the general to the specific. The researcher begins with a **theory,** an **explanatory** idea that can be generalized to predict what will happen in a new situation. Working from such a theory, or general proposition, the researcher derives a **hypothesis,** or specific proposition, that can be tested by collecting a certain kind of data. If the new data support the hypothesis, the theory is upheld. If the data prove the hypothesis to be wrong, questions are raised about the adequacy of the theory.

"Cultivation theory" is an example of a theory in media studies; this theory, from the work of George Gerbner and his colleagues, states that our perceptions of reality are "cultivated" or encouraged to grow in a certain direction by what we read or see in the media (Gerbner, Gross, Morgan, & Signorielli, 1986). A hypothesis that came from this theory was the assertion that the more violent television we watch, the more we would believe that the world is a violent place. This hypothesis has been tested extensively by collecting data on television-viewing habits and beliefs and then looking for a relationship between the two.

For the most part, the hypothesis, and therefore cultivation theory in general, has been supported by investigations of this relationship, although questions remain about the adequacy of the methods used by cultivation researchers (Potter, 1994). Over the next few decades, researchers will undoubtedly try to correct the short-comings they see in today's cultivation research and retest the theory using slightly different methods.

Inductive

Inductive logic involves reasoning from a specific case to a general theoretical conclusion. For example, a researcher who starts to work on the problem of how people in a particular community use various media but with no theory to guide the development of specific questions may be using an inductive approach to what is called **exploratory** research. If no general conclusions are drawn that might apply to some other community, the research is of use only in that specific community, which may be fine for some purposes (e.g., media management in that particular setting) but does not add to our accumulated social scientific knowledge in an important way. It remains just another **descriptive** study without making a contribution to general theory.

Often, however, the study of a particular case will stimulate thinking that will result in the formation of new theory, even though the researcher began with only a question—not with a specific, well-defined theory or hypothesis. The researcher in this example might conclude that media use seems to vary a great deal depending on ethnic group membership. This could lead to the development of a new theory that would explain media use in terms of cultural identity. This would be an example of inductive reasoning in research. The new theory could then be tested in additional communities—deductively.

Blurring the Difference

In reality, whether we are discussing the work of laboratory scientists, cultural anthropologists, or communication researchers, the inductive-deductive distinction is not as clear-cut as the preceding examples make it sound. Most good research begins with at least a general notion of what kinds of explanations the researcher thinks are likely (theory, at least of a sort) and asks whether the data found fit those explanations or not (hypothesis testing, at least of a sort). Strict adherence to the logic of the hypothetico-deductive model is probably not the norm, even in hypothesis-testing work. If the data don't quite fit, the theory is modified appropriately but not necessarily thrown out altogether or even significantly revised. Perhaps an explanation can be found that is consistent with both the theory and the new data, or an error is identified in the original deductive logic.

Negative results—those that don't provide clear evidence in support of a hypothe-sis—are very likely to be simply set aside; they are rarely published. Indeed, the logic of experimental design is such—as you'll see in a later chapter—that negative results only mean that a hypothesis can't be supported, not necessarily that it needs to be rejected. So out-and-out rejection of a theory is quite rare. However, the distinction between deduction and induction is still a useful one in trying to understand what research of any type is all about.

It should not be surprising at this point to learn that deductive, hypothesis-testing research is almost always quantitative, whereas inductive, theory-generating re-search is more often qualitative. But these are not hard-and-fast rules. *Most of today's social science research combines elements of induction and deduction.* And both qualitative and quantitative methods are usually useful for understanding any given real-world problem.

APPLIED VERSUS BASIC RESEARCH

One final distinction that is very important in mass communication studies is one between **applied** and **basic** research.

Applied

Applied research is research that is designed to find answers to questions that have arisen in making immediate, practical decisions. Examples include every-thing from questions about readership that might be asked by a newspaper editor to questions about the effectiveness of children's educational programming being asked by members of the United States Congress.

Good applied research relies on theory. Using theory well helps predict what range of answers is possible and therefore helps the researcher design a useful project. For example, the newspaper editor interested in readership might make good use of a theory that suggested it has something to do with cultural identity, and a congressional committee interested in the educational value of children's television might make good use of cultivation theory in understanding how TV can modify our perceptions of the world. Using theory also means that applied research can add to our accumulated stock of scientific knowledge.

Basic

Basic research is research that is undertaken to improve our general under-standing of how something works rather than in response to an immediate practical need, such as a study of the role that soap operas play in the lives of housewives or of the way in which the news reflects cultural values.

Good basic research also relies on theory and usually has some connection to real-world problems, without which it loses much of its meaning. The study of soap operas' role in housewives' lives might be of practical significance to those concerned with better understanding the stresses and frustrations stay-at-home mothers experience; the study of cultural values in news might tell a public relations practitioner how to get a story included.

Blurring the Difference

The best research always has both applied and basic elements; it draws from theory and contributes to our accumulated knowledge, whether it is primarily intended to solve a practical problem or to answer a theoretical question. Unfortunately, applied researchers sometimes think that basic researchers don't understand the importance of solving real-world problems, whereas basic researchers may believe that applied researchers ignore the importance of theory. The truth is that both are necessary and important, and the best of each is not so different from the other. Good applied research pays attention to theory and the thinking of scholars who are primarily basic researchers. Good basic research has not lost touch with important real-world issues, whether social problems or media management questions.

THE LIMITS OF SOCIAL SCIENCE RESEARCH

Throughout this book, you'll learn to take these abstract distinctions—qualitative versus quantitative methods, positivistic versus interpretive research, inductive versus deductive logic—and apply them to real-world questions and problems, both theoretical and applied. But there is always a certain level of frustration built into attempts to tease apart the relationship between mass media and society, no matter how simple the question and how well developed the research technique. This is because the mass media are, of course, *a part* of that society, and it is very hard to separate one part of a complex system for study. Think of how difficult it would be to figure out the purpose of a car's accelerator without understanding what the engine does. The extent of Comte's commitment to positivism may be outdated, but his recognition that societies are complex wholes has withstood the test of time.

Each particular piece of research that a social scientist does provides only a partial answer, and each has limits. Only by assembling the "big picture" does a larger truth begin to emerge. That's what is meant by the cumulative nature of scientific knowledge. Things that we believe to be true are constantly retested and reevaluated in the light of new evidence. When multiple approaches—qualitative and quantitative, inductive and deductive—lead to similar results, we have more faith in those results. (This is sometimes called **triangulation** of methods.) Meanwhile, however, society is changing and evolving rather than holding still for us to get a good look! One of the tricks of doing satisfying, useful research is to learn to pare down the "big questions" into smaller, researchable problems for study. Even then, some of these questions will never be answered to our satisfaction, and most research designs involve compromise.

However, some of the questions we would most like research to answer, like the question of the effects of television violence (see Box 1.2), may never be settled by the evidence. They remain matters of social conscience and collective judgment. It is an important characteristic of our culture that we would like scientific answers to important social questions, but that doesn't mean they are always available.

As the issues that we as a society consider most important shift over time, and as we gain new insights and develop new tools for understanding them as social

---

BOX 1.2
TV VIOLENCE AND CHILDREN

The perennial question of the influence of television violence on children is one on which literally thousands of academic studies have been conducted. How can this ever be answered? You can do laboratory experiments that expose kids to violent television and then observe their behavior, but this approach is limited by ethics and common sense. If you think there's a chance that the media do, after all, cause children to become more violent, how can you ethically carry out these studies? Nor can you isolate one group of kids from media influences altogether to see if they grow up any differently!

So compromises are made by using indirect evidence of media effects. The young subjects in these experiments are given dolls to poke instead of your watching to see whether they attack each other. But even this approach tells you only something about what the short-term effect in the laboratory might be, not the long-term effect on a child who is also influenced by parents, peers, and his or her own personality. Studies of long-

scientists, new research questions are constantly being invented. An individual study provides only partial answers. Social science cannot usually provide complete answers, but it can almost always provide useful insights. The process of creatively asking and answering new questions is ongoing; no one can expect the underlying issues to be settled "once and for all," but for those of us who have learned that social scientific research can be a lot of fun, perhaps this is not such a bad thing.

IMPORTANT TERMS AND CONCEPTS

Applied	Hypothesis	Reductionism
Basic	Inductive	Reification
Deductive	Interpretive	Reseach method
Descriptive	Method	Technique
Empirical	Positivist	Theory
Explanatory	Qualitative	Triangulation
Exploratory	Quantitative	

BOX 1.2 (Continued)

term media violence effects often look at whether children who watched a lot of violent TV when younger grow into violent adults. But teasing out the other influences on a growing child's life is extremely difficult. Perhaps the child was already frustrated, had a "fragile" personality, or for some other reason was predisposed to violence at a young age, so violent TV had more appeal in the first place—but did it "cause" the child to develop in this way?

This does not mean that there is nothing new or interesting to find out about this issue. Let's re-examine the question. Because the media reflect, as well as reinforce, our thinking, perhaps there is another way to state it. Why not ask instead why we as a society choose to develop and watch this type of programming, instead of what "effect" it has on us? What is it about the United States that makes us (in comparison to Europe, for example) so obsessed with violence, yet embarrassed by sexuality? In this way, media studies can add to our insights about our own culture and so add to—not just borrow from—the other social sciences.

EXERCISE

In this chapter, you learned that social science can be qualitative or quantitative, positivistic or interpretive, inductive or deductive, basic or applied. Using theory helps us do research that is explanatory rather than simply descriptive. It can rarely—if ever—provide complete solutions to important social questions, but it can provide important insights and often at least partial solutions.

Because this book is designed for students of mass communication or journalism, you already have some interest in the methods of journalistic work and have probably already taken some courses in this area. Journalists also use qualitative and quantitative methods, and they can be positivists or interpretivists.

To better understand the points of this introductory chapter, try to think through the answers to these questions:

1. Does the idea of "journalistic objectivity" sound like the idea of positivism? How are they similar (or different)?
2. Editorials are obviously interpretive, but they are not the only form of interpretive journalism. Can you think of some other examples?
3. In gathering information, do journalists generally rely more on qualitative or quantitative methods? Give examples of each.
4. Investigative journalism usually relies on observations, interviews, and documents to build a case. But it can also use statistical information. Can you think of a case where this has happened, or imagine a situation where this would be useful?
5. Do journalists ever make use of theories or hypotheses? What about triangulation? How and when?

And finally, on a different note:

6. What would an alien from outer space think of television? How would it report back to its superiors about this strange phenomenon?

Making ethnographic soup: Getting the ingredients of a description to blend together as they do in the culture is not easy.

Anthropology and the
Range of Human Experience

In the early 20th century, before the advent of today's "global village" in which nearly all human beings have access to information (in part through the mass media) about the rest of the world, a large proportion of the population around the globe knew only their own way of life. Many people practiced forms of marriage other than monogamy; some groups seemed peaceful and some perpetually at war; some, such as the Inuit or Eskimo of North America, had made extraordinary adaptions to extremes of climate, whereas others seemed to have an easier life.

Studying the variation in how people make their livings, how they are organized as societies, what their beliefs are, how work tasks and leadership roles are distributed, and how the differences between men and women, adults and children, leaders and followers are conceptualized is the subject matter of *cultural anthropology*. All of these things are often quite different from one group to the next, providing important evidence that much of human behavior is learned rather than inherited. Cultural anthropologists begin with the knowledge that all human beings are part of the same species; their genetic makeup is very much the same despite superficial variation in such things as skin color or body type. So how is the extensive variation in human ways of life to be explained?

DEFINING CULTURE

What is **culture**—or what is *a* culture? Many definitions have been proposed. Culture has been said to be the "way of life" of a people, for example, or to consist of "folkways." The most useful definition of culture for our purposes, however, is *the knowledge necessary to act as a member of a given social group.* This definition encompasses many of the more narrow ways of thinking about culture. To be a member of a social group, we have to know what's expected of us—what the **norms** or rules for behavior are, including what's expected on ceremonial occasions and in everyday interaction with others. This does not just mean we need to know the laws that we will be punished for breaking, but we must understand what subtle aspects of behavior everyone in the group "takes for granted." Even in hot weather, it's inappropriate in North American culture to wear bathing suits to, say, a wedding or a funeral. Those who break this kind of unwritten rule would immediately be recognized as "outsiders" even though their behavior wouldn't necessarily be illegal!

We also have to know a certain language. We have to know how to make a living, whether this means how to program a computer or how to net salmon running in Pacific Northwest rivers and dry them for the winter. We have to share something of the values and beliefs of those with whom we go through life—a special problem in modern, complex, pluralistic societies such as the United States. We have an understanding of what constitute acceptable religious beliefs in our culture, even though we may be taught to be tolerant of variations. We have the same basic beliefs about cause and effect (whether weather disturbances are caused by disagreements among the gods, for example, or by things like jet streams and fronts).

High and Low Culture

The preceding definition of culture is, of course, quite different from the common meaning of the word in ordinary language—the meaning we intend when we say that a person is "cultured" or an event, such as a concert or a play, is "cultural." In this sense, culture refers to the kind of knowledge held only by the most educated elite. It's assumed we can fully appreciate this kind of cultural activity only if we have learned a great deal about the intellectual history of our civilization; it's an important mark of high status in our culture to appreciate art, opera, or theatre.

Communication scholars sometimes write about **high culture** and **low culture** in the mass media; they have this other sense of culture in mind. High culture includes such mass media segments as the elite press (e.g., the *New York Times*), public television, and books written by and for intellectuals, as well as such things as symphony, art and "art films," and opera. Low culture (also called popular or "mass" culture—the culture of the masses) is the tabloid press (e.g., the *National Enquirer*), popular books such as romance novels, most movies and network television shows, and rock and country music.

Cultural Relativism

Not only is the definition of culture assumed in the use of the terms high culture and low culture different from the anthropologist's definition, it is in some ways its opposite. Anthropologists are often "cultural relativists" to at least some degree; that is, they explicitly avoid assuming that one culture is "better" than another or evaluating a particular group's value system by comparing it to their own but try to understand each culture on its own terms. **Cultural relativism,** in its extreme form, can generate ethical conflicts. If a culture says that murder, child abuse, the subjugation of women by men, or the existence of slavery is acceptable, is the anthropologist obliged to go along? Of course not. But holding moral judgments in abeyance for the purposes of understanding how a culture works is, at a minimum, an effective research technique; it's also a good exercise in tolerance and understanding.

Social Roles

Different cultures not only have different beliefs about the world around them, they also have very different expectations for how people should behave in a particular **social role,** such as mother or brother, soldier or healer, leader or outcast. For example, the definition of what constitutes mental illness and how the mentally ill person is expected to behave—let alone beliefs about what causes them to behave in unusual ways, be it childhood trauma or witchcraft—vary greatly from one culture to another. As you will see shortly, what are seen as appropriate roles for men and women also vary around the globe. In each case, there is some kind of biological foundation for the existence of different roles, but the forms these take are very much socially determined.

Ethnocentricity

At one time, scholars from North America and Europe thought of the world outside their own cultural boundaries as "primitive" or underdeveloped, but in time, this kind of **ethnocentricity**—the belief that all cultures should be understood in the light of one's own—faded. Life in the Australian bush or the frozen Siberian tundra is challenging; the social organization, the rituals and beliefs, and the knowledge and technology required to live successfully in such environments are extraordinarily complex. Modern cultural anthropology now uses the word

preliterate to describe peoples around the world who have no written language of their own. Although this term (which, interestingly enough, focuses on a communication variable) still implies that cultures have reached different stages of development, it is not as pejorative as earlier descriptions.

Still, how can anyone be sure that what an individual anthropologist says is anything more than subjective impressions? Could a different researcher come up with an entirely different perspective on the same culture? Indeed, this has occasionally happened. But the qualitative methods of cultural anthropology are still theoretically based, systematic, and produce accumulated knowledge—they are quite "scientific." As you will soon see in more detail, the subjective reactions, impressions, and interpretations of the researcher are important tools for understanding cultures—not necessarily just barriers to be eliminated.

BOX 2.1
MARGARET MEAD

One of the earliest well-known American anthropologists (and one of the earliest prominent women scientists in the United States) was Margaret Mead, recognized for her work in Oceanic societies. It's hard to imagine now what her work must have been like—living as a young woman among peoples of strikingly different heritage from her own and thousands of miles from home, recording field notes from interviews, observations, and her own experiences on ream after ream of paper, cut off from easy, regular communication with the outside world, and at a time when women with professional careers of any type were still quite rare in Western society.

One of Mead's best-known books is *Sex and Temperament in Three Primitive Societies*, published in 1935, in which she documented the wide variations in gender roles among three different groups of people who lived not far from one another. Not all societies, Mead argued, had the same ideas about appropriate behavior for men and women; women could be aggressive and men could be nurturant in societies where those behaviors were the accepted norm.

Mead, like other cultural anthropologists, used qualitative methods by necessity. Survey and experimental methods were still under development, but even so they are impractical for the type of field conditions that cultural anthropologists of her era encountered. Mead's work later came under attack for being "subjective," the standard critique of qualitative research.

Culture Shock

Many of you will have experienced at least small degrees of culture shock—whether dramatically from an experience with living in a radically different culture or more simply by sharing in a friend's religious observances, changing schools, or moving to a new neighborhood. The unsettling sense you get from being in a culture different from your own is not just a matter of getting used to new norms of behavior—learning when and whether to shake hands, what table manners are acceptable, and so on. Rather, behavior in cultures other than the one you are used to tend not to "make sense" in the same way your own does. You hardly notice this when the change is small, but when the change is great it can cause disorientation and homesickness.

Think about coming to college for the first time as a kind of cultural reorientation. Not only have most of you left behind your families and many of your close friends, you have joined a new cultural world, usually in a new city, often in a new region of the country. Expectations for behavior are subtly different and may not be completely understood. Freshman orientation sessions help in your **socialization** as a new member of the college culture by teaching you the rules of the game, just as children must become socialized into the culture into which they are born (and the mass media are, in modern society, an important socializing influence).

When adults are forced to adapt to new cultural expectations, perhaps as immigrants to a new country, the term **acculturation** is used to describe the process of adopting to the new environment. Similarly, Native Americans in the United States may be said to be acculturated in various degrees to the pervasive European culture that surrounds them. The mass media have an acculturating effect on immigrants, teaching them about the expectations of their new society.

Eventually, if persons stay in a new cultural environment long enough, they will probably become fully adapted to it. Their expectations for themselves and the expectations that others have for them are no longer at variance. Sometimes, such persons experience reverse culture shock on returning to their culture of origin. This is because they have unconsciously changed their way of thinking, or worldview, to be consistent with that of those around them; on returning home, life now seems strange, perhaps faster or slower, more abrupt or more polite, too materialistic or not down-to-earth enough. The need to readapt underscores the extent to which values and ways of doing things pervade individual cultures; they affect many different aspects of life in ways that no one notices on a day-to-day basis until forced to confront a different kind of cultural expectation.

LANGUAGE AND CULTURE

Languages around the world vary not only in the words and grammar used but in the concept of the world they reflect. We cannot translate jokes, poetry, or sometimes even simple statements successfully from one language to another simply by substituting words and making grammatical adjustments. Often, two languages lack equivalent vocabulary; often, other cultural knowledge is necessary to "make sense" of what is being communicated, or a message is inappropriate or incomprehensible if translated literally—an important principle for advertisers hoping to tap into the growing Spanish-speaking market in the United States! This

---

BOX 2.2
SAPIR-WHORF HYPOTHESIS

Early American anthropologists Edward Sapir and Benjamin Whorf were struck by the divisions of time and space they found in Native American languages. Many European languages divide all objects into male and female; adjectives and pronouns must reflect agreement with the gender of the relevant noun. But in North America, Sapir and Whorf found groups who divided objects into quite different classificatory schemes, based on shape, and who used verb tenses that suggested a quite different concept of time from that of European culture.

Sapir and Whorf hypothesized that by learning a particular language a child learns important things about the structure of the world and that this culturally derived lesson varies from language to language and from group to group. Learning to speak a language that makes particular distinctions structures the cognition of the speaker in

ways compatible with a particular cultural tradition. In the same way, a researcher's learning the language of a group of people can yield important clues as to how those people think about the world.

Sapir and Whorf, for whom Native American culture must have seemed extremely foreign, may have made too much of their findings. Languages do not reflect cultural tradition consistently. In traditional Chinese society, for example, women were without doubt subservient to men. Yet spoken Chinese makes no distinction between the pronoun referring to a man and that referring to a woman, and written Chinese characters began to make this distinction only after the influence of Europe had become strong. Sapir and Whorf's theory is usually interpreted as suggesting that the language someone learns not only guides but constrains their thinking about the world.

applies to **nonverbal communication,** such as gestures and "body language," as well as to what is spoken aloud. Naturally, the branch of anthropology that studies the relationship between language and culture, called linguistic anthropology, is of special interest for communication researchers.

Following Sapir and Whorf's hypothesis, it becomes difficult to imagine how new words would ever be invented. But this happens all the time as new needs arise. According to their thinking, people living in the far north would probably have many words for "snow," whereas those living nearer the equator would have fewer—perhaps none at all. But skiers have borrowed or created special words for snow that millions of speakers of English have no need for; if they had been literally constrained by the limits of their native language, how would this have been possible? Nevertheless, language—including slang, dialect, and specialized terminology—remains a powerful clue to the patterns of thinking characteristic of particular social groups. The ethnographer studying skier culture would surely want to find out what, exactly, the term "powder" means—and why it is important!

Dialect and Subcultures

The tradition of relativism in cultural anthropology (that is, the avoidance of judgments about the relative value of particular cultural perspectives) is compatible with the recognition that minority cultures and languages within a pluralistic society such as the United States are not somehow "lesser" just because they differ from the European mainstream. From this perspective, it is easier to see African-American dialect and culture as a rich tradition of its own rather than a "distortion" of the majority dialect and culture or strictly a matter of educational level. And this and other kinds of specialized variations of mainstream language—from the slang of teens to the terminology of physics—are important symbols of group identification, as well as a reflection of the specialized needs of the particular group. Students of the mass media who hope to understand the relationship between mainstream "mass" culture and the specialized communication of particular groups, or **subcultures,** need to understand this.

Although Sapir and Whorf may have been partially wrong to conceive of language as representing a culturally imposed restriction on thinking, language is an important tool of socialization, and paying close attention to special terminology can give us important insights into the worldviews of those who use them.

PARTICIPANT OBSERVATION AND DEPTH INTERVIEWS

Today, the tools of anthropology are often applied to groups within our own culture, whether by anthropologists, qualitative sociologists, or (as we will see) mass communication researchers. Two key research methods here are **participant observation** and the **depth interview.**

Participant Observation

Learning about a social group and its culture (or subculture) through acting as a member of the group is called participant observation. The researcher's reactions (and mistakes) are useful clues as to what is importantly "different" about the culture. Remember that early cultural anthropologists faced enormous practical problems: transportation, language barriers, isolation from colleagues and from sources of information, sometimes hostility or even violence, and always the uncomfortable role of "outsider." Perhaps these field conditions themselves are what caused **ethnography** to develop the way it did, elevating simple experience and observation to one of the important social science methodologies and using the reactions of the researcher to the "foreign" culture as one of its tools rather than seeing them as a liability.

Participant observers try to become a member of the group they are studying. They try not to impose their own cultural worldview—their assumptions about how things should be done or what they mean. They make systematic notes about

---

BOX 2.3
ADOPTING A CULTURE

Guests of the Sheik (Fernea, 1969), an excellent ethnographic description of life as an Arab woman, was written by the *wife* of an anthropologist visiting an Arab country. Like many ethnographies, it is well written and reads like a good novel. Left to her own devices because Moslem tradition did not allow her to travel freely with her husband as he conducted his own academic research, the author of *Guests* adopted her Arab hosts' norms for female behavior.

She covered her body and her face with the traditional gown and veil while in public; the rest of the time, she lived behind walls and closed doors in an almost exclusively female world. She struggled to reconcile her (temporary) acceptance of and adoption of this culture with her personal beliefs about the rights of women—in the Arab world and elsewhere. Her reward, however, was the discovery of—and the opportunity to share with her readers—a fascinating and rich reality to which she would otherwise never have had access: the cultural world of the traditional Arab Moslem woman.

their experiences and observations (what is said and done) as regularly as possible, although (unlike reporters) perhaps most often not until they are alone—for example, at the end of the day. They take note of things like how people spend their time, who seems to be in charge, who seems to be together, what order things are done in, and the explanations that people offer for their actions.

They may also take note of their own reactions; behavior that seems odd or unexplainable suggests an area where the expectations or beliefs of the culture being studied are quite different from those in the researcher's own culture. They try to note *what it is that they themselves have to learn in order to behave as a member of the culture,* that is, what they have to do not to be seen as odd themselves—for the same reason. They try to understand the various social roles that they observe: who the leaders and the followers are, what men, women, or children do differently, and how families and other subunits (e.g., clubs or work teams) are organized. They pay attention to beliefs and to important ceremonies.

Holism

A key principle of ethnographic work is the idea of **holism**—the assertion that cultures must be understood as whole systems, not isolated parts. All parts of a cultural system depend on each other, and cultural values and beliefs tend to be internally consistent even where individual aspects of them may appear irrational to the outsider. Perhaps this discovery was partially accidental, a result of the way that early field expeditions led by one or a few individual researchers were organized; a small group of individuals would capitalize on the research opportunity to study many aspects of a culture at once, rather than focusing on only one part, such as religion, agricultural practice, or marriage rites. Whatever its origins, however, this is a principle that has proved its usefulness over and over again. Isolated practices or beliefs may seem odd to the outsider, but to the insider (the member of the culture of which these practices or beliefs are a part) they will make sense. The researcher's task, then, is not to explain the apparent oddities but to look for the internal consistency that weaves them together—from an insider point of view.

Informants

Ethnographers often rely heavily on individuals who, for whatever reason, are willing to give great chunks of their time to explain what is going on. Such an individual is called an **informant**—not to be confused with the police informer—and can be invaluable. Imagine going to a country other than your own, one with a different language, without a guide or host! But one criticism sometimes voiced is that overreliance on the perspective of the informant can result in seriously distorted research. Some informants' **marginalization**—being in a position of lesser respect or power—in their own culture may prompt their speaking from a very special point of view. In fact, marginalized or powerless individuals "on the outs" with their own social group may be more likely to volunteer as informants, hoping to gain status (or at least the ethnographer's friendship) in this way.

Although this is not a trivial problem, the response is that the ethnographer is not trying to sample a population randomly like a survey researcher would but is trying to gain access to *shared cultural knowledge* that every member of the group commands. If I have never been to a football or soccer game, I can ask almost any fan basic questions about how the game is played and why it seems to be so important—what people are cheering at, what the uniforms mean, what the rules are, and so on—and I will probably get about the same answers. This is quite different from trying to determine who the fans think is the better team, a question to which there is always more than one answer and that would probably call for a survey! Ethnographers are systematic in the sense that they probe and explore all aspects of a culture, not in that they try to ask the same questions of everyone. So they do not necessarily need a random sample for the reasons that a survey researcher does.

Depth Interview

A second key ethnographic technique is the depth interview, which is an open-ended conversational exploration of an individual's wordview or some aspect of it. Unlike a survey questionnaire, the depth interview does not have a rigidly set structure; for this reason it is sometimes called a semistructured interview. Rather, although the interviewer may begin with a particular set of questions or concerns to be addressed, he or she is entirely free to ask follow-up questions in response to the informant's answers and interests, to rephrase a question to get a more complete answer, or to ask for clarification of interesting points. A linguistic anthropologist will be especially interested in how language is used and what it means; a cultural anthropologist will also be sensitive to specialized terminology that seems to have special significance. As in participant observation, researchers must work hard to be sure they are not imposing their own worldview but gaining a meaningful understanding of what might be a very different perspective.

ETHNOGRAPHIC DESCRIPTION

Writing up the results of an ethnographic project—even a small one—is a difficult task. Although you have learned that the ethnographer need not strive to be "objective" in the sense that a chemist, physicist, or experimental psychologist must be, there is still the obligation to be as systematic as possible and to be certain that the written description is as true as possible to the ethnographer's experience. Well-written ethnographies make good reading, but they are not constructed easily.

Constant Comparative Method

The task is to reduce a mass of descriptive detail into a coherent description that pulls out the key characteristics or themes of the research setting. This often means classifying observations or statements but without the aid of predetermined categories such as survey researchers might use—and without, in many cases, the necessity or desire to reduce the observations to a set of numbers that would do damage to the richness of description the ethnographer is seeking.

In the **constant comparative method** (Glaser & Strauss, 1967), the researcher starts out with a tentative set of themes or categories suggested by the data themselves, testing that tentative set against new data—additional observations or statements—and adding, eliminating, or refining categories, as necessary. This sounds (and is) somewhat like making soup without a recipe, with periodic taste tests!

Culture Versus Subculture

Anthropologists studying entire cultures for the first time often organized their written reports according to various spheres of inquiry, such as religion, work, family and children, social structure, technology, and so on.

Today, there are really no new unexamined cultures left to study. The modern ethnographer is more likely to be studying a particular subculture (e.g., a characteristic of an institution or profession, perhaps in the mass media), a particular social event, or in some other way to have a more limited research question in mind. Even though the principle of cultural holism still guides the work, the end product of the research is likely to be less comprehensive.

The task of writing is guided by the research interests of the ethnographer. Even so, there's no "recipe" for this, and ethnographic descriptions continue to be organized in different ways for different purposes. Here, ethnography, even though it shares the commitment to systematic inquiry and the accumulation of knowledge that we have learned are characteristic of the scientific method, might perhaps be said to become more art than science. The goal is to produce an honest description that is as true as possible to the researcher's understanding of the culture and as rich in detail as necessary for the reader to appreciate the foundations of that understanding. Later in this book, this problem is considered again but in more detail.

THE ETHICS OF ETHNOGRAPHY

Today, there is a new set of considerations that early ethnographers did not pay as much attention to. When anthropologists' descriptions were often of isolated groups with no written language and no access to today's mass media, an individual researcher's description would never be read by those described in it (and, often enough, never cross-checked by another researcher). This is now rarely, if ever, the case. What are the researcher's obligations to produce a description that will "ring true" to members of the culture being described? What if crime, immorality, or behavior acceptable in one culture but likely to be denounced by another (e.g., polygamy) are uncovered?

BOX 2.4
USING ETHNOGRAPHIC METHODS

• White's (1950) study of newsroom practices—one of the studies that helped develop the very important concept of "gatekeeping" in the newsroom—was conducted by a researcher sitting at the elbow of newspaper editors and observing their work from an "insider" perspective.

• One of the early "Payne Fund" studies of the influence of the movies on American life and values was conducted by sociologist Herbert Blumer (1933) using an innovative qualitative technique. He collected autobiographical accounts from over 1,800 young people in a study that Lowery and DeFleur (1988) list among the milestones of mass communications research. Blumer asked participants to keep diaries of their reactions to movies—not a traditional ethnographic technique but one responsive to the same objective of constructing a rich description from an "insider" point of view.

• Janice Radway, in her well-known 1984 book *Reading the Romance,* used ethnographic techniques to document the reasons why people read romance novels. She spent time in a bookstore that specialized in romantic fiction, using the storekeeper as a key informant, and with input from the readers of this fiction, trying to understand how the activity of romance reading fit into their daily lives and what its meaning was for them. Radway is only one of a growing number of media researchers who understand and use ethnographic techniques, many of whom base their work on that of anthropologists, such as Clifford Geertz (1973), and/or media scholars, like John Fiske (1978).

Modern ethnographers might choose to study such things as gang life, homelessness, or the world of prostitution or illegal gambling. What are their obligations to informants who are engaged in criminal activity? What if a published report is so specific that an informant's family can identify the individual described but the individual does not want to be found? What if law enforcement officials become interested? Although these situations are unlikely to arise in the study of mass communication using ethnographic practices, this is not impossible.

Generally speaking, anthropologists assume that they have strong obligations to respect the wishes of those who allow them into their lives. This should never be done under false pretenses; although the group being studied may not need (or want) to know all the details of the ethnographer's research interests, they must know what the ethnographer is doing and be given the right to refuse. Student ethnographers who are studying groups that might be engaged in illegal activities are sometimes given the advice not to keep written notes that they would not want to see brought into a court of law.

MASS COMMUNICATION APPLICATIONS

Qualitative methods in general, and ethnographic description using participant observation and depth interviews in particular, have enjoyed something of a renaissance recently in mass communication studies. These are ideal methods for understanding the role of media in everyday life in ways that experimental or survey research, without the rich contextual detail and holistic approach of ethnography, cannot duplicate. However, some of the earliest mass communication studies used participant observation and other qualitative techniques.

Why do people watch football games or soap operas? What roles do newspapers or computers play in individuals' everyday lives? Which of these are social activities, and which are solitary ones that in some cases might be substitutes for social activity? Above all, what meanings do these messages and these experiences hold for members of particular cultural worlds? Ethnography is a good way to approach answering these questions. Everyday social life is rich with opportunities to increase our understanding of the relationship between media and society—if you, the researcher, are a bit creative about finding them and can "step back" into the ethnographer's role in your own culture. Remember the earlier advice to try to think like an alien from outer space?

IMPORTANT TERMS AND CONCEPTS

Acculturation   Low culture
Constant comparative method   Marginalization
Cultural relativism   Nonverbal communication
Culture   Norms
Depth interview   Participant observation
Ethnocentricity   Preliterate
Ethnography   Social role
High culture   Socialization
Holism   Subcultures
Informant

EXERCISE

Now that you have had some introduction to ethnographic methods, let's
practice one of these techniques, the depth interview. Choose an informant
(a friend, classmate, co-worker, or relative, or even a friend of a friend)
who is active in a specialized group about which you are not especially
knowledgeable. We are going to treat that group as a subculture with its
own beliefs, organization, values, and specialized language.

Your informant can be someone involved with a hobby you're unfamil-
iar with or who is active in a political or social organization or belongs to
a religion different from your own. It can be a person majoring in physics
if you are the type who steers clear of science, or it might be an active artist
or musician. It can be someone who grew up in a small town if you're an
urbanite, a Hispanic if you're African American. It can be someone with
a job you don't know much about, whether it be a fast-food worker or a
corporate attorney.

Plan on about an hour for the interview and sketch out some broad areas
of questioning beforehand. The exact questions will depend on why you
chose this particular informant. Be sure to ask about different roles in the
organization, qualifications for membership, shared beliefs, and, above all,
special terminology. Be sure you follow up with a request for clarification
whenever your informant uses a word you're not familiar with or seems to
be using a common word in a special way. Don't be afraid to ask questions
that might sound dumb!

Take notes during the interview. Afterward, see if you have answers to these questions:

1. How is the worldview of a member of your informant's group different from your own? Are there special beliefs? What things are important to group members that are not so important to others?

2. What are the norms (expectations or rules for behavior) in this group? What are the qualifications for membership, and what are members supposed to do? How are leaders chosen?

3. What special terminology is in use in this group? What is its significance? If you can't find any special terms, look back over your notes to see if everyday words aren't sometimes being used in special ways.

It's hard to capture all the variables of interest in an experimental study of the mass media.

3

Psychology and
the Experimental Method

In some ways, experimental psychology is at the opposite end of the social science spectrum from cultural anthropology because it tends to be quantitative (sometimes elaborately so) rather than qualitative and tends to focus on the individual rather than on cultural or social influences. As is true for anthropology, however, there are historical reasons why psychological methods developed in the direction they did. So it is useful for mass communication researchers who want to borrow these methods to understand their original purposes and the practical and intellectual constraints that characterized them. This helps us make reasonable decisions about when to use them.

TWO SCHOOLS OF THEORETICAL THOUGHT

Psychoanalytic

Some theory in psychology, such as that of Sigmund Freud, was developed largely on the basis of observations of patients in clinical settings rather than data collected specifically for research. While many psychologists and psychiatrists, whose primary work is treating patients rather than doing research, continue to find Freud's **psychoanalytic** theories (and the related family of theories that came later) useful, others became increasingly concerned that these theories had not been tested against research data.

Critics argue that Freud's ideas and the ideas of those working in the same tradition are so fluid that they cannot be translated into statements that can be proved or disproved (hypotheses, as you'll recall). From this perspective, clinical observations of individual cases just don't have much scientific value; using isolated stories that have not been gathered systematically, it is too easy to focus attention on the ones that seem to fit the theory and conveniently overlook the rest.

This approach to evidence gathering is also influenced by unexamined prejudices and cultural presuppositions. Feminist scholars have pointed out that Freud's ideas about women were heavily colored by the Victorian times in which he lived. Besides, Freud's ideas were developed in an attempt to understand individuals with definite psychological problems; their applicability to other questions is sometimes not so clear.

BOX 3.1
FREUDIAN THEORY

Sigmund Freud, as many readers of this book probably already know, emphasized the importance of unconscious mental processes as important explanations of human behavior. We cannot study these processes directly, Freud asserted, but we can study the symbolism of dreams and the associations that people make between images and ideas when they are conscious but relaxed, as in therapy. The idea of the "Freudian slip," a verbal mistake that reveals such an association—often to the embarrassment of the person making it!—has even crept into our everyday vocabulary.

Freud felt that by paying close attention to symbolic associations a working understanding of unconscious processes and motivations could be constructed both for people in general and for specific individuals even though these unconscious phenomena cannot be seen or otherwise studied directly. Freud also developed the concepts of the *ego* (or conscious self), *superego* (or conscience, the socially imposed moral self), and *id* (or instinctual self, involving inherited drives such as sexuality) as somewhat independent components of each individual's psychology.

Behaviorist

The **behaviorist** movement in mid-20th-century American psychology was a reaction against the psychoanalytic type of thinking, based on the perception that theory-building in the Freudian tradition was not scientifically rigorous enough. Behaviorists such as American researcher B. F. Skinner argued that, regardless of the ultimate truth or falsity of Freudian-style propositions, it was best to limit the social scientific study of human behavior to factors that could be observed and measured under laboratory conditions.

Behaviorism was thus explicitly positivist in its orientation. How could psychology advance as a scientific discipline, these researchers asked, unless it could develop testable hypotheses? If there was no way to distinguish whether one psychologist's interpretation was better than another's, no accumulated body of accepted knowledge could be developed.

APPLYING EXPERIMENTAL METHODS IN MEDIA RESEARCH

Language, however, consists of culturally shared symbols and conventions for combining them. Even the visual symbols evidenced in painting, photography, television, and film can be thought of as a kind of language. Critics of behaviorism and "experimentalism" ask how anyone can understand communication without considering the processes of symbolic interpretation—processes that can't be directly observed in the laboratory. Behaviorism, at least in its extreme form, is not very likely to answer the kinds of questions that media researchers are most likely to ask.

Nevertheless, as you'll see later in this chapter, some types of media-related questions can be approached very effectively with experimental methods borrowed from American psychology, despite the legacy of behaviorist influence. Also, today's experimental psychology is much broader than the behaviorist tradition, encompassing many other theories that are potentially helpful for understanding how media information is received.

Influence of Freudian Theory

Some mass communication scholars do make use of Freudian theory in a general way. This approach is more common in European scholarship than in that of the United States, perhaps because the behaviorist reaction and the development of the experimental tradition in psychology occurred primarily in North America rather than Europe. Soap opera plots, for example, might be seen as reflecting the common but unconscious cultural aspirations and associations of their producers and their audiences. However, the use of experimental methods is a far more typical form of borrowing from psychology into mass communication studies, especially in the United States and countries heavily influenced by U.S.-style scholarship, than is the use of Freudian and other psychoanalytic theories.

Although behaviorism gave psychology part of its motivation for further developing these methods, they are useful for many other types of problems. Contemporary U.S. research psychology is no longer primarily behaviorist in orientation, and mass communication researchers similarly use experimental methods to investigate many other types of problems.

Influence of Behaviorist Theory

Behaviorism's influence can be seen clearly in American mass communication studies in the early (World War II and immediate postwar) years, however. What's now called "magic bullet" thinking in mass media theory—the mistaken idea that there is a simple, direct relationship between media content and what people think—has much in common with behaviorism's emphasis on the direct relationship between an observable **stimulus,** or environmental cause, and a measurable **response** made by an organism to its environment. However, researchers can use experimental methods without making the reductionist assumption that communication can be understood in terms of stimuli and responses alone.

Attitudinal Research

A strict behaviorist might not see much meaning in the idea of an **attitude,** usually defined as a positive or negative orientation toward some object, idea, or group. Attitudes can be measured only indirectly, usually through the use of questionnaires, or inferred through particular behaviors, such as attraction or repulsion, or answers offered to the researcher's questions. Yet both psychologists and media researchers work with attitudinal data quite regularly, using the methods of experimental psychology along with data from public opinion surveys.

Interpretive researchers may distrust attitudinal research for entirely different reasons; they feel that getting answers to survey questions is a poor way to understand someone's point of view in any meaningful sense. Whether from a behaviorist-positivist or an interpretive perspective, it's worth asking yourself from time to time whether things like attitudes are real or only reified.

Cognitive Modeling

Not all behaviorists ignore "invisible" mental processes. Some **model,** or represent, complex internal **cognitive,** or thinking, processes by imagining little s's and r's (internal stimuli and responses) that arise in response to big S's (observable, external stimuli) and result in big R's (external responses). Such mental factors as associations and reasoning can be taken into account in this way, but the interpretation of language and other verbal symbols is so complex and **nonlinear**—that is, it doesn't take place in a straight line but may involve many simultaneous mental activities, conscious and unconscious—that this type of modeling often is ill advised.

The study of cognition requires a different paradigm. The recently developed artificial intelligence (AI) systems that use entirely different models, such as the neural network model in which many points are interconnected and the connections themselves vary in strength, may prove more helpful to those exploring the complexity of human thought.

Methodological Limitations

However, whenever you are dealing with observable or measurable variables and are interested in fairly clear-cut, cause-and-effect relationships between two or more of them, experimental methods are a good choice. They can tell you, for example, whether men or women news anchors are more credible, whether viewing violent films results in physiological or short-term behavioral changes, or whether one computer interface takes longer to master than another. Creative use of experimental methods both in psychology and in mass communication studies can provide valuable answers to many questions, as long as you remember their limits and origins and don't try to apply them to questions for which they are inappropriate.

BOX 3.2
WHERE MODELS FALL SHORT

Even complex models such as AI-based ones are poor representations of human communication processes. Can they tell us why we laugh at a joke, or become absorbed in MTV, or find some news items vitally important while ignoring others?

Perhaps someday, but not now.

Can they show us how social values are communicated by children's television, or explain how kids learn grammar, or describe how some groups gain more power over communication processes than others?

Not likely anytime soon!

THE CONCEPT OF CONTROL

In the real world, each of you is subject to a multitude of influences at once as you move through a typical day. You operate under legal constraints, the contraints of acceptable social behavior, and institutional and professional norms. You act to please yourself, your family, your co-workers, or to live up to your parents' expectations. Whether you're male or female, Hispanic or African American or Anglo or Asian, old or young, you have certain expectations for yourself—and others communicate theirs to you, sometimes in indirect ways. You get information from the news media, from entertainment, from casual conversation. You're bombarded by advertising materials.

Children grow up under the influence of teachers, parents, friends, siblings—and mass communication. More and more evidence suggests that some aspects of personality itself—consistent patterns in an individual's behavior—are at least partly hereditary.

How do you sort out all of these influences? You need to look at them a few at a time. Even though you realize that in normal social life many influences are operating simultaneously, and the influence of two or three or a dozen things at once may operate quite differently from each of the same things considered separately, you can't study them all. The great advantage of the **controlled experiment** is that it allows you to look at the influence of one or a handful of factors, or **independent variables,** at a time.

You can assess a limited number of changes in things that you believe (on the basis of clear, theoretically informed, thinking) are affected by these independent variables; those outcomes that you think will vary as a result of variation in the independent variables are called **dependent variables.** For example, if you wanted to study the influence of parents' personalities on children's development, the parents' personalities would be the independent variables and the children's development the dependent variable. (Of course, you'd still have to figure out how to measure each of these—no easy problem in itself.)

Means of Control

Three approaches allow you to achieve control in your experiment: controlled laboratory conditions, choice of participants, and statistical analysis.

Controlled Laboratory Conditions

Most important is the use of controlled laboratory conditions. Participants in psychological experiments are usually tested in a special research setting, not in their homes. Each **subject** (the term used in psychology to refer to a research participant) is treated exactly the same, minimizing the chance that a difference in, say, room color, temperature, the order in which events occur, the way a question is asked or a task explained, or something else about the subject's interaction with the researcher or research staff has an influence on the dependent variable that is different from one subject to another.

Choice of Participants

The second means of control is through your choice of participants, the people who will participate in your experiment. For example, if you want to rule out the influence of gender, you might study only men or only women, but then your results would only apply to half of the population; results obtained for women might not be the same for men. Health researchers who have used government funding to study heart disease in men have recently come under fire from critics who point out that women also get heart disease, but it is less well understood. Thus, control achieved by eliminating whole categories of potential participants needs to be used with caution.

University researchers often use students as subjects. This helps eliminate the possibility that age or level of education is affecting the results but opens the researcher to the very common criticism that results are not generalizable to other groups. Indeed, a cliché joke among researchers is that a tremendous amount is known about the psychology of university freshmen but precious little about anyone else! Nevertheless, sometimes this form of control is convenient and appropriate.

Statistical Analysis

The third type of control is statistical. Modern techniques for statistical analysis can do a better job distinguishing between the effects of different independent variables than could older techniques. Provided you have measures of all the independent variables that you think might be important, you can sort out the independent contribution of each to one or more dependent variables in a variety of ways. (Analysis of variance, which you'll study in a later chapter, is one such technique.) Usually, these techniques require computer programs and people who know how to run them. But they are extremely useful and, for those of you interested in doing experimental work, very much worth the effort required to master them.

Problems With Control

Controlled experiments are often difficult to achieve or can be misleading, especially for mass media studies (see Box 3.3 for an example). Furthermore, experimental methods (although their usefulness is not limited to simple relationships) are designed to determine cause and effect, whereas mass media act as both cause and effect at the same time. One of the key characteristics of mass media is that they reflect what the members of a culture are thinking, doing, and feeling at the same time as they influence that thinking, doing, and feeling. The constraints of experimental design often encourage researchers to ignore this and to imagine instead that the influence goes in one direction only. So, although mass media experiments can be quite useful, it's important not to forget this problem. "Magic bullet" experiments ignore the active role of media audiences in choosing and interpreting mass-mediated information. Still, the power of the controlled experiment is substantial.

Experimental work is subject to two very important additional criticisms. It usually measures only short-term effects, whereas many important media effects are cumulative and take place over a lifetime of exposure. Also, the way that people react in laboratory situations, while these may satisfy the experimenter's need for controlled conditions, may not be very much like the way they react in everyday life. This is especially true for mass media studies. Persons watching TV at home while doing the dishes or surrounded by family or friends probably react to the programming quite differently than they would in a research setting.

BOX 3.3

Say you want to study whether information obtained from television or from print is better remembered. You would probably want to have one group of subjects watch a television program (or, perhaps, a commercial) and a second group read the same information in printed form. To control for in-formation content, you'd have to make sure that exactly the same information was presented in the printed and visual forms. But how can you? Visual media contain images that cannot be duplicated in printed text. Only the soundtrack can be made to match the text.

MORE ON CHOOSING SUBJECTS

Earlier in this chapter, you learned about controlling an experiment by choosing from a limited group of subjects, such as only men or only students. If you are interested in measuring the effectiveness of an interactive video presentation of college course material, it makes sense to use college students as your subjects. More often, however, you are interested in achieving broader generalizability than in this example. If, say, you want to know how a certain type of media presentation affects the general population, you would want to choose subjects with the same range of age and educational background as that general population and in about the same proportions.

That sounds easy enough. But in reality there are dozens and dozens of factors beside age and education that could affect our results: gender, ethnicity, religion, region or nationality, whether our subjects are urban or rural residents, their attitudes, beliefs, and political affiliations—the list is endless. Often, however, you don't have a good reason to eliminate many of these factors as possible influences on your dependent variables. To solve this problem, researchers typically rely on random selection of participants from a larger population.

Random Selection

Subjects are also usually assigned randomly to groups. You'll learn more about random selection and random assignment in later chapters. For now, just remember that its purpose is to assure, to the extent possible, that the makeup, according to demographic and other factors, of a group of subjects is as much as possible representative of the makeup of the population.

Because you don't know in advance all the possibly significant ways that subjects could differ from those who aren't subjects, you try to choose subjects randomly from among the population that you're interested in. There are many types of random sampling techniques, but the simplest, **probability sampling,** is probably the one that most people think of when the word "random" is mentioned. In a probability sample, each member of the population under study (say, all adults of voting age in the United States) would have the same chance of being included. Now, all you need is a list of all these folks. Then you'll put their names into a giant hat and draw out as many as you need!

Of course, such a list doesn't exist. Phone books are inaccurate, incomplete, out-of-date, and exclude those with unlisted numbers or no phones; some people may be listed more than once. And even phone books are only readily available city by city, not for whole states, regions, or countries. You might decide to choose a representative city (maybe your own!). What you've really done in that case is sample twice—once by choosing a city and then again by choosing subjects from within the city. Survey research, which you'll learn about in later chapters, often uses this type of sampling, except that more than one city or other area would be chosen. Survey researchers also commonly use computer programs that randomly dial phone numbers, taking into account the way that phone prefixes and area codes are distributed across the country.

Participant Persuasion: Representativeness Versus Bias

The biggest problem with choosing experimental subjects is not locating a random sample, difficult as that is, but persuading people to participate. Even if they are paid for participating, those who agree to do so will not be representative of the population as a whole. They may be more helpful, more bored, more interested in research, more in need of money, more easily led, or any number of other "mores"—but they won't be typical.

Medical experiments often ask for volunteers, who physiologically are probably enough like the rest of the population that it doesn't matter what their motive for participating is, but you can't make this same assumption about psychological differences. Sometimes, civic groups can be persuaded to get their members to volunteer, perhaps as a fund-raiser, but, again, their membership probably isn't representative. Your last resort—recruiting your own family and friends and friends of friends—means, of course, that your experiment will be biased toward people like you.

So, don't be too upset with your professors for occasionally asking you to be the subjects of their research! Finding people willing to participate in experimental research when they are not "captive audiences" in classrooms (or hospitals, or prisons) is quite difficult. It's hard enough for survey work, where people are asked to spend only a few minutes filling out a questionnaire at home. Finding experimental subjects outside of institutions is a tricky business.

HUMAN SUBJECTS ISSUES

All university-sponsored research involving human subjects requires approval by a Human Subjects Review Board. This applies also to research done by students and is true for ethnographic and survey research as well as for experimental research. Privacy considerations affect many kinds of research. Is it ethical even to observe someone's behavior and make notes about it without their permission? Here opinions vary, especially if the behavior occurs in public.

Ethical issues are, however, especially sensitive for psychological experiments because there is more obvious potential for psychological harm than in other forms of social science research. Some psychological research has involved putting people in difficult or embarrassing situations, and it's hard to guarantee that this will not have any lasting effect. The ethics of deceiving subjects about the actual purpose of an experiment or its conditions is also an issue. Wherever there is a potential for even the slightest or most unlikely harm, the value of the information to be gained from the experiment must be weighed against the risk to the subjects. Perhaps there is another way to gain the same information.

Ethics and Media Research

Do these issues apply to media experiments? Absolutely. Researchers who believe that exposure to violent or pornographic material has negative effects on people will be hard-pressed to establish that experiments with such material do not cause harm to those who participate. This is especially important when children are involved. Clever designs may help; for example, Bandura's (1977) classic study put children with dolls instead of other children to study how youngsters behave after watching violent entertainment. Still, could it be guaranteed that the experience did not have a lasting or even permanent effect on the children?

Some survey research also raises similar issues: asking people about their sexual behavior in the context of assessing an AIDS information campaign, for example, might cause them psychological distress. Furthermore, especially stringent procedures must be followed to ensure confidentiality of the research data.

DEFINING AND MEASURING VARIABLES

Definitions

Variables can be difficult to define. It's not easy to learn to think of the world as composed of isolated fragments that you can observe and measure independently. To compound the difficulty, variables come in many "flavors"—their distinctive characteristics must be identified so you can know how to measure them and what to make of the results. Variables can be independent, dependent, intervening, and interactive; a later section discusses confounding ones.

Independent and Dependent

Beginning researchers often have difficulty thinking in terms of independent and dependent variables. Independent variables are ones that you can change or manipulate at will; they can be thought of as varying freely, whereas dependent variables change only as a result of changes in the independent ones. It is this relationship that an experiment is designed to measure or test.

The relationship between independent and dependent variables is often assumed to be a **linear relationship.** This means that a given change in one variable produces the same amount of change in the other for all values of the variables. Another way of thinking about this is that a graph of the relationship would show a straight line. But the actual relationship may be curved in various ways. It takes some knowledge of advanced statistics to identify and compensate for complications of this kind.

Some experiments also involve intervening and interactive variables.

Intervening

A variable that changes the relationship between the independent and dependent variables is called an **intervening variable.** For example, if eating chocolate makes you sick *unless* you drink milk with it, milk is an intervening variable in the "chocolate effect." If watching the news makes you experience something called "information overload" *only if* you are paying particular attention, attentiveness would be an intervening variable in the "overload effect."

Interactive

A dependent variable whose changes are not attributable to changes in individual independent variables but to interactions among them is called an interactive variable. Say you have evidence that age affects people's preference for a certain television show. So does region of the country. In one region, older people may prefer a certain show, whereas in a different region the same show is preferred by younger people. If you put all the data together, the relationship between these three variables will not be apparent; you won't easily recognize any relationship between age and preference because the groups from the two regions will tend to offset each other in summarized data. Interactive relationships can be complex and very difficult to understand.

Measurement

Operationalization

Defining a variable in a way that allows it to be measured is called **operationalization.** Sometimes, this is pretty straightforward; for example, time spent watching television can be operationalized as the number of minutes per day spent in the same room with a television set that is turned on. Note that even this simple example represents a compromise, however. Actually measuring "watching" would be a bit trickier! Nevertheless, this is a simple problem in comparison to the problems posed by measuring abstract psychological variables such as attitudes, attentiveness, salience (perceived relevance), and so on. How would you measure loyalty, liberalness, or political power? And just what is an attitude, after all? The fuzzier the concept, the harder it is to come up with an operationalization that's acceptable.

Levels of Measurement

The way that a variable can be measured is classified into its **level of measurement.** Although at first this sometimes seems arbitrary to students, a variable's level of measurement is extremely important to understanding how data can be analyzed and especially what statistical tests are appropriate. Some variables can only be measured in terms of simple categories; they are not measured numerically. Others can be measured with greater precision using numerical scales, in the sense that a ruler measures a distance from one point to another. You'll learn more about levels of measurement in later chapters.

ELEMENTS OF EXPERIMENTAL DESIGN

Treatment

The heart of experimental design is that a different condition, or **treatment,** is applied to different subjects (or groups of subjects). You might think of this as analogous to giving out different kinds of medications to see which works best, which is presumably where the term came from. Treatments are the independent variables, the ones you are free to alter at will. You are looking for an effect (a change) in the dependent variables. To continue the medical analogy, do the patient's symptoms improve with one medication but not another? Usually, one group of participants is called the **control group;** this group receives no treatment but in all other ways is handled like the treatment group to help isolate effects attributable *only* to the treatment.

Remember the discussion of control earlier in this chapter? If the control group is handled as much as possible like the treatment group except for the action of the independent variable or variables, you can be more certain that a change in the independent variables (or treatment) is what's causing the change in the dependent variables (or outcome). In experiments that test medications, researchers often provide the control group with a "placebo"—a pill or injection that has no medicinal effect whatsoever—to make sure that any improvement observed is not just a psychological one resulting from the fact that the patients believe they are being cured, that they have received extra care and personal attention due to the experiment, and so on.

Confounding Variables

A variables that isn't part of the research design but might be causing an observed outcome is called a **confounding variable** because it "confounds" or complicates the interpretation of the experimental results. In the preceding examples, the psychological effects on patients of being involved in a research project or the effects on mass media experiment subjects of sitting in a room and watching a program, regardless of its content, are confounding variables.

Sometimes, the act of measuring itself acts like a confounding variable. Giving subjects a test or attitudinal questionnaire may give them an idea of the purposes of the experiment, sensitize them to certain issues, cause them to recall things they wouldn't otherwise have been thinking of, or teach them new information they hadn't had before. Hooking them up to apparatus to test their breathing or heart rate is bound to have both psychological and physiological effects.

The design of experiments can become extraordinarily complex, as can the analysis of the data that they produce. At this point, it's most important simply to remember that all of the many variations on experimental design are intended to do one thing: control for the influence of confounding variables, including variables involving the experimental procedures themselves.

BOX 3.4
USE OF A CONTROL
GROUP IN MEDIA RESEARCH

In a mass media study designed to find out the educational effects of a video presentation, for example, you might show the control group a video that has no educational content to make sure that any noticeable effects on your subjects are really due to the content of the test video. After all, just sitting down and watching any program could conceivably have measurable effects on subjects' knowledge, if only because it relaxes them or forces them to concentrate.

LIMITS OF EXPERIMENTS

All experiments, no matter how cleverly designed and carefully executed, have important limitations. You've already learned about two of these. Subject selection is difficult and usually not bias free; students and others who are readily available to university researchers are studied too often, others may not be studied at all. Also, experimental methods are specifically designed to explore cause-and-effect relationships. Many aspects of human cognition and human society are not best understood in simple cause-and-effect terms, however—especially communication aspects.

Two other important limits already discussed are these: Experimental (laboratory) conditions do *not* duplicate natural conditions, and almost all experiments are short term. Researchers are interested, of course, in how mass media communication actually works in real life; sometimes experiments carried out in laboratories, in which the number of confounding variables, such as alternative sources of information, are deliberately limited, are too artificial to be a good basis for generalizing to "real world" events.

BOX 3.5

Say you want to look at the amount of time that preschoolers in day care spend watching television, in comparison to preschoolers staying home with a parent. You would probably want to study children in their natural environments rather than trying to bring them into a "day-care-like" or "home-like" laboratory setting because you don't know enough about the conditions that occur naturally. In fact, that's what you're trying to investigate in your study!

Of course, you could put children for a short period of time in a room with a television and either a day care worker or one of their parents and carefully observe what happens. But you'd be hard-pressed to argue that you're observing the same things that would happen naturally if no experiment had been set up. Are the number of alternative activities, the daily schedule, the interruptions and intrusions, or the general character of the interactions going to be the same as in the children's normal day?

It's known from decades of media research that most of the important effects of the mass media are long term, subtle, and indirect, such as the effects on children's values or on political institutions or on attitudes toward particular professions or ethnic groups. One-shot, short-term, laboratory experiments are poor choices to capture all aspects of these effects, although they can add important insights to knowledge gained from other sources and occasionally provide the most definitive answers available to important questions.

Quasi-Experiments

To study real-world processes that cannot be easily duplicated in the laboratory and yet retain some of the advantages of experimental design, researchers sometimes do a **quasi-experiment** involving experimental-type measurements of variables that occur naturally. These are often field experiments.

Field Experiments

At some sacrifice in terms of experimental control, researchers often choose a **field experiment** carried out under natural (or "field") rather than artificial conditions. To apply this idea to a study of children's TV viewing (Box 3.5), you would try to arrange to study real-world homes and day-care centers instead. Field experiments are only one type of field study, however. The ethnographic approach you have already learned about is also a type of "field study." A field experiment, on the other hand, incorporates at least some elements of experimental design, such as a before-and-after or between-groups comparison.

MASS COMMUNICATION APPLICATIONS

Despite the limitations, experiments are often easier to conduct than ethnographic studies and therefore more common. Often, numerical results may be seen as less ambiguous and more persuasive (even though their generalizability or meaningfulness can also be limited); they can therefore be easier to publish in some academic journals. While this is gradually changing in mass communication studies, experiments remain a popular and highly respected way of investigating media-related problems.

Media Violence

Literally thousands of studies have been done of the relationship between such factors as exposure to media violence or pornography (usually defined not as explicit sexuality in and of itself but as the association of sexuality with violence or exploitation) and behavior and attitudes, especially the behavior and attitudes of children. Many of these studies, perhaps the majority, have used experimental methods.

The preponderance of evidence suggests there is some relationship, but can it be said to be a causative relationship, and is it an important—let alone the *most* important—one? The research on this question is not entirely clear-cut, partly because of the limits of experimental research for these purposes. Violence in real life occurs because children are neglected, because teens feel hopeless, because young people grow up in violent cultures, such as that of the United States—certainly not because of the media alone.

Public Persuasion

Studies conducted on propaganda and persuasion effects, beginning in the World War II period when we were concerned with effectively countering Nazi propaganda, have relied heavily on experimental methods. Such problems as the credibility of sources and the persuasiveness of one- versus two-sided messages on particular types of audiences have been thoroughly investigated using experimental methods.

This research continues today; advertisers and political candidates, among others, continue to be interested in how to construct the most persuasive possible message. Do we know how to persuade an audience to do what we want them to do—whether buy our product, be interested in our issues, or vote for our candidate? No, and this is probably fortunate! Yet, as for violence studies, the *partial* answers that experiments can provide have been interesting and useful.

Agenda Setting

Work on the process of agenda setting—how issues that are prominent in the media become prominent in the minds of readers and audiences—also commonly use experimental or quasi-experimental methods. Here, data on media content is often included in the same study with data on public opinion change. Agenda setting is now well established as a definite mass media effect. Whereas laboratory experiments are short-term and artificial and quasi-experiments suffer from a lack of control of confounding variables, the two taken together have provided strong evidence of agenda-setting effects. Research is ongoing to understand these effects in more detail, however, using the methods of experimental psychology in either laboratory or field settings. And other competing theories of the relationship between media content and public opinion are also in the process of being tested.

Everyday Events

Unusual real-world events—a labor strike at a media organization, or perhaps a parade, political rally, or demonstration—have provided special opportunities to look at the role of the mass media in everyday life using quasi-experimental methods. Similarly, the introduction of new technologies to work settings are logical targets of quasi-experimental work that attempts to assess associated changes in work style or productivity.

Electronic Communication

New media design is an emerging area of applied research where experiments and quasi-experiments are likely to prove extremely useful but are only just now beginning to be exploited. For example, what type of computer interface is actually most "user friendly"? Could multimedia systems really help children learn faster? What are the effects of the electronic newsroom, where wire news comes in and is processed electronically and where reporters and editors communicate by electronic mail?

These questions seem amenable to further experimental or quasi-experimental study. Some researchers (e.g., Rice, 1984) have already begun to take advantage of these opportunities.

IMPORTANT TERMS AND CONCEPTS

Attitude	**Linear relationship**
Behaviorist	**Model**
Cognitive	**Nonlinear**
Confounding variable	**Operationalization**
Control group	**Probability sampling**
Controlled experiment	**Psychoanalytic**
Dependent variables	**Quasi-experiment**
Field experiment	**Response**
Independent variables	**Stimulus**
Intervening variable	**Subject**
Level of measurement	**Treatment**

EXERCISE

This is an experiment that you can do on yourself! It is really a quasi-experiment because you can't control many of the conditions. Try this: decide what your favorite, most important daily source of media information or entertainment is. Do you always watch a certain television show or a certain kind of show? Do you listen to a certain news program or read a particular paper? Do you turn on your computer or listen to recorded music as a part of your daily routine?

Design a series of three to five simple questions that are based on what you think you get out of this particular media experience—whether a better mood or a feeling of being better informed about current events or a sense of involvement in your community. Make the questions ones that you can answer on a 1-to-10 scale. For example, if keeping up with current events is why you watch the news, your question should read something like this: "Today I feel as though I am knowledgable about current events." If relaxation is a goal of watching television for you, use a question like "I felt relaxed and comfortable at the end of the day today."

Pick one day, follow your usual routine, and then fill out the questionnaire before bed. The next day, skip your usual routine, and complete the questionnaire again. Try to answer these questions:

1. Are your answers on the two days different? Of course, using just two days does not give the most meaningful results, as there will be normal variations in your ratings and repeatedly answering the same questions could have effects of its own. Do the differences *seem* to you to result from the break in routine? Are there other possible explanations?

2. Are there other changes that you think might be caused by changing your routine but that are *not* captured by the questions you wrote? What are they? Can you write a few additional questions that would reflect them?

3. In a paragraph or two, suggest how you might design an experiment to test whether these conclusions would hold up as hypotheses using subjects other than yourself and a longer period of time. How would you change the questions you asked? Your general experimental approach? What, in your view, are the main limitations of such a study?

Theory provides the lens that tells social scientists where to look for data and how to interpret them.

4
___

Sociological Study of
Organizations and Institutions

ociology studies how modern societies work. Sociology is a complex and sometimes bewildering discipline, drawing sometimes from the experimental paradigm,
sometimes from the ethnographic paradigm, and, perhaps more often, using additional methods of its own, such as survey research.

SOCIOLOGICAL THEORY

Theory in sociology is quite diverse; it's necessary to understand a little bit about
this diversity to understand why sociological researchers choose particular methods for their studies. Sociology is built on the work of such influential early theorists as these:

- Emile Durkheim (1858-1917), who saw modern society as characterized by an
  increasingly complex division of labor;
- Max Weber (1864-1920), who looked closely at the changes introduced as societies
  became more bureaucratic and at the value system that seemed to be driving
  economic development in Western (European) societies; and
- Karl Marx (1818-1883), who looked at the way in which industrialization seemed to
  be accompanied by a concentration of power in the hands of owners at the expense
  of workers.

Practitioners Defined

One way to think about sociological theory is that a sociologist who more closely follows the thinking of Durkheim and Weber is a **functionalist,** asking questions about what maintains social organization and order, whereas another who more closely follows the thinking of Marx is a **conflict theorist,** asking questions about power and its distribution among various competing groups. Whenever you ask questions about the media's role in society, whatever method you use to investigate them, you are drawing in a general way from sociological theory. Some media researchers are particularly interested in the ways that media contribute to social stability, drawing from functionalist theory; these scholars ask what functions (e.g., surveillance or entertainment) the mass media serve for society.

Cultural Studies

Other researchers are specifically interested in societal-level conflict and the social distribution of power; the British **cultural studies** tradition, reflected in the work of scholars such as Stuart Hall, has been heavily influenced by this type of thinking as has the work of some American mass media scholars such as Todd Gitlin (e.g., his 1980 study of the media's portrayal of 1960s' U.S. activism). These researchers ask not how mass media might contribute to a smooth social order, but how they contribute to the maintenance of existing power relationships, legitimating some ways of thinking while ignoring others or labeling them as "fringe" points of view. These "critical" scholars use media material as evidence of how some ways of thinking are socially "privileged" over others, and they identify the media themselves as an instrument through which this is accomplished.

This is in sharp contrast to functionalist thinking in that conflict theorists see modern societies as incorporating evolving struggles over power distribution, while functionalists—even though they may not actively disagree with conflict theory—are looking instead at the factors that keep societies harmonious, including the mechanisms that allow for orderly change to take place.

Societal Value Systems

Every society seems to rest on a **value system** that is shared by its members to at least some degree. Sociologist Herbert Gans, as you may know, found a series of "enduring values," such as moderatism, pastoralism, and a belief in the importance of individual leadership, reflected in the way that news is presented in the United States (Gans, 1979). Work like his helps us understand the foundations of our own societies as well as the media's role within them. But the transmission of established values can be interpreted in two different ways: as a positive force contributing to social harmony and order or as a negative force inhibiting growth and change. Images of women in 1950s' sit-coms have often been criticized for holding back women from achieving professional careers, for example, by promulgating distorted and restrictive ideas about women's roles.

One of the values that Gans identified in news accounts was "ethnocentrism," the tendency to look at world events from a narrow, culture-bound perspective. This type of thinking may not be compatible with a society's success or even survival in an increasingly international economic and political world.

But social values—and their media reflections—are not entirely static; they change over time. Under some circumstances the media seem to transmit new positive values, contributing to the growth of social movements such as civil rights or environmentalism and to public awareness of issues like AIDS. Other mass media messages, such as the acceptance of violence as "normal" in both news and entertainment, are of concern because of their potentially destructive impact on the thinking of youngsters whose own value systems are still being formed. Studies of the relationship between the values in media and those of a society have important implications for professional work in mass communication, which has at least some power to shape the direction of social change.

Social Institutions

Complex societies incorporate **social institutions** (businesses, the legal system, schools, churches, the police, and so on—including mass media institutions), which are characterized by their tendency to endure even while specific individuals come and go. Social institutions represent units with ongoing traditions and important social influences that extend beyond their individual makeup at any given moment. Sociologists often study not only the external function of an institution but its internal structure. Some of the earliest and most influential media studies (e.g., White's 1950 gatekeeping study, discussed in Chapter 2) have been in this tradition.

In general, the study of professional roles is considered a specialty within sociology, along with the study of such related issues as occupational mobility, the ability of an individual to move into a higher-status or better-paying job. Some researchers interested in the mass media have asked questions about the typical socioeconomic backgrounds of those who go into such fields as journalism or television production. Studies like these also help you understand *which* values— or rather *whose* values—are most likely to be reflected in the media. Today's concern with ethnic diversity and the roles of women in journalistic professions results in part from an appreciation of the importance of this question.

SOCIAL PSYCHOLOGY AND SOCIAL INTERACTION

Much sociology of interest to those studying the media falls under the heading of **social psychology**—that is, the study of the psychology of social groups. (Social psychologists are found in academic departments of psychology as well as departments of sociology.) This includes the study of **collective behavior,** such as collective social responses to crises (e.g., a threat of earthquake or an environmental risk), crowd behavior, and social movements. Obviously, media are important influences on collective behavior.

Symbolic Interactionism

One branch of sociology that is social psychological in character is the study of human interaction as a source of meaning. These sociologists generally draw from the work of George Herbert Mead (1963-1931), particularly his notion of the "looking-glass self." Mead argued that our sense of self is derived through interaction (or communication) with others. We are social creatures, and our sense of identify is derived in part from our perceptions of what others think of us and expect us to be.

This subdiscipline is called **symbolic interactionism.** The media play an obvious role here; studies concerned with how women, ethnic minorities, or professional groups are portrayed in the media are in part concerned with how these images will shape both the self-conception and the general social expectations associated with each. Such expectations tend to become self-fulfilling prophecies. Women might learn from the media that they are expected to become housewives or "supermoms." They may reflect these expectations in their own life planning, measuring their success against a standard that comes in part from the media.

Labeling Theory

Also derived from the symbolic interactionist tradition is **labeling theory,** which is concerned with how some behavior (and some individuals) become classified by society as **deviant,** or unacceptable, whereas other behavior and other individuals are accepted as conforming to social norms (see Box 4.1).

Social Construction

Similarly, social interaction (including the kind of communication that takes place through the mass media, even though this isn't "real" face-to-face interaction) helps shape our notions of what's an environmental crisis, a crime problem, an instance of corruption, an acceptable or unacceptable political stance or religious belief. Those concerned with this process are said to be studying the **social construction** of reality (Berger & Luckmann, 1966). They argue that we live in a world literally defined by our own perceptions and expectations, perceptions and expectations derived from the society and culture in which we live as much as by the physical world that surrounds us.

This perspective is often applied in mass media studies; one of the best-known early examples is the work of Tuchman (1978), based in part on participant observation. Unlike social learning theorists, who are primarily concerned with behavior, constructivists are primarily concerned with the creation of perceptions and beliefs.

Ethnomethodology

A variation of social psychological theory that has recently received increased attention from some media researchers is **ethnomethodology.** This highly special-

---

BOX 4.1
EXAMPLES OF LABELING

One of the classic studies in this area was Becker's (1963) investigation of what it means to become a marijuana smoker—what the symbolic social significance of this deviant act is. Another related group of studies has been concerned with what it means to be mentally ill in this society: who is considered "ill" and who is considered "normal," what expectations follow from classifying someone as "ill" on the basis of their behavior, and what the consequences of this act of labeling are for the social role of the affected individual.

Others are concerned similarly with the "career" of juvenile delinquents. How does labeling someone "delinquent" affect their self-image and the expectations of those around them, and how do these, in turn, change their behavior? This research has been influential in shaping the way we treat youthful offenders, as it points out the danger of imposing punishments (e.g., prison sentences) that will further reinforce a deviant self-image, teach additional deviant behaviors, and result in lifelong criminal behavior rather than rehabilitation. Here, too, the media play an important role in shaping people's expectations of what is considered "normal" versus "deviant."

ized approach is a theoretical perspective, *not* a methodology, despite its name. Most closely associated with the work of sociologist Harold Garfinkel, ethnomethodology looks at how people make sense of their everyday lives. Whereas labeling theory questions our assumptions about what is normal and what is deviant, ethnomethodology tries to look deeper and ask how we go about making these decisions in the first place—how we identify a particular social situation or event as an instance of a more general category. How do you know you are now engaged in an activity called "studying"? More significantly, perhaps, how do the bureaucratic social institutions that collect official statistics decide what is a "suicide," or who is "unemployed"?

The term ethnomethodology actually refers to the study of what set of methods (that is, what methodology) members of a culture use to make sense of their everyday social worlds. It is parallel in meaning to ethnobotany, the study of how various cultures classify and understand plants, or ethnomedicine, the study of how cultures, especially non-Western cultures, understand and practice medicine.

Labeling Theory by Any Other Name?

Ethnomethodology sounds a lot like labeling theory, but its adherents argue that it is quite different and goes much deeper to examine the very roots of social organization. Labeling theory begins with the assumption that there are established social norms; "deviance" is what occurs when these are violated. Ethnomethodologists argue that, in practice, norms are quite fluid and flexible—that they don't necessarily exist as rigid rules independent of a particular social context but only emerge in practice. What *do* exist, and what social scientists should be studying (they say), are practices or strategies that allow the members of a culture to decide how to identify something as normal or deviant, suicide or death by natural causes, studying or "fooling around," and so on.

To think like an ethnomethodologist can be quite productive for mass communication researchers because doing so causes them to question their assumptions about how people "make sense" of the information and entertainment the media provide. Yet because ethnomethodology does not have its own method, ethnomethodologists often use conversational analysis (a methodology derived from speech communication studies) to look at how social meanings are negotiated in everyday speech (see Box 4.2).

That particular set of techniques is not covered in detail in this book, which focuses on methods for the study of mass communication rather than interpersonal (person-to-person) communication.

Choosing a Research Method

Generally speaking, specific sets of methods can't be identified as coming specifically from social psychology. Rather, symbolic interactionists, ethnomethodologists, labeling theorists, or researchers interested in collective behavior tend to interpret data in the light of their own theoretical understanding, which determines what kinds of questions they ask and what kind of data they intend to collect.

Many of these researchers prefer to use qualitative methods because the processes they are interested in cannot be easily captured in quantitative models, which have clearly defined independent and dependent variables. If they do use quantitative data, such as survey findings, they tend to supplement them with descriptions of the contemporary events and the complex social processes that they believe underlie the formation of answers to opinion questions.

Other social psychologists are more inclined to use the methods of experimental psychology, however, and prefer clean separations among measurable factors in studying the behavior of groups or organizations.

PUBLIC OPINION STUDIES

At the other end of the interpretive-positivist spectrum from most of the perspectives considered thus far in this chapter, sociology is also concerned with the precise measurement of public opinion. Researchers influenced by the symbolic interactionist tradition do not necessarily dismiss public opinion data but (as mentioned earlier) interpret them in the context of how opinions are formed in social interaction and, at least potentially, in response to how the mass media present particular issues.

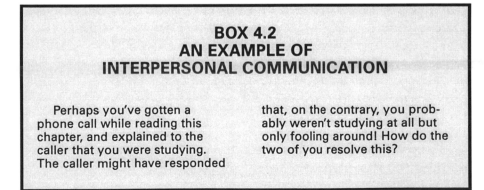

**BOX 4.2
AN EXAMPLE OF
INTERPERSONAL COMMUNICATION**

Perhaps you've gotten a phone call while reading this chapter, and explained to the caller that you were studying. The caller might have responded that, on the contrary, you probably weren't studying at all but only fooling around! How do the two of you resolve this?

Some argue that public opinion surveys are a fairly superficial means of understanding complex social phenomena. Meanwhile, however, other sociologists have set these questions to one side and worked on refining techniques for assessing exactly what public opinion is at any given moment. In practice, an opinion is defined as what people express when they are asked an opinion question in a survey.

Value of Opinion Research

Problems of conceptualizing what is meant by "public opinion" aside, the techniques of public opinion research have been extremely useful in media studies, as well as in other newer fields of study such as political science, and are included in this book. Studies of media effects often combine data on media content with data on opinion change. In addition, many journalistic stories (especially around election time) include opinion data.

It's worthwhile pausing from time to time to consider whether "opinions" are real or only reified. Nevertheless, public opinion research methods constitute an important contribution from sociology to other fields—perhaps even the single most important methodological contribution in terms of their broad social impact.

Respondent Sampling

Where ethnographic studies refer to their participants as informants and psychologists call them subjects, sociologists and others doing public opinion surveys refer to each participant as a **respondent**—one who responds to their questions. Choosing respondents is extremely important because the goal of a public opinion survey is almost always to be able to make statements about what some population as a whole (e.g., all U.S. citizens, all British voters, all elementary school teachers in the state of Texas) think about a given issue or topic.

The question of sampling, which you first read about in the chapter on experimental methods, becomes even more critical in survey research. In an experiment, different treatments (perhaps including "no treatment" for a control group) are usually applied to different groups of subjects. The most important sampling consideration is whether you can assume that your various treatment groups are equivalent (see Box 4.3).

Representativeness

With survey research, the primary goal is to have a **representative sample**—the group of people who actually respond to the survey. An unrepresentative survey sample yields results that are meaningless. The goal of saying something about the larger group from which your respondents have been drawn can only be achieved if this condition is met—difficult to accomplish because people have been surveyed so often (and, sadly, approached so often by salespeople and political activists masquerading as survey researchers) that most refuse to respond to even a short telephone interview.

How many people should be included? A typical telephone survey published in a good academic journal or high-quality news medium will often contain information from 1,000 or more respondents. Such surveys often use techniques such as **multistage sampling,** which involves first choosing a representative sample of cities or counties, for example, and then choosing a sample of individuals who live in the chosen geographic areas. But statisticians say this reduces the accuracy of results and to call them in such cases!

A good rule of thumb for a simple survey using only one "layer" of sampling from a single **sampling frame,** or list of possible respondents (e.g., everyone listed in the Chicago phone book, or all registered voters in Smith County, or whoever answers the phone at any household that has a sixth grader enrolled in a particular school district), is that between 200 and 400 responses are needed, which often means that at least 400 to 800 surveys must be mailed or phone calls made. Smaller

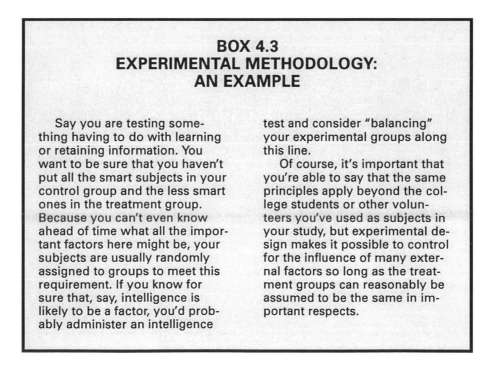

BOX 4.3
EXPERIMENTAL METHODOLOGY:
AN EXAMPLE

Say you are testing something having to do with learning or retaining information. You want to be sure that you haven't put all the smart subjects in your control group and the less smart ones in the treatment group. Because you can't even know ahead of time what all the important factors here might be, your subjects are usually randomly assigned to groups to meet this requirement. If you know for sure that, say, intelligence is likely to be a factor, you'd probably administer an intelligence test and consider "balancing" your experimental groups along this line.

Of course, it's important that you're able to say that the same principles apply beyond the college students or other volunteers you've used as subjects in your study, but experimental design makes it possible to control for the influence of many external factors so long as the treatment groups can reasonably be assumed to be the same in important respects.

numbers may work, especially for exploratory research; however, the smaller the sample, the harder it can be to draw definite statistical conclusions. No matter how large the sample, applying conclusions beyond the population actually included in the sampling frame (to other cities, counties, school districts, and so on) is a risky business—and, technically speaking, *never* justified on statistical grounds.

How should respondents be chosen? Ideally, the sampling frame should include everyone in the population, or group to which you hope to generalize your conclusions. But recall the discussion of sampling in Chapter 3: There is no master list of the population of a particular country. Phone books are available for almost all areas, but not everyone is listed. Furthermore, it's not always easy to tell businesses from individual home numbers. Computer programs now in common use that generate random numbers and dial them can reflect the distribution of area codes and local prefixes among the population of interest, although of course this solution doesn't help for mail surveys.

Samples drawn from lists, such as phone books, are commonly determined by **systematic random sampling.** Typically, the researcher chooses a random starting point (usually by consulting a random number table), then skips a certain number of names and takes the next one, then skips the same number and takes the next one, and so on. The number to be skipped is determined by the number of names in the sampling frame and the number the researcher wants in the sample (see Box 4.4).

Many other sampling schemes are used. The goal is always to get an unbiased, representative sample of the population. **Quota sampling** adds respondents who fit certain characteristics until the proportions in the sample are like those of the population in terms of age, gender, ethnicity, or other demographic factors of particular interest. This technique is used to overcome sampling conditions in which the sample would otherwise be particularly unrepresentative, such as surveys that recruit respondents from among shoppers in a mall. Surveys designed specifically to understand differences among ethnic groups may deliberately oversample particular minority groups who would otherwise make up only a small percentage of the respondents.

Regardless of what sampling technique is used, there is always the possibility that your sample may include those who are especially gullible, who have extra time on their hands, or who just like to talk.

Response Rate

By definition, response rate is the percentage of acceptances among those asked to participate in a survey. A low response rate means the sample can't be assumed to be unbiased. But there's no easy rule of thumb about what an acceptable response rate should be. Some marketing surveys achieve only very low response rates, perhaps less than 10%. People are a bit more willing to participate in surveys when the purpose is identified as academic research, but the goal of having a response rate of 60% or 70% is not realistic anymore. Between 40% and 50% is more typical, even for a well-presented and carefully conducted survey.

Professional survey firms, such as Gallop and Harris, whose polls are well known, and survey specialists working at major universities use elaborate techniques of sampling and statistical analysis to compensate for possible biases introduced by imperfect response rates and other sampling problems.

Choosing a Survey Method

Should surveys be conducted in person (door-to-door) or by mail or telephone? Each method has its advantages and disadvantages. Door-to-door surveys are relatively rare these days; obviously, they are more expensive, and the possible advantage that a person appearing on the doorstep might be harder to turn down is diminished in these days of crime and the fear of strangers. Mail surveys are too

---

BOX 4.4
A SAMPLING EXAMPLE

Say there are 20,000 names in the local phone book and you want to draw a sample of 400 names for a telephone survey. You would need to take every 50th name (20,000 divided by 400) to come out about right. Research of this type should be as precise as possible, but the number of names in the phone book can be estimated by counting several pages and averaging them and then multiplying by the total number of pages. Similarly, the amount of distance to skip can be estimated—in this example, you might find that 8 column-inches contain about 50 names and so could use a ruler to skip down 8 inches between names to be included.

If the sample turns out to have a few more or a few less than the desired number (say, 398 or 403 instead of 400 names), it's not as important as ensuring that there is no systematic bias. For example, you would not want to use the membership roster for a local civic group as a sampling frame for a study of general public opinion on a community issue, and you certainly would not want to use the membership of a local political party for this purpose!

easily tossed in the trash with all the other junk mail. And telephone surveyers must be carefully trained to give each respondent exactly the same introduction and to ask exactly the same questions in the same order, or the results may be difficult to interpret. Experienced telephone survey workers may have some control over the refusal rate, and surveyors are sometimes compensated on the basis of number of interviews completed to encourage them to develop this skill further. There is, however, the danger that a dishonest worker will make up answers that respondents declined to give. In short, each approach has its limits.

Public Opinion Quarterly and other similar academic journals publish many methodological studies that investigate the effects of different approaches to survey research—in other words, it's a whole field of study in itself! For example, such factors as the ethnic appearance or accent of the interviewer definitely make a difference in how people respond to questions about public policy on civil rights, affirmative action, and other issues about which particular ethnic groups might be expected to be particularly sensitive.

There also is a tendency for survey respondents to give answers they feel the researcher would most like to hear. This influence is called **response bias** and might help explain why exit polls (surveys conducted of voters leaving polling places that ask questions about who they voted for) don't always agree with election outcomes. Another possibility is that respondents might simply lie, even when there is no response bias. This is probably unusual, but nobody knows for sure what the rate of misrepresentation might be in a typical national survey.

Identifying Causation

Whether based on participant observation and reported in words or on survey research and reported numerically, much sociological research is descriptive, but its ultimate goal is theoretical explanation—the identification of causes. Is labeling theory a good explanation of how juvenile offenders become juvenile delinquents? Does public opinion change as a result of political advertising? Is a good education or the socioeconomic status of parents a more important key to professional success? Surveys of public opinion cannot answer these questions directly; neither can observational studies.

Modern statistical techniques, including some you'll study in this book, can help "tease out" causative relationships from complex sets of quantitative data. Careful, systematic comparison of qualitative observations with the tentative ideas of the researcher can help develop and test the adequacy of particular theoretical explanations. But in either case it's important to start with sound theory.

Even for a study intended to be inductive or exploratory, you need a clue as to what kind of data to collect and analyze. These clues come from theory, an existing idea about causation, which is why this chapter began with an exploration of the diversity of theory in sociology.

A WORD ABOUT OTHER METHODS

As you've seen, sociology is theoretically and methodologically diverse. Sociologists and other social scientists use many methods other than the popular ones that you'll study in more detail.

Unobtrusive Observation

Some researchers use **unobtrusive observation** in which they do not become a part of the research setting, as in participant observation, but try to remain anonymous and unnoticed, thus not altering the normal social routine by their presence, a criticism directed at participant observation studies. Unobtrusive observation often involves important ethical issues, just like investigative journalism in which the journalist is not identified. It is usually perfectly legal to observe and study people's public behavior—for example, in a bar or club, in a shopping mall, or in a college dormitory—but in many cases it may not be ethical (see Box 4.5).

More generally, unobtrusive measures of all kinds have been used in sociological studies (for discussion and ideas, see Webb, 1966). What workers bring from home for lunch could conceivably be studied by looking in garbage cans. Methods of this type can be used in media studies. What newspapers or magazines are discarded by office workers in a certain location? This would be useful information

---

**BOX 4.5
UNOBTRUSIVE STUDIES:
AN EXAMPLE AND JUSTIFICATION**

One student study using this method involved spying on women in a public restroom; it produced the conclusion that the women using the restroom were more likely to wash their hands if others were present. This seemingly innocent study still involved an obvious degree of invasion of privacy.

Whether this approach is justified in any given case depends on the value of the data collected. *If* you can learn something new, *if* you can answer an important question, and *if* the invasion of privacy is relatively minor and no specific individuals are identified, then the research may be justified. *If* you also learn something important about how to do research, that's a benefit to be taken into account. Still, there is no particular need for you as a student to do unobtrusive research that involves spying on private behavior when so many alternative opportunities exist to practice observing others.

ser trying to reach that particular group with a new product. Which
en most commonly checked out of the local library? Do these pro-
to the social or psychological needs that reading most commonly
times the necessary data might already be publically available, such
r newspaper circulation figures or audience figures for television
programming.

Often, unobtrusive measures are indirect measures of the variable the researcher
is most interested in. For example, the percentage of the eligible population voting
in a particular election might be used as a rough approximation of the degree of
political interest that election aroused.

Focus Groups

Sociologists and other researchers also make use of a qualitative technique
called the **focus group** in which questions are asked of an assembled group rather
than an individual. Sometimes described as a sort of "group interview," the real
advantage of a focus group is that the researcher can gather data on participants'
interaction with one another. A richer picture of how information is processed and
conclusions are drawn can be constructed in comparison to what can be understood
from the narrower data produced in an interview situation. Participants may say
things to one another that they would not bring up in a one-on-one conversation,
such as arguments they consider persuasive and associations they make in response
to others' comments. They may also more easily forget that the researcher is
present, so their conversations and reactions more closely approximate normal
conditions.

Focus groups are not easy to conduct effectively, however, and should not be
thought of as a simple way to get a lot of interviews over with in a hurry!

Content Analysis

One extremely important type of research in mass communication studies is
content analysis, the systematic description of the content of some part of the mass
media. Content analysis is also sometimes used by sociologists and occasionally
by psychologists. While it is really the method (or set of methods) that most clearly
"belongs" uniquely to mass communication research, it is based on concepts
originally developed in the other social sciences.

Content analysis can be quantitative, borrowing sampling techniques from
survey research, or qualitative, much like the inductive analysis of open-ended
interview data. The goal of characterizing a particular type of content by looking
at a representative set of data is very similar to the goal of describing the opinions
of a population based on those of a sample or to that of gaining insight into the

cultural knowledge of an entire social group based on information obtained from a limited number of group members who act as informants.

Research is, above all, a creative activity. Researchers have used essays and diaries written by those participating in the study, data available in the public record (e.g., census data or congressional voting records), other researchers' data gathered for a different original purpose, and a host of alternative methods for answering questions about people, the mass media, and the relationship between them.

This book discusses only a few of the most common ones, but these should not be considered a "closed set" of all the techniques from which you, as a researcher, might choose. What should dictate the choice of method, or the development of a new method, is the demand of the particular theoretical question being asked; what should limit this choice is only your imagination and the practical constraints of data gathering, not the preferences and priorities of textbooks about research.

Research requires caution and common sense. Call-in surveys (where listeners are invited to call a television station or, more typically, a radio station or a newspaper with their opinion on an issue), reader mail-in surveys (once common in magazines, now reemerging in a new form on electronic mail systems), or "man (or woman!) on the street" interviews are not good ways to assess public opinion. Today's new media—electronic mail on commercial videotex and the Internet system, for example—provide new opportunities for both research and expanded public dialogue, but "surveys" conducted by electronic mail can result in very biased samples indeed if only the computer literate have a chance to respond!

None of these should ever be represented or interpreted as reliable indicators of public sentiment—and describing them as "nonscientific" or "just for fun" surveys doesn't take care of this problem, as the average person who reads or hears about the results may not understand what's entailed. They certainly shouldn't form the basis of business decisions by media organizations or others. And many probably shouldn't even be conducted, since they undoubtedly contribute to the general survey "burn-out" that has made today's response rates for legitimate surveys by qualified organizations so low.

MASS COMMUNICATION APPLICATIONS

You've already learned of many common mass communication applications of sociological methods. New ones continue to intrigue us. Public opinion data can be used to relate shifts in public thinking to media influences of all kinds, although cause-and-effect relationships are difficult to establish because studies of this type cannot usually done under controlled laboratory conditions—and even if they were, they'd be open to the charge of being untrue to *natural* conditions!

Some important public opinion theory used in mass media studies is relatively independent of theories in anthropology, psychology, or sociology, even though it is tested using methods derived from those fields. For example, agenda-setting theory, media dependency theory, cultivation theory, and various selective influence theories—which you may have studied in a media theory class—have all been tested by social science methods to various degrees, often in studies that incorporate opinion data. Some have been tested and largely rejected, such as the "bandwagon" theory of political behavior, which suggested that voters would tend to support the candidate portrayed as most popular. But media theory continues to reflect the influence of the other social sciences (as well as the humanities) in a general way.

A practical application of survey methods is found in studies that ask questions about the media themselves. How credible are they? Which are preferred? Which are used most often? These can be local (see Box 4.6) as well as more global media.

Similarly, editors and producers may be interested in a well-designed survey of their readership or audiences that will help them do their jobs more effectively.

BOX 4.6
UNIVERSITY COMMUNICATION:
A STUDY EXAMPLE

A student research project conducted at Texas A&M University involved a survey of students, faculty, and university staff that asked about the adequacy of the information they received. The results were intended to help a university committee improve on-campus communication. Unexpectedly, respondents liked most forms of on-campus communication, including newspapers, newsletters, and electronic communication. But they seemed to suffer from information overload—the most common barrier to better information access was simply a lack of time to keep up with all the information already available. (You'll look at data from this survey later on in more detail as an example of quantitative analysis.)

New theories of public opinion and its formation are also being developed and tested using survey research at least in part, such as Noelle-Neumann's (1984) "spiral of silence" theory, which asserts that your perception of majority opinion will influence your willingness to voice your own—if you think you're in a minority! Exploring this and other emerging theories in detail would require a whole other book, but new theories are critically important to media researchers because they can open up new ways of thinking about the media's influence to guide tomorrow's research, whether these theories are unique to media studies or come from the "parent" social sciences.

IMPORTANT TERMS AND CONCEPTS

Collective behavior   **Representative sample**
Conflict theorist   **Respondent**
Content analysis   **Response bias**
Cultural studies   **Sampling frame**
Deviant   **Social construction**
Ethnomethodology   **Social institutions**
Focus group   **Social psychology**
Functionalist   **Symbolic interactionism**
Labeling theory   **Systematic random sampling**
Multistage sampling   **Unobtrusive observation**
Quota sampling   **Value system**

EXERCISES

1. Choosing a sampling frame and drawing a sample from it are not terrifically difficult, but they often present practical problems that are not apparent in textbook discussions! How would you sample the student population of your college or university? Be extremely specific in your answer! What biases would be present? Which do you think should concern you the most? (Hint: If you've found a completely unbiased way to do this, you've made public opinion research history!)

2. As a class exercise, using for your sampling frame the roster of membership in the class in which you are using this text, draw a random sample of 10% of the class members. Does the sample appear to be representative of the class in terms of gender? Ethnicity? Age? Draw another sample of 25%. Is this one better?

3. Sociologists understand data from a variety of theoretical perspectives. Next time you are at the library, find a journal specializing in sociological research (your instructor or a friendly librarian can help). Pick an article that looks interesting. Can you tell what the theoretical perspective of the author or authors might be? Are they conflict theorists, functionalists, or symbolic interactionists? What methods did they use? And *why?*

PART II

DIGGING UP ANSWERS
Asking Questions and Collecting Data

Methods without theories are like horsemen without heads. Where does this researcher think she's going?

5

Developing a Research Question

y now it should be clear that the choice of method depends a lot on the theoretical perspective of the researcher and the type of question being asked:

- Those who conceptualize the mass media as a causative factor in the acquisition of knowledge or the formation of individuals' attitudes, perceptions, behaviors, and opinions are more likely to use *experimental* methods.
- Those concerned with the media's important role in everyday social life and its meaning within a particular cultural context are more likely to choose *ethnographic* methods.
- Those interested in the interaction of media information with general public opinion will usually combine *public opinion* survey data with data from *content analysis*.
- Those interested in the mass media's role as a social institution will focus their attentions, whatever method they choose, on *institutional structure and function*—or on the media content that is itself an outcome of institutional processes.

None of these perspectives is "wrong" or "right." Mass media research has become an important academic field because of the pervasiveness of the media in modern culture and society. Important studies can be done on many different aspects of the media's social roles. Practical questions about the media are also posed by media managers, educators, advertisers and public relations practitioners, and policy specialists. Different questions call for different means to answer them.

73

Often, the choice of theoretical perspective and preferences about research questions, when not determined by particular practical issues, reflect the researcher's training—the ways that he or she has been taught to think about the media—more than anything else. As a student, your understanding what media research is all about is complicated by the fact that communication researchers have borrowed both theories and methods from fields with widely differing histories and purposes.

But this is also a great advantage. As a mass communication student, you have the opportunity to develop a better sense of the relationship between theory and method and a deeper understanding of why some methods are chosen over others than students who are taught only how to do experiments, or only how to do surveys, or only how to do qualitative studies.

DETERMINING THE PROJECT

Usually, researchers begin with a general interest in a particular problem. Perhaps it has been unsolved for years and there's a certain irresistible challenge in it. Perhaps new research on a related problem has suggested a new way to attack an old one. Perhaps a government agency or private philanthropic foundation has a special interest in solving a particular problem and makes funds available for research projects in that specific area. Or a manager in a media organization is faced with practical decisions that call for a better knowledge of the target population.

In any event, the first step in any research project (after identifying a general direction) is reviewing the academic literature on the issue.

REVIEW OF THE LITERATURE

A review of other researchers' work helps clarify conceptual issues, identify fruitful theories and methods, and rule out "dead ends" that appear to have been thoroughly investigated already, which is why it is first on the list of essential steps in the research process. Sometimes, even experienced researchers may be so excited about a project that they want to complete it first and look at the literature later. This is a mistake: It can lead to a lot of wasted work.

Absence of Published Research

If there seems to be no previously published research on a topic, there are two possible explanations:

■ The topic may be difficult or even impossible to investigate using empirical research methods. In other words, it may be a matter of opinion or policy rather than a researchable question.

■ The research question may be truly new—an exciting discovery! In this case, you must determine that other research on the question is not "hiding" somewhere in the library. Because media questions interest researchers in a broad range of academic disciplines (from political science to engineering), this search can be unusually challenging. A knowledgeable librarian can help enormously here.

It's also important, even if there seems to be no published research available on the specific subject of interest, to identify closely related or analogous studies. These still serve the purpose of helping to clarify theory and suggesting an appropriate method, providing a conceptual foundation on which to build.

Why Researchers Publish Their Work

The "publish or perish" imperative in modern universities is sometimes misunderstood and often the subject of debate. It's true that poor-quality research sometimes comes from professors who are less interested in the research question they're studying than in getting promoted. Also, the amount of time that professors devote to writing research articles can interfere with the time they have available for teaching. Yet the most productive researchers are sometimes the best teachers, with access to the very latest information.

The requirement that university professors publish their work in books and academic journals arose for important reasons and has a long history. It is through publishing—making public—research results that science is able to build upon previous results and others' thinking, thus producing an accumulated body of knowledge. This applies equally to social science. Results that have been made public can be tested again, using the same or perhaps a slightly different approach, by other researchers. Each generation of researchers is not required to "reinvent the wheel" but can create new work that rests upon—although it sometimes reverses—the old.

The Academic Journal

The term **academic journal** usually refers to a periodical that is devoted primarily (often exclusively) to the publication of research results in a particular area. Before being published, each article typically undergoes a **peer review.** The journal editor sends the article out for evaluation by other researchers (the author's "peers") who are specialists in the particular subject matter and methodologies (or general types of methods) used. To ensure an objective review, the title page of the manuscript is removed so that reviewers do not know whose work they are looking at. This is called a **blind review.**

The Review Process

Often, reviewers will not accept or reject an article outright but will ask for clarifications, revisions, additions, or even a total rewrite to bring the material up to an acceptable standard of quality.

Despite genuine concern with fairness, the review process does not necessarily select articles on the basis of quality alone but also reflects the particular interests and priorities of the journal and its editors. Some publications are more likely to print qualitative work, others primarily quantitative work. Also, each is more interested in studies on some types of research questions than others.

Like the commercial mass media that appeal to a broader audience, academic journals must consider their readership and strive to present research articles likely to be of keen interest to those readers. This situation can be frustrating to beginning researchers trying to figure out where to send their work—or to understand rejection of what they consider a good paper. Unlike the commercial print media, academic journals have no "query" process in which authors inquire of editors as to their interest in a particular piece. Because publication is intended to be the

---

BOX 5.1
COMMUNICATION (AND RELATED) JOURNALS

Among the most important journals in mass communication studies are *Critical Studies in Mass Communication, Journalism Quarterly, Journal of Broadcasting and Electronic Media, Journal of Communication,* and *Media, Culture, and Society.* More specialized journals exist in such areas as feminist scholarship, journalism history, and international and intercultural communication. Even highly specialized areas like science journalism scholarship have their own academic publications.

Important research of interest to mass communication scholars is also published in journals devoted to sociology, psychology, and, occasionally, anthropology, as well as those that cover the fields of rhetoric, technical writing, political science, English, education, public policy, law, and even engineering—in the case of new media technologies.

result of open competition, this could even be considered unfair. Instead, authors must make a judgment based on past issues or published guidelines, which are often quite brief, as to where to send their work.

The ultimate authority over acceptance or rejection rests primarily with the reviewers rather than the editors, and the process is supposed to be as open and fair as possible. Editors' preferences are reflected in decisions on borderline cases; editors often encourage researchers they see doing interesting work to consider submitting to their journals; and sometimes, special "theme" issues are put together with work from researchers studying closely related areas. Still, *all* articles intended for journal publication are subject to the peer-review process and cannot be published just because an editor likes them!

Articles in many of these journals are written in a very dense style that is quite difficult for the inexperienced researcher to penetrate; this is especially true for journals outside the communication fields. Because journal space is at a premium, researchers are trained to write as tersely as possible. Unfortunately, even experienced researchers have trouble writing tersely yet clearly, which may be one reason why research articles have a reputation for being dull and tedious. They are also written with highly educated readers in mind, often with a minimum of background explanation. Try to overlook the style and reach instead for the important information and ideas they offer.

Guides and Indexes

The Iowa Guide

A publication called the *Iowa Guide: Scholarly Journals in Mass Communication and Related Fields* (published annually by the School of Journalism and Mass Communication at the University of Iowa) lists each academic journal that publishes a significant proportion of articles on mass communication questions along with the special interests of each and the procedure for submitting manuscripts. Most of these are peer-reviewed journals; a few are not. This guide is an excellent starting point if you want to understand where the literature you're looking for is likely to be found.

Indexes

As noted earlier, the task of reviewing mass communication literature is especially complicated because of its interdisciplinary nature. The fields of sociology, psychology, anthropology, and so on have developed indexes that list articles from all the peer-reviewed journals in their respective areas; most of these indexes, available at any university library, are now also in electronic database form. These can be searched by subject terms, author, or title—a key advantage of conversion to electronic formats.

At present, the best central index to mass communication research is *Communication Abstracts,* not yet available in electronic form. This "hard copy" index is likely to be found in the library of any university with an academic communication or journalism program. Increasingly, general-purpose indexes to periodical literature may include articles from important communication journals—check with your librarian to be sure and always be cautious.

An important strategy for locating relevant material is to look at the citations in a few of what appear to be the most important recent articles on a subject, locate the references that appear to be the most crucial in each case, and continue this process using *their* bibliographies until the question seems to be exhausted.

When the Review Is Completed

How do you tell when a review of literature is complete? There's no magic trick, and there certainly is no accepted number of citations that's considered appropri-

---

BOX 5.2
ELECTRONIC INDEXES: USE WITH CARE

Modern electronic library indexes have greatly simplified the process of locating appropriate articles and books—but at some danger. Electronic indexes are often incomplete—especially for older material. It's also altogether too easy to turn out a bibliography consisting of 100 or even 1,000 references overnight. But what are you going to do with 100 references? You still need to be able to identify which ones are the most important. Those are the ones you should invest the time to read and digest and to mention in the introduction to your own research report.

No electronic shortcuts are available here, although a good reference librarian can help you choose appropriate keywords to narrow an electronic search appropriately. Usually, there won't be more than a dozen or two truly important, truly relevant pieces that should be included. But these can't be chosen by throwing darts at a list of 1,000.

ate. But there is an important rule of thumb: In doing a thorough review, you'll eventually find that you keep seeing citations to literature that's already been examined. The key academic sources on a specific question are usually reasonably limited in number and often refer to one another.

The Literature Review as Part of Your Research Report

Writing the review of literature as a section of your final research report is a major task in itself, but it can also be an exhilarating one. Putting the existing literature together in summary form, showing how it relates to a new problem (or a new interpretation of an old one), and identifying gaps and opportunities in the existing research record is both demanding and creative. It's a skill that's at the heart of scholarship, and it's every bit as difficult as running a complicated statistical analysis properly or designing the perfect survey. Looking at the literature reviews in a few of the important mass media research journals can give you

---

BOX 5.3
DIFFICULT-TO-RESEARCH PROBLEMS

Some extremely interesting problems are simply not researchable by the methods of social science. This includes legal and policy issues—*should* televisions be allowed in courtrooms, for example, or *should* children's programming be more aggressively regulated, or *should* newspapers reveal the identities of sexual assault victims?—on which social science can shed considerable light but which are ultimately matters of judgment.

It also includes a great many questions about long-term media influences. Does growing up with mass-mediated violence—or with Saturday morning cartoons or with MTV—affect children in negative ways that last into later life? How about positive ones? How has the availability of modern media and the use of political advertising changed the political systems of modern society? What will the eventual influence of the "information superhighway" on public access to information be? Will the advertising campaign you've designed for this product really work?

Questions like these are researchable only if reduced to smaller, more specific ones; decades of research, tempered by judgement, are required to actually answer them, and even then the answers will not be certain.

a good idea of the format (which varies considerably from journal to journal) and style typically used.

Guidelines for writing the review are presented in a later chapter; there are a number of different approaches to organizing this material. For now, the trick is to access, understand, and think about what others have done so as to clarify your own thinking about a problem that interests you. Here, experienced researchers often have an edge, as they try to "keep up" with new publications related to their research interests. As a student researcher, you must more often start from scratch. If you find a good, recent textbook in the specialized area of mass communication research that most interests you, the book's bibliography is often the best way to get started.

DEFINING A RESEARCHABLE PROBLEM

Once you've chosen a general area of interest—say, the role of soap operas in the lives of your fellow students, the effectiveness of interactive video presentations of health information, the change in a public figure's popularity following media disclosure of official impropriety, the interaction with sources characteristic of modern journalism, or readership patterns for a local weekly—and once the relevant literature has been identified, located, and digested, the next task is to turn this general interest into a **researchable problem.**

Usually, defining a researchable question means narrowing down a bigger problem and choosing only one aspect of it for immediate study. Are you interested in how the roles of women, as portrayed in popular media, have changed over time? Will you study this in print or on television? Better to focus on a thorough study of one particular publication (or at most a few) during a specific time period (or, say, a comparison of two time periods that you believe, on theoretical grounds, will provide an especially interesting contrast).

Logistical and Practical Hurdles

There are also logistical and practical questions to consider. If you're doing a magazine study, which magazines will you choose, and for what time period? Are copies even available to you? Not all libraries archive old publications, particularly popular ones, so your study is likely to be limited to what's available. Perhaps your grandmother has a collection of pre-1950s women's magazines stashed away in her attic! Your study will be limited by what she decided to read and keep. If you decide to study how broadcast content has changed, where will you get data for previous years? The Vanderbilt Television Archives, with indexes and abstracts in most major university libraries, contain some of this information, but it is largely limited to news and documentary presentations. Likewise, your study of entertainment programming may be limited to current cable reruns!

Newspaper Databases

Electronic indexes of leading national newspapers, such as the *New York Times* and the *Washington Post,* are now available, especially for recent years' issues. Older issues are indexed only for a few papers and only in "hard copy" form. Perhaps your local newspaper has its own index, but you may or may not be given access to it because of the costs involved—space for researchers to work and staff to help locate and then refile old material—and so the newspaper might not be comfortable saying "yes" to student researchers who promise to put everything back just as they found it.

The commercial "Newsbank" newspaper indexing service includes regional papers from across the country but only for fairly recent years. It is not necessarily a systematically drawn sample of either papers or articles because the index was not designed for social science researchers.

Some social scientific studies of the media have used articles available in the Lexis/Nexis database. But deciding whether the contents of any electronic resource are a reasonable sample for social science purposes can be difficult. For example, sometimes it's hard to determine exactly what criteria and procedures were involved in entering the material into the database in the first place, so it's hard to know how comprehensive the system's coverage might be.

Research on People

Research on people rather than media content has its own problems.

- Are you interested in what programs today's preschoolers most enjoy, or how familiar they are with current events? Getting access to a group of kids in a school or daycare center requires official permission and human subjects board approval. You may have to use kids in your own family instead—an obvious bias!

- Would you like to survey sports fans to find out what they think of today's media coverage of sports? Fine, but where will you find them?

- Do you want to know what newspapers or which television newscasters are believed the most? This raises complicated research design issues because you can't answer this kind of question with certainty just by asking people. They may say they believe only what the *New York Times* prints but pick up "facts" from the tabloids just as readily; they may not think they are more easily persuaded by men than by women, but an experimental design might prove differently.

■ Do you want to determine if journalists pay attention to press releases? Most will likely answer no; journalists don't want to appear to be relying on public relations practitioners for their stories and may actually believe they never do. But a participant observation study of journalistic practice, or a content analysis of the news that results, might well tell a different story.

Your Role as Researcher

Asking—and answering—a researchable question generally requires tremendous amounts of both caution and creativity, crystal-clear thinking, often a willingness to track down obscure resources, persuade others to participate in and support your study, and sometimes even raise money. Still, asking a simple, if small, question that can be researched on a student budget with readily available tools and resources *can be done*—and also can be a lot of fun!

A good trick is to write your research question on a scrap of paper or a 3 × 5 card and put it somewhere where it's constantly in view. One characteristic of a good researcher is a broad interest in all kinds of possible research questions and all sorts of available theories and methods. Of course, *finishing* a research project requires focus, too!

BOX 5.4
EXAMPLES OF ALTERNATIVE APPROACHES

The influence of docudramas on people's perception of social issues, for example, could be studied by participant observation, interviews, public opinion surveys combined with content analysis, or an experiment. You might begin with a well-defined hypothesis about how such an influence might work (a deductive approach) or decide to take a more exploratory, inductive approach—beginning from a particular theory, perhaps, but not with a specific hypothesis.

Say you are interested in evaluating the effectiveness of a health promotion campaign designed to encourage regular exercise among the members of a specified target group. You could do a survey of the problem or use a design involving a before-and-after survey (a type of field experiment). You could develop informational materials and ask focus groups to respond to them. Or you might do a laboratory experiment involving a systematic comparison of subjects to test a hypothesis about the influence of certain types of persuasive arguments.

CHOOSING AN APPROPRIATE METHOD

Thinking of the right method to answer a question and phrasing the question so that it's researchable are intertwined jobs. Part of what makes a question researchable is whether a method is available that will generate the required data. So, by the time the final research question has been chosen, the research method has probably already been determined—at least in part. But don't get the cart too far ahead of the horse here. Most research questions can, in fact, be answered by different methodological approaches (or, at least, each of several approaches would give a partial—if incomplete—answer).

As you've already learned, the theoretical assumptions derived from reliance on a particular research paradigm will have a big influence on both the questions seen as important and the methods seen as appropriate—as will the question of whether the research has been inspired primarily by scholarly curiosity or a pressing practical (applied research) need. The review of literature can—in fact, *should*—lead the researcher to reframe an earlier interest and perhaps to discard one theoretical framework for another that others have found more fruitful. So it's unrealistic to expect that the research steps described here always occur one after another in a nice, neat, linear sequence.

Research on People Versus Content

Nevertheless, some methods are better for some types of problems than others:

- *Experimental* methods are the first choice for problems about short-term influences that involve clearly defined causes and measurable effects.
- *Participant observation* is a better approach for understanding the role of a medium in normal social life.
- *Interviews* provide the best window on how people think and feel, allowing you to probe into areas that aren't immediately understood.
- *Surveys* are a more accurate measurement of public thought when the goal is to be able to generalize to a bigger population rather than take a snapshot of a particular cultural world.

You'll note that all of these methods provide information about people. Where media content itself is the object of study, content analysis—whether quantitative or more qualitative—is the logical choice.

Remember, you can't answer questions about media content by asking people— you answer them by looking at content. Conversely, you can't answer questions about how people think or feel or how they are influenced by looking only at content—you need to have data from people. In other words, there's much more to mass media research than asking survey questions. Yet that's what many beginning researchers think of when asked what research is.

IMPORTANT TERMS AND CONCEPTS

Academic journal
Blind review
Peer review
Researchable problem

EXERCISES

1. Choose any media-related question that you believe is researchable by social science methods. Write it in as few words as possible. What methods would you use to research it? *Why?* What problems will you encounter in gathering your data? Do you know how to begin to solve them? (Your instructor might allow class time for you to ask for your classmates' help here!)

2. Say you've carried out the research chosen above. Write a short paragraph summarizing the project you had in mind. Where would you publish a full report on this project? What peer-reviewed academic journal would be most likely to accept it? What objections do you think the editors and reviewers would be most likely to raise? Use the *Iowa Guide* to identify a potential journal, and then take a look at a few issues to see how the articles are like—and unlike—the one you've proposed.

Measuring the important things about media content isn't easy.

6

Counting
A Quantitative Methods Primer

Whether collected by means of a survey, experiment, or content analysis, quantitative data must be as reliable and valid as possible.

Reliability means that repeating the same procedure would be highly likely to generate nearly the same result. If a survey question is so ambiguous that answers to it might be different at different times, or if an experimental effect can't be measured with some degree of accuracy, or if content analysis uses categories that mean entirely different things to different people, the results lack reliability. Sometimes, reliability is explained by analogy to a simpler measurement instrument—a ruler. Using an unreliable measure is like using a ruler that stretches or shrinks or changes shape when you're not looking.

Validity refers to whether you are measuring the things you think you're measuring—those that interest you on a theoretical level. If you're interested in violence in children's television but measure only the number of screams on the soundtrack, your measurement is invalid. If you're interested in attitudes toward higher education but actually measure only whether people like a particular university program, your measurement is invalid. This is like trying to measure length by using a scale or determining inches by using a ruler calibrated in centimeters.

Reliability and validity are extremely important measurement concepts for all quantitative studies; they have many forms and variations. Although different experts emphasize slightly different aspects of these concepts, all agree that they are critical to meaningful measurement. The more abstract a concept, the more difficult it is to achieve a reliable and valid measure. Social psychologists interested in attitudinal research or other complex quantitative studies often spend large proportions of their time and efforts on just this issue.

The goal of all quantitative research is to measure something (whether opinions, knowledge or beliefs, attitudes, or media content) as precisely as possible. In this chapter, you'll learn some of the tricks of the trade that will help you get started with writing survey questions, designing experiments, and doing content analysis. Numerous books have been written on each of these subjects; this chapter provides only the basics—all you need to successfully design a meaningful small-scale research project, along with common sense and careful planning.

WRITING SURVEY QUESTIONS

Perhaps because everyone's familiar with answering survey questions, survey methodology seems easy and straightforward. Yet writing good survey questions is extraordinarily difficult. Many factors influence the results of a **survey.** One of the most important is having a clear idea of what the survey form, or **instrument,** is intended to uncover. Say your underlying idea is to assess people's opinions on why today's talk shows seem so popular. What, exactly, are you going to ask them? This is not as simple as it seems!

Professional survey research organizations often ask questions that are not directly related to one another in the same survey. Why? Because the size and complexity of surveys these groups conduct make them very expensive, and so the same project must often serve multiple research needs to make ends meet. Under other circumstances, it's much wiser to organize survey questions around a clearly defined research topic and to write (and edit and then rewrite!) the questions with as much care as possible.

Question Order and Wording

Question *order* and exact question *wording* have important influences on how people respond.

Order

One question can suggest a context for interpreting the next in a pattern that is quite leading, even though the researcher may not intend it to be. For example, a survey on foreign policy opinion might ask a question like this: "Do you believe that world trade has an important influence on the domestic economy?" If the next question asks whether international trade policy is an important national issue, the answers might be quite different than if the question order here was reversed. Respondents will have been introduced to the idea that international trade might have something to do with the local economy. Perhaps they'd never thought of this before or wouldn't otherwise have thought about this argument in answering the second question.

Wording

Very small differences in wording that a reasonable person might not expect to make a difference certainly *can*. Consider this example: Asking people whether they are "pro-choice" with respect to abortion decisions might produce results that are quite different from asking them whether they are "in favor of" abortions. No wonder abortion opinion surveys produce such contradictory results! But the differences in wording don't have to be this great. Any small variation can produce an unexpectedly large effect. Also, your own biases can creep in very easily, producing questions almost certain to generate predictable answers without your being aware of your influence on the results.

Furthermore, questions must be absolutely unambiguous, which is almost impossible. Multiple interpretations are likely for even the most carefully worded question. People with different political or religious beliefs and those from diverse ethnic or cultural backgrounds may interpret the same words differently.

Pretesting. The careful researcher can at least be certain that the questions used are as simple as possible and have been read and checked by a broad range of people before embarking on the survey itself. This is the purpose of what's called a **pretest.** Here, a group of people, as much like the potential survey respondents as possible, are asked to read the proposed questions critically and identify any that are unclear, ambiguous, or overly complex.

Watch out for "loaded" questions: "Are you in favor of increased federal regulation of broadcasting, or would you rather see children's television deteriorate even further?" Don't ask them. And don't ask "double" ones: "Are you in favor of increased federal regulation of broadcasting, *including* increased congressional involvement in PBS?"

Awareness of cultural/social diversity. Occasionally, researchers overlook the cultural and social diversity characteristic of most modern nations. Asking questions that assume that all respondents are part of the college-educated middle class is an example; another is surveying respondents in English when it is not their native language (also see Box 6.1).

Response Formats

Forced-Choice Questions

A question that requires the respondent to select an answer from those provided by the researcher is called a **forced-choice question.** Answers should be in the form of numerical rating scales (say, from 1 for "strongly disagree" to 5 for "strongly agree") or simpler verbal categories (yes, no, undecided) may be used. Which is better?

Generally speaking, rating scales produce more precise results and more can be done with them statistically, as you'll see later in this book. The argument against their use is that they are less meaningful for some respondents and more difficult and time-consuming to convey in a telephone survey. Where a simple, straightforward assessment of public opinion is the goal, yes-or-no questions are preferable, especially for a phone survey. Scales may be better when data are being collected for a more complex analysis of, say, what factors might be influencing this opinion.

Some survey questions give respondents a choice of answers—not just "agree" or "disagree." For example, the respondent could be asked to choose from among a list of adjectives which ones most closely describe an advertised product, or to choose among a list of reasons or issues or feelings. Lists of choices should always

---

BOX 6.1
TWO PROBLEMATIC STUDIES

One recent survey of economically marginal migrant farm workers in south Texas asked them how often they used hot tubs; in addition, the questions were worded in English and only translated on-the-spot into Spanish for this largely Hispanic group.

Another study asked respondents whether newly available genetic information would be likely to be used in a way that discriminates against minorities—without explaining what kind of new science was involved.

Both of these studies were done by professional researchers.

be as exhaustive as possible of all of the answers that might be offered, even though "other" is also generally included as a choice.

Open-Ended Questions

A question that has no predetermined choice of answers is called an **open-ended question.** Respondents provide comments and opinions on questions of this type, which are asked when the researcher can't easily (or doesn't want to) "prejudge" what respondents' possible answers will be. These are a form of qualitative research, and the data should be handled in the same way as other qualitative data are handled, which you'll learn about in more detail a bit later on. However, because surveys are usually administered to a considerable number of people (indeed, one of the main advantages of surveys is that they *can* be given to large numbers of respondents relatively quickly and easily), it's especially important to be able to categorize and count answers to open-ended questions in some systematic way. (It's unethical to invite people to go to the trouble to offer comments and then just ignore them in analyzing the results!)

Demographic Questions

Questions on **demographics** are often saved to the end of the survey because respondents might resent questions about personal matters such as their ethnicity or income or religious beliefs. This resentment may be less after the interviewer and respondent have had a short history of interaction in the process of the interview. Even for mail surveys, demographic questions put at the end of the survey form and described as being necessary "to make sure we have reached people from all walks of life" or some similar phrase are probably less likely to "turn off" someone who has just invested time in completing the rest of the questionnaire than someone who is still deciding whether it should go in the trash.

What demographic questions should be asked? Age and income are standard; choosing among categories for either of these may be less threatening than having to fill in a blank. Include "under $1,000" as an income choice so that most lower-income respondents won't have to choose the bottom category. Gender and ethnicity are also important; today, these terms are generally preferred to "sex" (which is a physical rather than a social characteristic) or "race" (which does not have much of an agreed-on meaning at all).

Ethnic categories are problematic. Some people in the United States who are of African descent prefer to think of themselves as "African Americans," others as "black." People with Spanish-speaking family backgrounds might not like having to choose between calling themselves "white" or "Hispanic"—they may consider themselves both. Changing "white" or "Caucasian" to "Anglo" might solve this problem but confuse—or even offend—some non-Hispanics of European descent. Some Native Americans have returned to preferring being called "Indian," once considered offensive.

The easiest solution may be to leave ethnicity as an open-ended category and let respondents suggest how they should be described. Presently, the terms "African American," "Hispanic," "Anglo," and "Native American" seem to be generally accepted. However, in some areas, especially those with only small proportions of Hispanic residents, the term "Anglo" might be poorly understood.

For some surveys, factors such as political or religious affiliation, marital status, occupation, where a respondent was raised, and so on may also be important. It's certainly not necessary to always ask everything you can think of about your respondents. Ask yourself what's minimally necessary to assure that your sample is reasonably representative of the population of interest—usually, age, gender, ethnicity, and perhaps income are sufficient. Add only those questions that are important in terms of your particular research question.

Don't ask *any* question for "no particular reason"—that's unfair to the respondents who have volunteered to spend time helping you! Remember also that personal questions (e.g., about sexual behavior or even knowledge of issues related to sexuality) may offend some respondents, whereas others (e.g., about media preferences or family interaction patterns) may be difficult for respondents to give candid answers to on the basis of their own memories or perceptions.

Response Rate

Survey Appearances Count

Experienced survey researchers have a lot of tricks to increase response rates. Providing mail-survey respondents with stamp-affixed return envelopes rather than business reply envelopes may increase response rates because people are believed to be less likely to throw a stamped envelope away. Sometimes, a token payment is added as an incentive. Respondents might be offered a chance to be included in a free drawing—but this could bias the sample in unknown ways.

Coding return envelopes so that respondents who have not answered can be sent reminder letters has been a common practice for some, but it is less likely to be considered ethical today because it allows the researcher to "match up" responses with the identity of the respondent. Instead, a follow-up letter can be sent to all of the original sample with instructions to ignore it if the survey has already been returned.

A carefully designed cover letter and a questionnaire that looks professional help response rate a lot. The cover letter should promise anonymity to the respondent, briefly describe the purpose of the survey, and give a name, address, and phone number where the researcher can be reached for more information or a copy of the survey results—and, of course, thank people in advance for cooperating. Some respondents *will* check with the university or company described as sponsoring the project to be sure the survey is legitimate. Instructions for those helping with a phone survey should include a written-out introduction that gives all of this same information (except, perhaps, the address and phone number, which could be given on request). This way each respondent is approached in exactly the same way. The answers given should be written verbatim on a standard form or entered directly into a computer program designed for this.

Survey Timing

Timing of a survey is very important. Should questions be asked at a certain time of day? A lot of people resent survey workers who call in the evening when the average person is relaxing after dinner. Yet it's almost the only choice, as calls made during the day will reach a disproportionate number of housewives, retirees, night workers, and so on—a very biased sample!

Perhaps even more important, current news events can have a dramatic effect on responses to survey questions, even though their long-term effect on public attitudes is likely to be weaker. Data on public opinion about nuclear power gathered right after the Chernobyl or Three Mile Island disasters, for example, can't be represented as typical.

Sharing Results

Sharing survey data with other researchers in an open way (without revealing the identity, of course, of individual respondents) has been consistent with the ethical obligation in scientific research to share information and results. Science, as you've learned, builds on this kind of open sharing; reanalysis of old survey data using new questions and theoretical insights can yield important new conclusions. But remember, respondents have the right to refuse to participate in any survey—especially if its purpose doesn't appeal to them. This raises a new ethical problem when old survey data are reused for a new purpose that is radically different from the old one.

DESIGNING EXPERIMENTS

The simplest kind of experiment involves two groups: treatment and control. The treatment group is exposed to some experience, whereas the control group is not.

The groups should be as similar as possible, whether this is achieved by random (or systematic random) assignment of subjects to groups or by measuring some particularly important variables (e.g., intelligence, age, computer familiarity, or whatever might be especially critical for a particular research purpose) and balancing the groups along this dimension.

Design Types

Posttest

Following treatment, some measurement is made of the two groups (e.g., what they know or what their attitudes are toward something), and a comparison is made of the scores or measurements. Differences between the groups can reasonably be attributed to differences in their experience during the course of the experiment—the treatment variable. This is called a **posttest**-only control group design.

Sometimes, there's more than one treatment variable. For example, say you want to compare newscasts, newspapers, and interactive video as alternative media for conveying important health information and then measure your subjects' knowledge. Here there are three different treatment conditions. You would also want a control group. Varying (say) the vocabulary used or the topic considered would make things more complex yet. This is called a **multifactorial** design and

---

BOX 6.2
USE OF TREATMENT AND CONTROL
GROUPS: AN EXAMPLE

Say you want to find out if a newscast is effective as a means of conveying important health information, such as warning signs of cancer. The treatment group would watch the newscast; the control group would not. However, whatever the control group experiences in the course of the experiment should be as much as possible like what the treatment group experiences. For example, if the treatment group watches a newscast that includes a story on signs of cancer, the control group might watch some other kind of informational broadcast or perhaps a newscast that does *not* include the story the researcher is interested in assessing.

involves more subjects and a more complex statistical analysis of the results, but the principle is the same.

Pretest/Posttest

But what if, despite great care on your part to achieve equivalence among the various treatment groups, more subjects who are already health conscious (and knowledgable) end up in one of the groups (say, the newscast group)? Then the results from that group would make it appear that one treatment (watching a newscast) is more effective than the others, even though this may or may not be the case in reality.

The solution here is to pretest subjects on the important variable (in this case, knowledge of cancer signs). This serves as a check against the possibility that the groups are extraordinarily unbalanced. Also, because the scores of several different groups on such a measure will never come out exactly the same, the procedure provides a "baseline" measurement for each group. The important test of the treatment's effectiveness (that is, of the effects of watching the newscast on knowledge of cancer signs) is not based on the amount of knowledge in each of the groups but on any changes between the "before" and "after" amount of knowledge—the apparent *gain* in knowledge. This is called, simply enough, a **pretest-posttest** design. If a control group is included, it's called a pretest-posttest control group design.

However, giving subjects a test gives them a chance to practice; they might do better on the test the second time around even if they've learned nothing new in the meantime! It also focuses their attention on the subject of the experiment (cancer warning signs), so they could become especially sensitive to information presented to them on this subject shortly thereafter, learning more than they otherwise would. Here there are a variety of solutions. The pretest might include questions on a wide range of subjects so that the key questions about the subject of the experiment (questions about cancer signs) are "buried" in a host of others. Use of a control group would help you assess the amount of change between the first administration of a test and the second regardless of treatment exposure.

Solomon Four-Group Design

An even more satisfactory solution is to pretest only *some* of the subjects in each treatment or control group, so that their posttest scores can be compared to those of subjects who *weren't* pretested. The result is four groups: one treatment group that is pretested, one that isn't, one control group that is pretested, and one that isn't. This is called a **Solomon four-group design:**

	Pretest and Posttest	*Posttest Only*
Treatment	Group 1	Group 2
Control	Group 3	Group 4

You can then make comparisons between Groups 3 and 4 to determine the effects of the pretest on the posttest, between Groups 1 and 3 to establish the equivalency of the groups at the beginning of the experiment, and between Groups 3 and 4 versus 1 and 2 to determine the actual effects of the treatment variable itself. Of course, if other groups are added, the time and money required to conduct the experiment increases. The likelihood of pretest effects must be weighed against the costs of a more complex design. If, for some reason, a control group is not used, you would simply pretest only half the subjects. For example, a test of the effectiveness of a classroom presentation in changing the attitudes of university students in a large lecture class might use this kind of approach.

Applying Designs

As a beginning researcher, you can do most of your work with these simple designs (posttest only, pretest-posttest, or Solomon four-group). Advanced methods texts will suggest many more that can be very useful under special circumstances. Remember that the same principles apply to quasi-experimental designs, such as research carried out under natural ("field") conditions but conceptually designed as though it were laboratory research. For example, to test the effects on office worker productivity of piping in news or music during the workday, you would want to use a real office setting, not a laboratory substitute, but controlling the experiment and measuring productivity would be done as much as possible as though a laboratory design were used.

Causal analysis using survey data is always a risky business—again, there are too many uncontrolled variables. Carefully constructed hypotheses and a well-supported theoretical understanding of the problem help. But many media effects studies have attempted to use survey methods to relate television viewing to either attitudes or behaviors, in particular to either violent or criminal behavior or to violence-related beliefs or attitudes. A common criticism of these is that people with violent tendencies might watch more violent television than those who don't; it doesn't prove that television changed them! (Nor does this criticism imply that violence in the media is not a source of concern—only that its impact is hard to measure by the tools of social science.)

As a beginning researcher, you should consider using surveys primarily as descriptive tools that can be helpful in exploring relationships and perhaps in identifying hypotheses inductively. Hypothesis testing should be done with a true experiment (or something as much like one as possible).

Measuring Variables

Up to this point little has been said in this book about actually measuring experimental variables; you'll learn more about this in later chapters. Some variables are straightforward. Worker productivity in the above example can be measured in terms of the number of pages written or typed, forms completed or filed, calls answered, or whatever the day-to-day activities of that particular office are. Knowledge tests are likewise relatively simple to construct, although of course the items must be chosen and the questions written with the same care given to survey questions. Other variables, such as attitudes or beliefs or reasons, that may be of great theoretical interest may be much more difficult to conceptualize and to assess or measure. Some demographic data should also be collected on experimental subjects, just as for survey respondents.

BOX 6.3
PROBLEMS WITH CONTROL

Sometimes survey research is treated as though a controlled experiment were being conducted. For example, you might conduct a survey to determine public opinion on the importance of street crime before and after a major television documentary on this subject. This is a form of quasi-experiment; it's tricky because, of course, respondents will have been subject to many other influences between the two surveys—not just the television presentation. In other words, this type of experiment is not well controlled.

Alternatively, you might assume that some variables within a single survey are important influences on others. You might survey all graduates of a mass communications program and determine that job satisfaction is highest among those working in a certain field—say, the magazine industry. It's tempting to conclude that working conditions in that industry are responsible. But what if the personalities of those who choose this particular occupation are simply different in the first place? Perhaps some other factor altogether is responsible. You can hardly assign some graduates to work for magazines and others to other jobs on a random basis to be sure.

Importance of Ethics

Experimental research can involve some of the most serious ethical questions of any type of research. Deception, however slight, or exposing subjects to physical or psychological harm or stress, however short-lived, are simply not appropriate unless there's a clear justification in terms of gaining important information that cannot be obtained in any other way. *Remember, all research involving people, but especially all experiments, conducted as part of the activities of a college or university requires approval through the special committee or board charged with making these judgments.*

CONTENT ANALYSIS

Quantitative content analysis is an important tool for studying what's actually in the media. It borrows much from survey research. Content analysis takes many forms; you must begin with a well-defined research problem that determines the questions and categories of interest. For example, if the research question asks how much front-page space in major national newspapers is typically devoted to coverage of political events, you probably need a ruler to check column inches. On the other hand, if the research question asks what types of sources are most commonly quoted in political stories, you would need to read each story included in the study and classify sources according to some predetermined list of categories (e.g., government employees, elected officials, political party spokespersons, and ordinary citizens).

BOX 6.4
EXAMPLES OF CONTENT ANALYSIS

Say you are interested in the "themes" typically present in television news coverage of international conflicts. What's a "theme"—and what kind of list of possible themes should be used in the analysis? How do you recognize an instance of a particular theme, or decide when one ends and another begins? Such issues as the level of violence in media content or the amount of educational material are equally problematic. What "counts" as either of these? Elaborate instructions must be constructed for research of this type spelling out how these decisions are to be made.

Some questions that you might try to answer through content analysis are subtle and complex, and the resultant research task is demanding (see Box 6.4). Studies using complex content analytic schemes are often descriptive and inductive rather than hypothesis testing, but a meaningful quantitative study must still use some kind of consistent categories.

Sampling

The purpose of sampling in content analytic studies is the same as for surveys and experiments. But truly random sampling of the stream of media content is rarely accomplished. First, it's hard to decide what to include in the population:

- Should a study of children's television include all options available on cable, or only popular or network programming?
- Should a study of newspaper agendas involve all stories anywhere in the paper, or only those appearing in the first section, or the front page? What papers should be included?
- Should a study of the proportion of broadcast news that centers on environmental issues include local as well as national news shows? What about documentaries, or all-news cable stations, or public broadcasting?

Then there's the logistics of sampling itself. You've already read that historical collections of many media materials are rare. As a practical matter, truly random sampling of the stream of media material is also quite rare. Most content studies are guided by an interest in a particular type of programming and limited by practical considerations.

Coding

In content analysis, as well as for the analysis of responses to open-ended survey data, various measures of **intercoder reliability** are used to assure that everyone involved in the research (everyone, that is, who is **coding** data by assigning it to categories with numerical labels) understands the categories in the same way. Intercoder reliability is measured by having different researchers code the same body of data. In its simplest form, it is the percentage of the time that two or more researchers agree on the appropriate classification or classifications to be used. More complex indexes are available in most advanced methods texts.

If there is only one person involved in coding the data, intercoder reliability is not a factor. But other measurement considerations still apply, just as they do for survey and experimental data. Are the content categories reliable, or is assignment too arbitrary? Are they valid assessments of the abtract concepts that the researcher is really interested in (whether "violence" or "educational content" or "political themes")?

Using a Codebook

Regardless of how the data have been collected, what do you do with it next? The great advantage of doing a quantitative study is that your results will be easily coded (or converted into simple numerical form) for analysis. Coding is as simple as assigning a number to every answer, even those in the form of verbal responses. "Yes" answers can be coded 1 and "no" answers coded 2, for example. To keep track of what all the numbers means, researchers create a *codebook* that simply describes the meaning assigned to each numerical value for a survey, experiment, or content analytic study. (It's in the codebook that the researcher records exactly how "educational content" or "political themes" were identified.)

Using a Computer Program

Most numerical data today are analyzed quickly and easily by computer. SPSS® (Statistical Package for the Social Sciences) is probably the best-known computer software for this purpose in mass communication studies. This software is available for use on both personal computers and big university mainframes. It was used for the examples presented in the remainder of this book.

IMPORTANT TERMS AND CONCEPTS

Coding	**Pretest**
Demographics	**Pretest-posttest**
Forced-choice question	**Posttest**
Instrument	**Reliability**
Intercoder reliability	**Solomon four-group design**
Multifactorial	**Survey**
Open-ended question	**Validity**

EXERCISES

1. Design three or four survey questions within a specific research topic. Pretest them on your fellow research students. Are they simple and unambiguous? Can they be made any simpler? Do they all have something to do with the research question? Be critical of one another's work; first-draft survey questions *almost always* need revision!

2. As a group, design a simple test with five or six questions that will assess whether someone has read the front page of your local paper (or student paper) for the previous day. Add a question at the end asking whether that edition of the paper was actually read and administer it to the members of your class. Did those who'd read the paper actually score higher? Is there more than one possible explanation of your results?

3. Measure the proportion of content devoted to various kinds of news in your best-known local paper and in a popular local television newscast. What kinds of sampling and measurement problems does this present? Are the two media about the same in content, or are they different? Can you provide possible explanations for any differences?

Leading an effective focus group discussion requires skillful orchestration.

7

Interpreting
Introducing Qualitative Methods *Meaning*

ll qualitative research in some ways follows the model established by participant observation because the goal in each case is access to the "insider" perspective characteristic of members of a culture (or subculture). What does it mean to be a participant observer? Unlike unobtrusive observation, where the researcher strives to be either invisible or as much as possible like a quiet mouse in the corner, the key to *participant* observation is to become a "regular" member of the group under study. The researcher's own feelings, reactions and mistakes provide important data.

VALUE OF PARTICIPANT OBSERVATION

Participant observation is a good way to study the day-to-day operations of media organizations; if you are working as an intern in a communication organization or expect to, you can use this method to do a meaningful research project at the same time. What important work roles are there, and how do these seem to be thought of? How are decisions actually made in the organization? How do members talk about their work? Who is really in charge, and how is their influence communicated?

Studying a single organization in depth like this is one kind of **case study.** Although its results aren't perfectly generalizable to other, similar organizations, the data obtained are still valuable. Case studies might also be done of a particular event or series of events, such as how toxic waste from a local factory became an issue on the evening news; such studies usually involve a combination of interview and content analytic data rather than participant observation.

Participant observation is also a good way to study the social meaning of the mass media. Sports fans seem to agree that watching a game "live" on television (that is, at the time it is actually being played in real life) adds something to the experience; for many, watching it with a group of fellow fans is also important. (In the United States, after-dinner football is often a standard component of holiday celebrations, making it one aspect of a socially significant ritual.) The group character of these experiences is important. Similarly, college students may watch soap operas or movie thrillers as a group. What's going on here? What's different about watching with a group as opposed to watching alone? What do group members seem to get out of the experience? How do they talk about what they're watching, and how does their interaction with one another seem to be influenced by the "presence" of a mass medium?

Steps to Take in Observing

All right, so here you are, either an honorary or actual member of a social group you've decided it would be important or interesting to study. You've obtained permission from them to use them for your research. There's a date and time for the event, or a schedule of work, and it's agreed you'll be there. What next?

You want the group being studied to forget that you're there as a researcher to the extent possible, just as you would want someone you're interviewing to forget about a tape recorder running in the same room once you have their permission to tape the conversation. So your first objective is to blend in. Relax and try to be as natural a group member as possible. This probably means that you won't be able to take notes, an activity guaranteed to make your informants self-conscious in their actions! So plan on remembering as much as possible and save your note-taking for later on.

Notes

If you're doing a study that lasts over a period of days, weeks, or months—rather than studying a one-time event—be scrupulous about recording your observations at the end of each day, as soon as possible after you've left the group. Otherwise, it will be remarkably difficult to reconstruct what you learned and observed and how you reacted on the first day after several days have passed.

What, exactly, do you take notes *about?* Observe who's present, what they do, and what they say. Write down as much detail as possible; don't do too much screening or filtering of what seems important and what doesn't. Make notes about points at which things seemed confusing, surprising, interesting, or novel to you as an outsider—even if you don't especially understand *why* something strikes you as significant at this stage. Notes about how people dress, what they might eat or drink, when they come and go might also be important. What seems to be important about what they are doing, from your respondents' points of view? How do you know? Above all, don't overlook the apparently obvious.

BOX 7.1
THE EYE OF THE OBSERVER: EXAMPLES

Say your college roommates watch the same videotaped soap opera together every day at 6 p.m. They may be using this experience to cement their friendships with one another and to "switch gears" after a day of classes and studying, signifying a transition from work to play and smoothing over any friction in their relationships. They may also use the opportunity to talk over significant issues that arise on the show in a light-hearted way. They're unlikely to *say* these things in so many words, but their interaction, verbal and nonverbal, can give you a lot of clues. That's why participant observation is an improvement over just doing interviews in terms of understanding the social importance of events. The results of such a study will uncover and document an important aspect of modern social behavior, even though in retrospect you might be tempted to think nothing new was learned. How is this group strengthened by its use of entertainment television programming? How are its social norms solidified by talk about television?

Or say you're doing participant observation of a work group within a computer firm that writes and publishes technical instructions for software. You're likely to discover a clear division of labor between editors, writers, graphic artists, and typesetters—and important status differences between them. There may be conflicts here. Does the editor or the writer make final decisions? Who has control over how the final product looks? What's the role of the computer programmers who actually created the software in the writing-editing end of the business? Do they have more authority than the publishing group? How is it exercised? How do group members think about their potential audiences, or markets? How are they described?

Computer firms that produce mass-market communications products are a relatively recent institution and may seem especially appealing for a participant observation study, but more traditional media institutions can yield new insights, too, especially as business conditions change over time. For example, how do today's community newspapers actually function? How much news seems written locally, and how much is repackaged from wire reports? What are the work roles, and how are editorial decisions made? What seems to be important to the employees? You may think that the answers to these questions were found in research done decades ago. But in recent years community newspapers in many areas have become shorter on resources; many have been purchased by larger companies that own whole chains of small papers. Indeed, the whole concept of a "local community" is undergoing transition in today's mobile society. How have community newspapers changed as a result of these trends? Or, alternatively, how do local television stations operate today, now that cable service is so common? The answers obtained 20 or 30 years or more ago aren't adequate anymore. So you have many opportunities to discover and describe something truly new.

Choice of Setting

Begin, as always, with a clearly defined research problem—and, for participant observation, a carefully chosen setting. If you're trying to locate a setting for this type of study, be alert to groups and organizations where you already have an "inside track" that will make it easier for you to get permission to do your study and easier for you to be accepted as a natural (or nearly natural!) member. Perhaps a family member works in an organization that interests you, or a friend has mentioned that she always watches a certain show with her roommate. Do you have a younger brother or sister who plays videogames? Odds are they do this as part of a group! Perhaps that same younger member of your family is in a school that makes use of special video material in the classroom. Can you get permission to sit in and observe a class? We live in a media-saturated society; opportunities to study the relationship between media and everyday life are everywhere around us.

INTERVIEWS

Some aspects of the social world of someone not exactly like ourselves, and some aspects of what it means to be a member of a certain group, are simply not visible to us as observers, however. When the goal is to understand the "insider's" perspective, a quantitative design is just not the way to go either. You can't write effective questions for a survey without a better understanding of the worldview of those you want to study, for example, nor can you can very well do an experiment to find out how the invention of personal computers has, say, changed the lives of freelance writers! You need a holistic, inductive approach—but you're not confident you can observe everything that's of interest. Or perhaps your research questions concern individual use of media rather than group use or the structure of media organizations. You can't be a participant observer in a group of one! Either as a supplement to participant observation or as the primary method for a particular study, use of the "depth" (or semistructured) interview is an equally important qualitative approach.

Flexibility: The Benefit of Depth Interviews

The key thing that distinguishes the depth interview from survey research is the researcher's flexibility to explore interesting things that come up. (This is the direct opposite of the goal of survey questions, which is to ask each respondent exactly

---

BOX 7.2
HOW MANY INTERVIEWS ARE ENOUGH?

Most studies using qualitative interviews include interviews from at least a handful of people. Sometimes, hundreds might be interviewed for a particular purpose, such as finding out about the typical paths that communication careers might take or the reasons why people think they listen to talk shows. A student study done with just a few interviews can still be meaningful; it just shouldn't be considered the "final answer."

Sometimes, it's necessary or important to interview only a few people, as when a case study of a particular small, individual media organization is being conducted and the number of people with important roles in the organization is quite limited. You can interview just one individual in some cases and still come away with important information from a social scientific point of view, especially when the research goal is to understand the world from another's vantage point. Just one interview with a homeless former mental patient, for example, would give you a lot of rich information about what this way of life—very different from, say, that of the average person reading this book—involves. Of course, it would be better to have interviews with half a dozen or more, even though the sampling considerations characteristic of quantitative studies are not usually applied to qualitative interviews.

the same thing so that the results are reliable and valid measures.) By definition, the interviewer here does not know enough about the social world of the informants to make up a definitive list of what to ask. Of course, a clearly defined research problem is still important. Qualitative interviews begin with something called an **interview schedule** (or interview guide) that lists the most important topics to be covered—perhaps with tentative question wording suggested.

Let the research question guide the construction of the interview guide. (Good feature reporters often employ a similar interview style to that used in the social scientific depth interview.) If depth interviews are being used as part of a larger study based on participant observation, results from the observation (unanswered questions or things that need to be clarified) will, of course, contribute to the list.

Pay particular attention to *specialized terminology,* whether professional vocabulary, slang words or phrases, or special uses of everyday language. Ask for definitions or clarification: "What do you mean by that?" "Why is that important?" "What's the difference between a 'good guy' and a 'bad guy'?"

Tailor your language to the respondent. If you're interviewing a professional, it helps to sound as professional as possible, but if you're interviewing a child, use simple language.

Try to be sensitive to the same kinds of differences of perspective you'd be looking for as a participant observer. When an answer puzzles you, ask about it. Chances are your informant's response makes sense from their point of view—here's a chance to understand why! Be patient and don't be satisfied with simple answers. Be ready to shift the line of questioning if the answers you're receiving don't seem to be helping, but don't give up on trying to understand the informant's perspective.

Plan on spending an hour or more on each interview (a half-hour is about the minimum). Remember, when you express a sincere interest in how people think or what's important to them, and when you've been successful in making them relax and trust you a little bit, most are more than happy to talk.

Try very hard to avoid making assumptions about how your informant looks at things; keep your questions as neutral as possible—for example, "Can you tell me a little bit more about that? It sounds interesting, but I don't quite understand it." It can help, however, both to relax your interviewee and to verify that you are understanding correctly to repeat the answers you receive in different words: ("So you are saying that the managing editor doesn't make that kind of decision?") Let your informants know you are listening and care about what they have to say; maintain eye contact and offer them some neutral feedback ("I see" or "All right") from time to time.

Explain that you are conducting the interview as a student of social science research methods. Otherwise, if your interviewee knows that you are a journalism or mass communications student, your persistent questions about some points might violate your informant's expectations about how journalists are supposed to act—and perhaps even create some suspicion.

As with journalistic interviews, using a tape recorder has advantages and disadvantages. Most people who agree to be interviewed will probably agree to be taped, and they'll soon forget that the recorder is running! Then you don't have to be distracted by the necessity of getting everything down in your notes and can concentrate on listening and understanding. But it's still helpful to take at least some notes, especially on points that you want to follow up on later in the interview. Some informants might be less candid when they know they're being recorded; others will appreciate your interest in having an accurate record of their comments. Since depth interviews in social science are usually not designed to investigate any kind of wrongdoing or probe in sensitive political, ethical, or legal areas, tape recording is unlikely to upset anyone and is usually preferred.

FOCUS GROUPS

Focus groups can actually be designed in many ways. As you'll recall, the advantage of a **focus group** over an individual depth interview is that the respondents or informants involved (let's just call them focus group participants here) react to one another, as well as to the interviewer. In a one-on-one interview situation, the relationship between the interviewer and the person being interviewed is always a bit unnatural and one-way; often, the researcher is perceived as more powerful and the informant may feel pressured to give a certain kind of answer. In a focus group situation, the participants are likely to relax and interact more naturally. Furthermore, they have the opportunity to "pick up on" and react to one another's comments and responses, creating a richer set of data than can sometimes result from a single interviewer's interaction with a single respondent.

Some Uses of Focus Groups

Market-oriented focus groups made up of consumers are often used to assess reactions to a new product, service, program, or advertisement (see Box 7.3). Focus groups can be used to identify the problems that exist among various professional groups within a complex organization or to study how public opinion on important social issues is formed. Those who study small-group interaction and communication patterns may use focus group data to study such things as how leadership patterns emerge, regardless of the actual subject of the discussion.

Locating Participants

Recruiting subjects for focus groups is a special problem, however. Usually, there is at least some intent to produce results that apply beyond the group of individuals who actually participate in the study. But it's not practical to try to create a random sample for the purpose. Most people who are asked to participate in a focus group are going to refuse because they must disrupt their normal, daily routine—and perhaps lose part of a paycheck in the process. Even when research funding permits paying focus group participants for their cooperation, many will not find any reasonable amount of pay sufficient incentive, and many others will simply not have time. Those who accept will be less busy, more cooperative, and perhaps poorer (where financial incentives are offered) than the population from which they are drawn.

However, focus group work done as part of a case study of an organization can solicit the organization's cooperation in recruiting a good mix of participants. Sometimes, outside organizations, such as a local civic group, can be persuaded to recruit participants from among their members; volunteers pool their earnings

---

BOX 7.3
MARKET RESEARCH AND FOCUS GROUPS

Elaborate physical facilities are often used for focus group work, especially when this method is used for market research. Video cameras allow participants' body language as well as their comments to be recorded; one-way glass allows others interested in the research to observe participants' reactions directly. But analyzing the rich visual data recorded on videotape in a meaningful way is difficult, time-consuming, and may not yield definite conclusions. In fact, a general danger of using focus groups in market research is that too much faith is invested in the conclusions without consideration of whether the participants constitute a representative sample of the general population. For example, consumers who are especially fond of a company's line of products—the most likely focus group volunteers—may be wildly enthusiastic about the latest ad campaign but highly unrepresentative of the general consumer market for the product!

Tape-recording focus group discussions is probably at least as reliable as videotaping and certainly much easier and cheaper. Most of the analysis will probably focus on the verbal statements of the participants anyway.

as a fund-raiser for the organization even where they would not have been induced to participate for the small amount they could have earned individually. If the group is not too atypical in terms of its political orientation or social makeup, this probably produces a more nearly representative group than an attempt at truly random sampling.

Market research firms often maintain files of people who are willing to participate in focus group research, but it's hard to argue that these individuals will be representative—they are, again, likely to be those who need the money and have time on their hands and probably are more interested in new products than the average consumer or they would not have volunteered.

When focus group work is designed to find out what members of a particular group think or feel—for example, if a government agency is studying the needs and concerns of farmers so as to design a better communication campaign aimed at them—the membership of organizations in that particular professional, recreational, activist, or other social group is the logical place to turn for focus group recruits.

Conducting the Group

Leading a focus group discussion is an art—like conducting a depth interview, only more complex! As with surveys, it's often considered important to introduce the question, problem, product, or message that the group will consider in a consistent way. Even though focus group research is a qualitative technique, the direction of the discussion may be very heavily influenced by the way the problem is presented, so it's important to use a carefully worded introduction that is the same for each group. Some specially designed focus groups assign a mock task to the group. For example, they might be told to imagine they are being asked to act as a citizens' advisory board on an important planning issue. Other studies might simply seek reactions: "Tell us how this product (or message, or issue) makes you feel" or "What do you think about when you see this picture?"

Leader's Influences

The most difficult thing for the focus group leader is to keep discussion going as long as possible (perhaps an hour if this can be done) without directing the discussion in ways that will contaminate the information the research is designed to uncover. For example, say a group is asked for its reaction to a front-page newspaper story on local government corruption. The purpose of the research is to see if the participants believe the story or think it is overblown sensationalism and how they arrive at this conclusion. If the discussion leader keeps asking things like "Is there anything else about this story that makes you believe (or disbelieve) it?"

then the participants might be led to overstate their own point of view. As with response bias in surveys, it's natural for focus group participants to want to please the researcher, and they'll try hard to come up with the kinds of arguments they think are desired without even realizing it. Instead, the leader should use questions like "Is there anything else anyone would like to say?" or "Are those all of the things that come to mind?" without in any way directing the discussion. (These are sometimes called "neutral probes.")

Remember that the leader's tone of voice or facial expression can influence participants, and so the leader needs to appear pleasant, friendly, interested, professional, and objective. An important advantage of having at least a tape recording of the discussion is that the leader's performance and use of probes can be reviewed.

Multiple-Viewpoint Discussion

Sometimes, several groups are chosen to represent various points of view; for example, a group or series of groups might be created to represent student, faculty, and staff points of view on university communications problems. In this case it's important not to mix the participants, not only because their separate points of view are being sought but because having groups involving participants of mixed status may put a "damper" on the discussion of some members. Students might not speak as freely in front of faculty, for example, as they would in a group composed only of their peers. In fact, some authorities recommend that focus groups contain participants that are as much alike as possible, although "general population" focus groups are also quite useful provided the sampling problem can be solved in some reasonable way.

Value of Pretests/Posttests

Sometimes, focus group participants might be asked to fill out an attitudinal or other survey before or after participating. As with experimental design, pretesting participants' opinions can have a sensitizing effect; posttesting reflects only their opinions after having participated in the discussion, however, not the perspectives they had coming in.

Because focus group data can be summarized quantitatively, the purpose of pretesting or posttesting is to assess in an approximate way important characteristics of the participants to rule out the possibility that they hold extreme views on the subject under discussion. Demographic data should be collected to be sure the participants are roughly representative of the population of interest, often a target population intended to be reached with a particular communications campaign.

Because precise measurement, as in an experimental design, is not the objective, pretest and posttest effects may be of less importance. Logic and common sense should prevail; think about the research question when constructing a questionnaire for participants and about how pretests and posttests might influence the results, but don't try to analyze focus group data in the same way that experimental or survey data are analyzed. Precise measurement of either opinions or effects is not the objective of this method.

QUALITATIVE CONTENT STUDIES

Remember the example from Chapter 6 about content-analyzing the "themes" present in news coverage of international conflict? The participant observer or the depth interviewer begins with a clear research question but without a rigid notion of what to expect. Similarly, content analysis can be inductive and qualitative as well as quantitative; this is preferable in cases where the particular aspects of content being studied are difficult to capture in quantitative analysis schemes or are not definable with certainty in advance of conducting the study.

Means of Analysis

The qualitative methods used in such cases are sometimes referred to as **discourse** or **rhetorical analysis.** Faculty in university departments of speech communication and English are often the experts in these techniques, as they draw from the same intellectual traditions underlying the analysis of literary fiction or public speech. These more interpretive humanities traditions are often different from the traditions of social science with which this book is primarily concerned. The social science norm of being rigorously systematic in procedures for sampling content, for example, may not be relevant to these studies.

Although a few researchers originally trained in the social sciences still tend to discount rhetorical or discourse-analytic studies, these qualitative means of assessing content can be just as empirical and just as rigorous as, say, ethnographers' qualitative methods of studying people. And although interpretive methods cannot directly answer questions about cause and effect, the mutual influence of social scientific and humanities approaches is increasingly apparent in media studies.

Rhetorical and literary theory can help guide the researcher in deciding what to look for, just as social science theory is needed to help guide the construction of other types of studies. Sometimes, both are used: A conflict theorist may use discourse analysis to suggest how power relationships within society are reflected in the way the mass media portray certain issues.

Method of Sampling

Sampling is not an important consideration for all media content studies, just as it is not an important consideration for some ethnographic studies; rather, the intent is to gain a "window" on a particular worldview, whether represented by one or a few human informants or by a limited set of media messages selected by the researcher. A few media researchers talk about using the feelings and reactions of the researcher as a tool of content analysis just as ethnographers have used their own feelings and reactions as tools to discover what other cultures are like. This is often part of what is meant by a "close" (or ethnographic) "reading" of a mass media text.

Historically, part of the distrust in interpretive content analysis that has come from the social scientific community has had to do with the fact that without training in humanistic methods it can be hard to distinguish opinionated essays illustrated with examples from more rigorous, yet still qualitative, scholarship. Essays may make interesting and persuasive reading, but they are not always scholarly "research," which should represent something beyond personal opinion.

Good qualitative content analysis requires an open-minded researcher, a specific research question, and a systematic way of looking at whatever content is chosen—even if only a relatively small, selected set of messages is used in the analysis. The trade-off between using small message samples and analyzing them in depth versus analyzing larger samples is similar to the trade-off involved in doing a limited number of depth interviews versus survey research.

It's important to remember that qualitative content studies that follow the basic principles of social science are not "unscientific" just because they are more interpretive than positivistic in their approach.

IMPORTANT TERMS AND CONCEPTS

Case study
Focus group
Discourse/rhetorical analysis
Interview schedule

EXERCISES

Qualitative research can be time consuming. Your instructor will probably want you to choose *one* of the following two exercises:

1. Choose a situation in which a group you know watches television together. This can be football fans on a Saturday afternoon, a college dormitory crowd watching soap operas, or a family group getting together for a favorite sitcom, for example. It can be a group you are already a member of, although this project might be easier if the group is not quite so familiar—you won't be tempted to take so many of the answers for granted!

   Become a participant observer for an hour with the group you choose and, afterward, write notes on as much of your experience as you can remember. Try and respond to the following questions:

   - What seems to be appealing about the particular show?
   - What purpose does it seem to fulfill for the group—sheer escapist entertainment, or perhaps a chance to get together with others and relax?
   - Is the group all men, all women, or mixed? Do you think that anyone could join it who just happened along, or does the group have something special in common to begin with?
   - What kind of social interaction (comments and conversation, body language, sharing of food or drink) do you observe among the group members?
   - Does the experience seem to strengthen "social bonds" among group members? Does it bring a family closer together, help a group of dorm residents feel more like their own family, increase solidary among a set of friends?

2. For another type of experience with ethnographic methods, find a friend, classmate, relative, coworker, or a friend of a friend who has had some special type of direct experience with mass communication that you have not, either professional or as a media consumer. For example, can you locate a reporter for the student newspaper? Someone who had a student internship in radio, television, advertising, or public relations? How about a musician who has played professionally, a 10-year-old video game addict, or a computer programmer? Someone with television acting or newscasting experience? An electronic mail buff?

   Do a "depth" interview with this person. In the case of a professional experience, what was the setting (media organization) like? What were the important work roles? Who made the decisions, and how were they communicated? How were good and bad work distinguished, and how were they rewarded? In the case of specialized media use, when does the person use the medium? Why? Alone or with others? What seems to be the attraction? In either case, pay special attention to any specialized words or phrases that the interviewee uses. How does a magazine editor describe a great story? Or a mystery movie fan a terrific show? Write a two- or three-page summary of the interview that tries to capture what you've learned.

PART III

TOOLBOX
Quantitative Analytical Techniques

194039853985896471325739309589647132579403985398739309589
930958964713257325739309589647132579403985398739309589647
958964713257393095896471325739309589647132573930958964713
896471325739309589674921023098964713257393095898374387317
713257393095896471325794039853987393095896471325739309589
398539873747283338957732227749936458964713257393095896471
539873930958964713257393095896471325776552199568776489647
958969403985398747132573930958964713257393095896471325793
393095896471325739309589647132573930958964713257393095898
309589647132573930958964713257393095896479403985358964713
896471325794039853987393589647132573930958964713257940398
958964713257393095896471325709589647132573930958964713257
930958964325739309589647132579403985398739309589647132579
713257393095896471325739309589647132573930958964713257393
325739309589671325739309585896471325739309589647132579403
309589647132573930958964713257964713257932573930958964713
539873930958964713257393095896471325739309589647132573933

Descriptive statistics help summarize complex data sets.

Describing a Data Set

You've learned about samples and populations, independent and dependent variables, and something about the challenges of measurement in previous chapters. Quantitative studies, in short, measure variables in a sample to draw conclusions about a population and, especially in the case of studies based on cause-and-effect hypotheses, about the relationships between independent and dependent variables.

In this chapter, you'll learn about what to do with data once you have them (which, for many researchers, is the fun part!) and look briefly at a few more advanced techniques for both variable measurement and **statistical analysis** that you might want to use later on. You'll work through some of the arithmetic and algebra only for the most simple statistics as illustrations of what these calculations are all about. Many good textbooks and courses are available to help you pursue this type of analysis further, and computer programs like the SPSS® package will do most of the complex arithmetic for you. The goal here is to get you started thinking about what the purposes of statistical analysis are and to give you some of the tools to begin.

LEVELS OF MEASUREMENT

Because studies of the mass media and their relationship to society can take many forms, a broad range of statistical techniques are used, and it's sometimes especially difficult for beginning researchers to figure out which ones apply to a particular case. An important key is the distinction between types (or *levels*) of measurement.

Categorical

It's not possible to calculate an average (or many other statistics) on data that have been reported in **categorical** form only. The simplest example of categorical data is eye color. People are usually classified as brown-eyed, blue-eyed, green-eyed, and so on. You really can't talk about "average eye color" in any meaningful, precise sense. Nor can you talk about one eye color being "twice as much" or "half as much" as another. All you can do is talk about the number, or frequency, and percentage of people falling into each category.

Nominal

To talk about "average gender" or "average ethnicity" (like "average eye color") makes no sense. This kind of category is called **nominal.** Choosing a name, not making a measurement, is actually involved in assessing this variable. Even though you might assign numerical values to make computer analysis easier, the assignments are completely arbitrary. "Male" might be coded as 1 and "female" as 2 for such purposes, but you can just as well make "female" a 1 and "male" a 2.

Ordinal

Another kind of category for data is called **ordinal.** Here, the categories used can be ranked (or ordered) in a logical way. If you divide a sample of college students into freshmen, sophomores, juniors, and seniors, it makes sense to put them in a particular order, say, from those who have completed the least amount of college work to those who have completed the most. As with nominal data, you can talk about the numbers and proportions of students who are freshmen, sophomores, and so on, but you can't calculate "average class membership" anymore than you can calculate "average eye color." So while you hope that seniors have more education than freshmen, it makes no sense to say that a senior is exactly "four times as educated" (or "twice as educated," or "half as educated") as a freshman!

Continuous

In contrast, such things as weight, height, and hours of coursework completed are measured on **continuous** scales in which the distance between one number and the next has a consistent meaning. A 150-pound person is 5 pounds heavier than a 145-pound person just as a 105-pound person is 5 pounds heavier than a 100-pound person. Similarly, a 5′6″ person is 2″ shorter than a 5′8″ person just as a 5′4″ person is 2″ shorter than a 5′6″ person. Each 3-hour course completed adds the same amount to total coursework; someone who's completed 40 hours of coursework has completed precisely one third as much as someone who's completed 120.

Not all continuous measurements can be treated exactly the same for statistical purposes, however. Some have "true zeros" (a meaningful zero point) and some do not. The standard example is the difference between temperature as it's normally measured on a centigrade or Farenheit scale where "zero" is set arbitrarily (at either the freezing point of water or 32° below that point, respectively) and temperature in degrees Kelvin, the scientist's measure based on an absolute zero point where there is no heat (or molecular motion). To say that 30° is twice as warm as 15° does not make sense in the Farenheit and centigrade scales in everyday use, but the same statement is meaningful if the measures are made in degrees Kelvin.

BOX 8.1
AN INTERVAL SCALE?

Do you think that the course you are taking is an excellent one? Say you're asked to indicate your level of agreement with the statement "This is an excellent course." You're asked to answer this using a 5-point scale where 1 means you strongly disagree and 5 means you agree completely. Are the people who choose 4 twice as much in agreement as those who choose 2? Not really, because the scale has no zero point.

Some experts argue that this type of scale isn't really an interval scale because the "psychological distance" (the distance in respondents' minds) between 1 and 2 may not be the same as the distance between 2 and 3 because 3 is the neutral category on a 5-point scale of agreement; it is for middle-of-the-roaders who neither agree nor disagree. It may be psychologically easier for people to choose 2 or 4 on such a scale than to choose the extreme categories 1 or 5.

Technically speaking, these scales might better be treated as ordinal rather than interval ones for statistical purposes. But it's common practice to treat this type of scale data as representing an interval level of measurement. This means that researchers assume that summary statistics such as "average level of agreement" are meaningful calculations.

Ratio and Interval Scales

Because you can calculate meaningful ratios using continuous scales with a true zero point, they are called *ratio* scales, and the measurements made using them are called ratio measurements. Continuous scales for which you cannot calculate meaningful ratios are called *interval* scales; the intervals between one number and the next still have meaning (72° is 2° warmer than 70°, just as 16° is 2° warmer than 14°), but the ratios between them do not (72° is not "twice as warm" as 36°).

Weights, heights, and hours can be divided by one another in the same way as degrees Kelvin. A 150-pound adult weighs twice as much as a 75-pound child; a two-story house with a roof 50 feet off the ground is half as tall as an office building 100 feet high; someone who spent 2 hours reading has spent twice as much time as someone who only spent 1 hour. But not all interval measurements behave in this way, including many of the measures used in media research, such as scales of agreement, importance, satisfaction, and so on.

Of course, if you converted the usual eye color categories into some kind of precise physical measurement (perhaps of the wavelength of light that produces an appearance of "brownness," "blueness," and so on), you would have a continuous, at least interval-level measurement that you could treat much differently for statistical purposes. You could calculate average wavelength and many other important statistics. If you used a measure such as number of course hours completed to categorize a group of students (rather than the categories "freshman," "sophomore," and so on), you would—similarly—have a ratio-level measurement that would give you the same kind of statistical flexibility.

In general, the level of measurement of the data—whether categorical (nominal or ordinal) or continuous (interval or ratio)—determines what types of statistical analysis can be done.

Choosing an Appropriate Level of Measurement

In the early stage of designing a research project, decisions must often be made between one level of measurement and another—what type of categories to offer in a forced-choice questionnaire, for example. Experienced researchers think ahead and generally choose the scale that will give them the most flexibility later on.

However, there are exceptions. Income in actual dollars is a continuous (ratio) measurement; income chosen from a list of categories is only ordinal. But where income is used as a demographic variable to characterize the sample, and not a key independent or dependent variable in a causal analysis using more advanced statistical techniques, categories are often chosen anyway. It's believed that respondents are less embarassed, threatened, or offended by having to choose among a list of categories than by having to state their income in dollars. As always, this type of research decision involves a trade-off between the ideal world (in which, it seems, some statisticians live!) and the practical constraints of gathering data from real people.

DESCRIPTIVE STATISTICS

Probably the most straightforward statistics, intuitively, are **descriptive statistics,** which simply allow you to summarize the data you've collected in a meaningful way using numbers. For categorical (nominal and ordinal) data, there isn't much you can do except list the frequencies of the various categories and calculate the percentages that fall into each. You can't go any further to calculate, for example, the "average" gender or ethnicity in your sample; this has no meaning for categorical data. You probably want to figure out the percentage of women versus men and of various ethnic groups, income groups, and of any other categories for which you thought it was important to collect data in your study to provide a "snapshot" of the sample, but there's not much more you can do. Sometimes, categorical data can be used in advanced analyses concerned with cause and effect, as you'll see later on, but the options for presenting a descriptive picture of a **frequency distribution** (how many cases fall in each of a number of categories) are quite limited.

Measures of Central Tendency

For continuous data, however, you can do much more to summarize your results—your distributions—numerically. For example, say you've measured the perceived importance of multicultural issues for a sample of 15 mass communication students at your university on a 5-point (interval) scale from "not important at all" (1) to "extremely important" (5) as part of an agenda-setting study. Two students chose 1, three chose 2, seven chose 3, three chose 4, and none chose 5. Reporting these **raw data** is useful, but for most people who read your report not as easy to grasp as the overall **mean,** or arithmetic average: $(2 \times 1 + 3 \times 2 + 7 \times 3 + 3 \times 4 + 0 \times 5)$ divided by 15, or 2.7. A mean is the **measure of central tendency** with which you are likely most familiar. Other common measures of central tendency are the **mode,** or most common answer (in this case, 3); the **median,** or the middle answer if all the answers are placed in rank order (in this case, the median would be the 8th answer because there are 15 answer scores, or—again—3). In some cases, the **midpoint,** the point halfway between the highest and lowest scores, is also used; here it's less useful as a description because it was set arbitrarily when a 5-point scale was chosen.

Measures of Dispersion

A second, very common type of descriptive statistic is the **measure of disper-sion.** Such measures are shorthand ways of capturing the difference between a set of scores that cluster closely around a center and those that are more spread out, or variable.

Range

The simplest measure of dispersion is the **range,** the distance between the highest and the lowest scores. Using the example described in the preceding section, the scores vary from 1 to 4, so the range is 3. But range doesn't tell you as much as you'd like to know about the variation in a data set; it takes into account only the two most extreme scores.

Variance

Variance measures dispersion by calculating the amount that *each score* differs from the mean, squaring the difference, and dividing the total of the squared differences by the total number of scores *minus 1*. Algebraically, this is written as

$$S^2 = \frac{\Sigma (X - \overline{X})^2}{N - 1}.$$

Here S^2 stands for variance, Σ means "summation" (the total for all cases of whatever follows), X stands for an individual score, $\overline{X}$ for the mean score, and N for the total *number* of scores. So the variance for our example is $(2 - (1 - 2.7) + 3 \times (2 - 2.7) + 7 \times (3 - 2.7) + 3 \times (4 - 2.7))$ divided by $(15 - 1)$, or .93.

You'll remember from high school that two negative numbers multiplied to-gether produce a positive result, so you probably can see that each score here (as *none* of the scores is exactly equal to the mean of 2.7) makes a positive contribution to the total variance. The higher the variance, the more variation there is in the entire data set.

Why is variance calculated this way? Using the *square* of differences from the mean gives additional weight to extreme scores. A single score some distance from the mean can make a much bigger contribution to the total variance than several scores very close to the mean. Statisticians consider a calculation that is sensitive to extremes in this way to be a better representation (or description!) of the total variation in the data than a calculation without this property. If you work out the arithmetic for the above example, you'll discover that most of the variance comes from the 1 and 4 scores, with relatively little from the 2 and 3 scores that are nearer the mean, even though there are more of them.

Standard Deviation

Another common measure of dispersion is called the **standard deviation,** which is simply the square root of the variance. It is typically symbolized as S, whereas variance is S^2. The square root of .93 (from our example) is .96. It's easier for most of us human beings (being not, after all, *really* aliens from outer space!) to think in terms of the units of the original measurement, and standard deviations are stated in those units. To say that the distribution has a mean of 2.7 and a standard deviation of .96, then, is a standard way of describing a data set in "shorthand" terms to those with some acquaintance with statistical techniques.

Correlation Coefficient

If you want to describe the relationship between two variables, the degree to which the change in one is related to a change in the other, a statistic called the **correlation coefficient** is used. Remember, though, *correlation is not causation!* Yet even experienced researchers are often tempted to use correlations as "proof" of causative relationships (see Box 8.2 for an example). Correlation coefficients can help test hypotheses about causation that have strong theoretical justifications. Nevertheless, they are still essentially descriptive tools.

BOX 8.2
CORRELATION VERSUS CAUSATION:
AN EXAMPLE

Let's assume we found a close relationship found between people's degree of preference for elite newspapers versus, say, popular tabloids and their knowledge of current events, it is quite inviting to conclude that reading elite newspapers *causes* people to become better informed. However, it's also likely that people who are better informed in the first place are the ones who prefer the elite papers.

Some advanced methods, such as path analysis and time-series analysis, can help "tease out" this kind of chicken-and-egg question, a common one in media research.

Many different types of correlation coefficients are used with different types of data measured at different levels. A standard convention is that all range from −1 to +1, with "zero" indicating no relationship whatsoever, +1 indicating a perfect **positive correlation** (every time one variable increases, there's a known *increase* in the value of the other variable, too), and −1 a perfect **negative correlation** (an increase in one variable is always associated with a predictable *decrease* in the other variable).

Pearson's r

By far the most commonly used correlation coefficient, however, is **Pearson's *r*.** This statistic is used for measuring a linear relationship between two continuous variables. (Other correlation coefficients are available to assess relationships even when variables are not measured on a continuous scale, but Pearson's *r* is the one most commonly in use.) In practice, correlation coefficients (including Pearson's *r*) are almost always less than perfect; the meaning or importance of a less-than-perfect correlation is a matter of judgment and depends on the research question and how it is understood theoretically. Calculating *r* is not difficult, but it is tedious and the formula is a bit cumbersome; all standard statistical software can handle it with ease, however.

What's a linear relationship? This is a relationship that's essentially the same along the whole range of values of both variables. If you graph two variables that have a linear relationship and a perfect positive correlation, the graph should look like Figure 8.1.

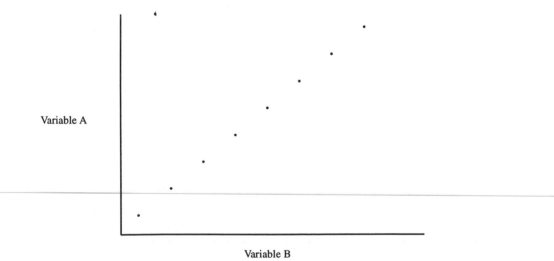

Variable A

Variable B

Figure 8.1

This relationship can reasonably be described as a straight line. (Incidentally, the algebraically minded may be interested to know that Pearson's *r* also describes the slope of the graph line. The line is steeper when the correlation is high, nearer to flat when the correlation is low.) A perfect negative correlation for two variables that are linearly related would look like Figure 8.2.

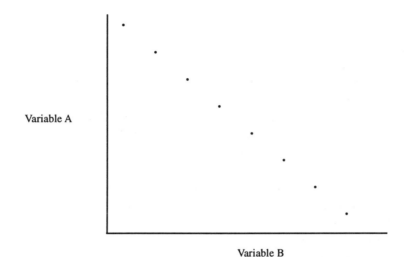

Variable B

Figure 8.2

A nonlinear relationship might look like Figure 8.3 or even like Figure 8.4.

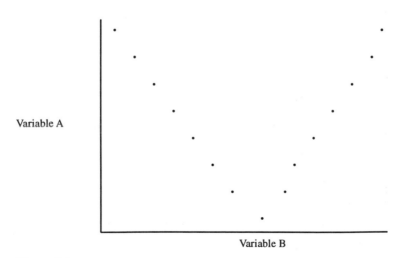

Variable B

Figure 8.3

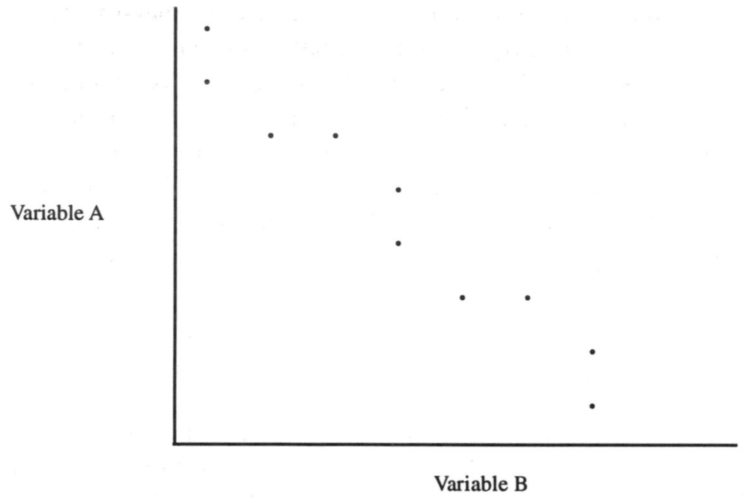

Variable A

Variable B

Figure 8.4

In fact, a nonlinear relationship can consist of *anything other than a straight line!* This situation is complicated by the fact that actual data never fall as nicely and neatly on *any* line (straight, curved, or zig-zag!) as these examples suggest. When there is any question that a relationship could be expected to be other than linear, though, you should graph the data you are looking at to be sure it seems reasonable to make an assumption of linearity. Otherwise, a correlation coefficient may give very misleading results; it will miss many nonlinear relationships altogether, leading you to overlook an important part of the picture, and it may understate others (see example in Box 8.3).

BOX 8.3
LINEAR RELATIONSHIPS: AN EXAMPLE

Assume that as children grow older and spend more time in school they watch less television. As older people retire and become in general less active they watch *more* television. Calculating a simple correlation between the two variables of age and hours per day of television watched might not "see" these important relationships. Because the relationship between the two variables is positive for part of the range of one (age) and negative for another part, the overall correlation would probably be low.

Of course, two variables can be related less than perfectly in either a negative or a positive direction, in other words, a correlation coefficient such as Pearson's r can take any value between -1 and $+1$. Very small correlations may or may not mean much; it depends on the purpose of the study and the theoretical significance of the variables. Even high correlations may not mean as much as they appear to. If two attitudinal items turn out to be highly correlated, you must decide (on the basis of theory and common sense) whether an interesting new discovery has been made, or if the two items are actually just measuring the same underlying idea using slightly different wording!

Coefficient of Determination

Another way of thinking about Pearson's r is that its *square* (r^2) tells you the proportion of the variance in one variable that can be predicted on the basis of the other. This is sometimes called a **coefficient of determination.** If there's a high correlation between two variables and you know the value of the first variable, you can make a good prediction of the second. The higher the correlation, the better your prediction—whether the relationship is negative or positive.

Say you've seen data indicating that there's a high correlation between a child's degree of preference for a particular TV program and the number of times that the child gets in trouble at school in an average week. When you meet a new youngster and find out that his or her TV viewing includes that particular show, you might feel sorry for the child's teachers, but there is no evidence that the show *causes* the behavior.

The goal of descriptive statistics is to enable you to present your data (to yourself and to those who will listen to or read your research results) in a simplified form that characterizes the data in a meaningful way. Generally speaking, these statistics give you a better "grasp" of what's been collected than poring over stacks of individual survey or experiment results! You can't keep all those numbers in your head, so descriptive statistics are helpful tools for summarizing and communicating larger data sets in an easily "digestible" form.

IMPORTANT TERMS AND CONCEPTS

Categorical	Negative correlation
Coefficient of determination	Nominal
Continuous	Ordinal
Correlation coefficient	Pearson's *r*
Descriptive statistics	Positive correlation
Frequency distribution	Range
Mean	Raw data
Measure of central tendency	Standard deviation
Measure of dispersion	Statistical analysis
Midpoint	Variance
Mode	

EXERCISES

1. Divide the following variables by the level of measurement each represents (nominal, ordinal, interval, or ratio). Explain your answer in each case.

   Political party affiliation

   Approval ratings for the president of the United States (is he doing a good job or not?)

   Health (excellent, good, fair, poor)

   Favorite TV show

   Educational level

   Knowledge of nutrition (test score)

   Miles per gallon for a particular model of car

   Intelligence quotient (IQ)

2. The following frequency distribution represents the results of a survey of the incomes of recent college graduates. (Of course, the sample is artificially tiny— only 13 respondents—but you can ignore that for this exercise.) Calculate appropriate descriptive statistics and write a one-paragraph news story summarizing the data. Did you include the unemployed respondents and the part-time worker in your data? Why or why not? Would it be better to report just the mean, or the mean and modal incomes? Why?

Unemployed (no income)	3
$ 5,500 (part-time work)	1
10,200	1

14,500	1
18,000	3
18,200	1
20,800	1
24,000	1
49,600	1

3. Let's assume that there is a correlation (Pearson's r) of $-.55$ between test scores on your instructor's exams for this course and amount of time spent reading the textbook. How much of the variance in test scores could be predicted by knowledge of the amount of time each student read the book? How would you interpret this result—what possible explanations come to mind? Would you conclude that students in your class shouldn't read the textbook at all? Why or why not?

Making population inferences from sample data can seem a lot like pulling a rabbit out of a hat.

From Sample to Population

eturn for a minute to the study example in Chapter 8, where the mean perceived importance of multicultural issues among a student sample was 2.7. It's a pretty good bet that had you actually asked all mass communication students in your university, the mean score would not have been exactly 2.7. It might have been 2.6, 2.9, or even 1.0 or 5.0. The goal of sampling is to be able to generalize to a population; that's why sampling procedures for survey research are centered on achieving representativeness.

SAMPLING RULES OF THUMB

But what's a reasonable estimate of the population value for this variable? Intuitively, it seems likely that the value would be somewhere around the 2.7 you obtained for your sample and that it's probably not either 1 or 5. This is only a good guess. But statisticians and social science researchers have developed rules of thumb for making this kind of reasonable, informed guess about population values based on sample results, which give you some guidelines for what's an acceptable inference from a social science point of view.

Parameters

The objective in working with descriptive statistics about sample values is to make reasonable guesses about the value of a population **parameter,** or characteristic (in this case, the true value of a population variable) that you are reasonably certain is accurate. How accurate? This is defined in terms of the probability that you're wrong! Generally speaking, researchers aim for at least a 95% probability that their results from a sample actually represent the population accurately. The greater the sample size, the more reasonable it is to aim for a 99% probability of accuracy, so larger studies routinely aim for this higher level.

Conversely, for exploratory research—a smaller **pilot study,** aimed at gaining some initial understanding of a new problem—a 90% level may be considered quite satisfactory. Pilot studies are usually not published in the academic literature unless subsequent research with a higher degree of confidence confirms their findings, so higher levels are typically seen in published work.

Naturally, it's easier to be confident that a population parameter is *close* to a sample value—within some range—than it is to be confident that a particular sample measurement represents exactly what the population value would be. That is, in the example, it would be easier to state with confidence that the population value is in the range between, say, 2.6 and 2.8 than to state with confidence that the population value is exactly, say, 2.7. The only way you could be completely certain that you know exactly what the population value would be would have been to survey everyone in the population; this is called a **census** rather than a sample.

Inferential Statistics

The objective of **inferential statistics** is to be able to determine, with some degree of confidence, what range the true value of the population parameter is likely to be within, based on a certain value that you've achieved with sampling, and to be able to state what the probability is that you're right. Researchers have agreed—arbitrarily—that this value should be at least 95%. When survey results are reported in the mass media, stories often use language like "results are accurate to within 3 percentage points"—language often found in fine print in the corner of a graph or in the closing paragraphs of a news story. So, if, for example, 25% of the survey sample agreed with a certain statement, the researchers are stating in this case that they are reasonably confident that the true population value for that parameter is between 22% and 28%.

They also believe that there is a known probability (usually either 95% or 99%) that their statement is correct. Because this statement is an assertion about the true values lying within a given range, or interval, with a known degree of confidence, that range is called a **confidence interval.**

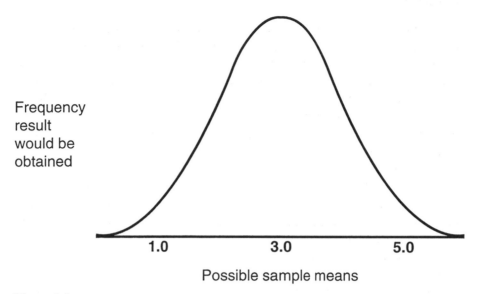

Figure 9.1

Before getting into the statistical justification for making such statements, you need to think a bit more about what this means. A probability can be determined in at least two different ways: logically and experientially. For example, you know that dice have six sides. By reasoning logically that the probability of any one side turning up is the same as for all other sides, you can therefore conclude that the probability of turning up, say, a 4 is one in six, or 17%. The other way is to throw a die 1,000 times, observing that a 4 turns up about 17% of the time. It doesn't matter whether you've even counted the number of sides on the die or whether you understand the logical thinking behind choosing 17% as the likely probability; you're basing your estimate on your experience.

Normal Distribution

One way to determine the accuracy of a survey result is to repeat the survey many times and examine the variation (or variance!) in your results. Sometimes, your sample value might be 2.5, or 2.6, or 2.7, or 2.8, or 2.9, and so on. Occasionally, you might come up with a value as low as 1.0 or as high as 5.0. (Remember, this question used a 5-point scale, so 1.0 is the lowest and 5.0 the highest possible value for the sample result.) If you did repeat a survey like this many times, you'd have a distribution of different results that would probably look like Figure 9.1.

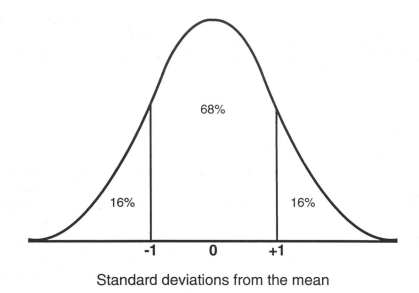

Figure 9.2

This basic shape is called a **normal distribution,** sometimes referred to as a **bell curve.** Bell curves can be pinched or stretched horizontally in shape and they can lean to the left or right, but they are a very typical shape for all kinds of naturally occurring continuous (interval or ratio) variables, such as weight and height. It is the shape that educational psychologists aim for when they design intelligence, aptitude, and achievement tests. The mathematical properties of normal distributions are very well understood by statisticians. Fortunately for your purposes, it is also the shape taken by the distribution of possible sample-based measurements of a population mean. *Usually, although not always, this is true regardless of the shape of the distribution of the actual individual values.* Most of the values in our example would cluster around a middle point, but a very few could be as low as 1.0 or as high as 5.0. Note that the *area under* such a curve represents the probability that results within a certain range will be obtained. There's a great deal of area under the curve between any two points close to the middle but much less out at the ends.

One of the things known about normal distributions is that if you go out one standard deviation from the mean in either direction, you will be including just over two thirds of the area, as Figure 9.2 shows.

Similarly (and conveniently enough!), if you go just about two standard deviations out from the mean, you will include 95% of the area. (Actually, the correct value here is 1.96 standard deviations to encompass 95% of the area.) And if you go out about another .5 standard deviation in either direction (actually to 2.58

standard deviations), you'll have include 99% of the area under the curve. Going out just 1.65 standard deviations, on the other hand, would take in 90% of the area under the curve. So you know a lot about what a distribution of possible sample results would be likely to look like, if you had one!

USING SAMPLING DISTRIBUTIONS

Where does the sample in the example given earlier in this chapter fit in? The mean sample value for answers to the survey on a five-point scale, you'll recall, was 2.7. Even if the survey was repeated 1,000 times using different samples, the average result would surely be almost exactly the same as the population mean for this particular parameter—and it certainly would be *exactly* the same if you had an infinite number of sample means to work with. But there's only one, the value of which is 2.7. Is the population mean really, say, 2.9, and the sample mean lower, or could it be, say, 2.5, and the sample mean higher? No one in the sample chose 5 on the scale, for example—was this just a matter of luck?

A "best guess" about the mean of the sampling distribution of possible sample mean values is based on the information available. Because the mean value for the sample is 2.7, and there's no way of knowing whether it's higher or lower than the population value (which is the same as the mean of all possible sample values), 2.7 is going to be the best guess of the mean of all possible such values.

What is the standard deviation of this distribution? Following the same logic, you'd probably want to use the amount of variance in the sample as the basis for an estimate of the amount of variance in the **sampling distribution of means.** However, the larger the sample size, the more certain you'll be of the accuracy of both the sample mean and the sample variance with respect to the values that really exist in the entire population. If you drew a lot of random samples of only 2 respondents each, there'd be a lot more variation in the means than if you drew a lot of random samples of, say, 100 or 500 respondents each!

Standard Error

For reasonably large samples (samples of, say, 100 or more; Minium, 1970), the formula for the standard deviation of the sampling distribution of means—also called **standard error**—turns out to be the standard deviation of the sample divided by the square root of the sample size.

However, the smaller the sample, the less accurate you can assume your population estimate to be, so you must adjust your estimate of standard error accordingly. (Remember, you had only 15 students in your sample.)

Student's t

Unfortunately, the shape of the curve on which your adjusted estimate will be based is not the well-known normal curve and is slightly different for every possible sample size. Actually, this forms a whole family of distribution curves of the statistic known as Student's t. (The mathematician who first described these distributions wrote under the pseudonym "Student.")

Degrees of Freedom

Any statistical or quantitative methods text will give the values for Student's t for various **degrees of freedom.** This term reflects sample size and refers to the number of scores in the sample that could be assigned any arbitrary value (that's the "freedom" part—they are "free" to vary) and still come up with the same mean. Both the distribution of t and the number of degrees of freedom are automatically taken into account by statistical analysis programs. For a problem like yours, degrees of freedom (abbreviated df) would be 1 less than the sample size (that is, $15 - 1$, or 14, in this example).

Probability

Your hypothetical multicultural issues variable had a mean of 2.7, a standard deviation of .96, and was based on 15 scores. So your best guess regarding the sampling distribution of all possible such results is that it would have a mean of 2.7 and a standard deviation of .96 divided by the square root of 15, or .96/3.9, or .25. Now, if the sampling distribution of means were a normal "bell curve" distribution, you could begin to draw some useful conclusions. You know that 95% of the area under a normal curve is between −1.96 standard deviations and +1.96 standard deviations from the mean. So, on average, 95% of the sample values that you might come up with by repeating the survey over and over again should fall within ± 1.96 standard deviations of 2.7. That means they'd be between 2.21 and 3.19 ($1.96 \times .25 = .49$, and $2.7 \pm .49$ specifies a range between 2.21 and 3.19). It would still be possible, of course, that your sample value was way off—but you'd be justified in asserting that there's only a 5% probability that it's so far off it won't even be in this range.

But your sample size is *not* 100 or more, so the sampling distribution of means is not normally distributed. Instead, you must substitute the shape of the distribution of Student's t when $df = 14$. In *that* distribution, 95% of the area under the curve falls in the range ± 2.15 standard deviations from the mean. So, you estimate the population value of your variable as $2.7 \pm (2.15 \times .25)$, or $2.7 \pm .54$, or the range from 2.15 to 3.24. Notice that this is not too terribly far from the range you would have estimated assuming a normal sampling distribution. But it certainly seems logical that the precision of your estimate is at least a bit smaller than it would have been if your sample had been larger, doesn't it? You can now state, with good justification, that you believe there's a 95% probability that the population value of your variable is between 2.2 and 3.2. In statistical studies, this is often abbreviated to something like $2.7 \pm .5$ (95% confidence).

Margin of Error

The preceding statement should remind you of the survey research reports in the media mentioned earlier in this chapter in which the results are said to reflect a **margin of error** of so many percentage points. The idea is exactly the same. Actually, big national surveys often use complicated sampling schemes, not just simple random sampling, and their statistical analysis can sometimes be much more complex than the example used here. But the principle is the same, except that survey data usually come in the form of proportions or percentages, not mean values.

BOX 9.1
CAUTIONS REGARDING DISTRIBUTIONS

Aside from the special case of percentage data, your analysis would apply only to data measured on a continuous (interval or ratio) scale in a sample drawn in true random fashion from a population. The results apply only to the actual population used. Because you drew your sample only from students at your own university, the results apply only to the population of students at your university, not to students at all universities and certainly not to the population as a whole!

There's one other important caveat: The sampling distribution of the means is, alas, *not* always normally distributed, even for large samples. Most of the time the assumption of a normal distribution is justified for large samples, regardless of whether the actual values of the variable form a bell-shaped curve or not. (Using Student's *t* provides the appropriate adjustment for smaller samples.) But sometimes when variable values themselves are nonnormal, the sampling distribution is also nonnormal, and you can't draw inferences of the type illustrated here.

Many researchers therefore routinely check their sample data for confirmation that the values seem to be distributed normally. A friendly statistician (or the handbook for a good computer-based statistical package) can suggest a procedure for this and approaches to making necessary adjustments before proceeding with the analysis.

Surveys are often based on agree/disagree or yes/no questions—questions with answers that fall into **dichotomous** (or two-valued) **categories** rather than continuous scale measurements. Under these circumstances there's a reasonably simple procedure for calculating the standard error of the percentages.

This procedure produces different answers depending on the proportions of the respondents in each of the two categories for a given question, but the largest error exists when the proportions are 50-50, with half the respondents in each group. So making the assumption that the respondents' answers are divided equally will produce the largest estimate of error, minimizing the chances of overstating accuracy. The error estimate based on this assumption is the one used to suggest a margin of error for an entire set of survey data in which the results are expressed as percentages.

Using the large-sample assumption that the sampling distribution of means is normal and choosing a 95% confidence interval, this formula is $\pm 1.96 \times \sqrt{0.25/N}$. (A 99% confidence interval would use $\pm > 2.58 \times \sqrt{0.25/N}$, and so on.) For a random sample of 500 respondents, then, the margin of error would be stated as either $\pm 1.96 \times \sqrt{0.25/500}$, or $\pm .044$ (4 percentage points) using a 95% confidence interval; it would be $\pm 2.58 \times \sqrt{0.25/500} = \pm .058$ (6 percentage points) using a 99% confidence interval.

Before continuing, pause for a minute and consider the significance of what you've done. Isn't it a bit like magic? Yet it has a real-world significance for mass communication students that goes beyond application to research problems. *Remember, though, that whenever survey results are reported to the public the sampling error needs to be taken into account* (see Box 9.2).

BOX 9.2
THE IMPORTANCE OF SAMPLING ERROR

In the case of political races, a candidate with a 52% "lead" in the polls is not necessarily going to win. If the sampling error (or margin of error) is 2% or more, it's a toss-up, even if the election were held immediately and everyone voted exactly the same way they answered the survey questions! And, regardless of the size of the sampling error, there's always a chance that the results reported are more inaccurate than the range suggested by the error term. How big a chance? This depends on the confidence interval chosen. With a 95% confidence interval, for example, there's still a 5% (or 1 in 20) chance that the sample misrepresents the population value by an amount greater than the range specified. With a 99% confidence interval, there's a 1% chance of greater error, and so on.

TESTING A CORRELATION'S SIGNIFICANCE

Confidence intervals can be calculated for any population parameter, not just for means but for variances, standard deviations, and so on, including correlation coefficients. The procedure's logic is the same; a sampling distribution of the possible values of the statistic in question is the basis of the inference in each case, just as it was for estimating a mean. However, the sampling distribution of Pearson's *r* is a nonnormal distribution with a shape that varies depending on both the size of *r* and the size of the sample. So calculating confidence intervals for a correlation coefficient is not so straightforward.

Statistical Significance

Fortunately, researchers are usually most interested in the question of whether a relationship does or does not exist in the population between two variables that (in your sample) are correlated. In other words, you want to know whether the population value for *r* could reasonably be assumed to be zero, or whether your sample *r* is so extreme (either in a positive or a negative direction) that this would not be a reasonable assumption. In this case, the standard procedure is to test the hypothesis that there is no correlation. If you can't support it because your value of *r* is too far from zero to be reasonably attributed to chance variation, you assert that the correlation has **statistical significance.** (Stating and testing hypotheses are explained in more detail in Chapter 10.)

It turns out that if you assume that the true (population) correlation is zero, you can calculate a value from your sample *r* that has a distribution just like Student's *t*. (Statistical methods are peppered with such seemingly strange coincidences!) The relevant degrees of freedom are defined as $n - 2$, where *n* is the number of score pairs.

Confidence Level

Say you have a sample consisting of 30 subjects and you've measured both level of interest in current events and years of education for each of them. There are 28 degrees of freedom ($30 - 2$). You calculate a correlation of .60 between the two variables. The formula for calculating *t* from *r* is $r \div \sqrt{(1 - r^2)/(n - 2)}$ and gives you a value for *t* of 3.97.

You decide on an acceptable **confidence level** (probability that your result was not obtained by chance variation) of 99%. A *t* value table (from a statistics or quantitative methods text) tells you that for $df = 28$, you need to go out to a value of 2.76 in either direction from the mean to include 99% of the area under the curve. Because your *t* value of 3.97 exceeds that value, you can reject the assumption there isn't an actual correlation between interest and education in the population you've sampled and conclude instead that there probably is!

By now you're begin to understand the logic of hypothesis testing and how it is similar to the logic of estimating population parameters. (Incidentally, confidence intervals *can* be constructed for a correlation coefficient; additional "tricks" are required to get around the nonnormal character of the sampling distribution, however.) Today's statistical software will report the statistical significance of a correlation as effortlessly as it calculates the correlation itself, so you probably won't actually have to follow these steps very often!

Real-World Limitations

A very small correlation (say, less than .10) can have high statistical significance if it's based on a large enough sample. That is, you can be almost completely certain that there's some correlation, which sounds impressive! But, as you've learned in Chapter 8, a .10 correlation means that .01 (only 1%) of the variance (change or variation) in one variable can be predicted on the basis of the other. Shouldn't you be more concerned about the other 99%? Sometimes, the interpretation of results like these can have important social significance (see Box 9.3).

BOX 9.3
WHAT CORRELATIONS CAN
REALLY MEAN: AN EXAMPLE

Say a researcher reports having evidence at a 99.9% confidence level that there's a relationship (positive correlation) between the age at which children begin to spend their days away from home in day care, preschool, or regular school and their scholastic aptitude at age 18. That is, the longer children stay at home, the smarter they are later on. This might be taken as important evidence that leaving home too early somehow limits a child's development. But if the correlation is quite low, however significant, other factors are certainly vastly more important, and social policy designed to leave children at home longer is not likely to make an important difference—and may divert attention from the importance of other influences. A higher correlation between the two variables—even one with a lower level of statistical significance—might be a more serious source of concern.

In other words, it is possible with very large samples that even very small correlations will be statistically significant. But this does not necessarily translate into significance in the real world because factors *not* represented in the correlation are likely to be much more important influences.

IMPORTANT TERMS AND CONCEPTS

Bell curve

Census

Confidence interval

Confidence level

Degrees of freedom

Dichotomous categories

Inferential statistics

Margin of error

Normal distribution

Parameter

Pilot study

Sampling distribution of
   means

Standard error

Statistical significance

EXERCISES

1. Do a minisurvey of the total number of credit hours of college coursework completed by those in your class. Draw a random sample of 5 students and use the data from these 5. Calculate the mean, standard deviation, and standard error, using a 95% confidence interval. Each class member should complete this ministudy separately; then, as a group, figure out the true population mean. (The population here is the entire class.) How many of the individual estimates from each class member's sample of 5 define a range (confidence interval) that includes the actual mean for the class?

2. Find a news story (magazine or newspaper) that features survey data. Are the sample size and margin of error reported? Try to estimate the margin of error based on the sample size, using the formula in this chapter. (You may not achieve the same result, however, because the sampling procedures used in some major national surveys can increase the error, and this may have been taken into account in the published margin.) Now, read the story carefully. Are all of the statements in the story justified in terms of the data presented? Edit any inappropriate statements to better conform to what the data really do and do not show.

Statistical tests allow us to make informed judgments about whether things are alike or different.

10

Testing Hypotheses

 statistical test helps you determine whether conclusions based on sample data are warranted. The term "confidence level" in hypothesis testing, introduced in Chapter 9, is related to the probability that a hypothesis supported by your data is actually true (more about this shortly). Naturally, you want this likelihood to be high, but if you set it *too* high, you may miss important inferences. The general approach used in hypothesis testing is similar to that used in inferring population values based on sample results. As was true in calculating confidence intervals, typical values for confidence levels are 95%, 99%, and sometimes 90%.

TYPE I AND TYPE II ERROR

Type I

There's always some chance that your experiment or test will provide data supporting your hypothesis by random accident, not because the hypothesis is really true. Statisticians call this **Type I error;** it is the complement of the confidence level (in other words, a 95% confidence level carries a 5% probability of Type I error, and so on).

In the correlation example in Chapter 9, you were able to conclude that there is indeed reasonable evidence of at least some positive correlation in the population between the two variables that interested you. The confidence level was 99%, which means that the probability of Type I error—the estimated probability that there really isn't a correlation in the population at all, regardless of what your sample data suggested—is believed to be only 1%. Had you set the confidence level higher, you might not have been able to assert that such a relationship exists, even though your evidence says that there seems to be no more than a 1 in 100 chance that it doesn't!

Type II

There's also a chance that your experiment (also by random accident) won't provide data supporting a hypothesis even though that hypothesis is actually true. Statisticians call *this* **Type II error.** The lower the Type I error (the more rigorous our criteria for hypothesis-testing, in other words), the higher the Type II error, although there's no simple formula that describes this relationship.

The possibility of Type II error always exists, even at more typical confidence levels. What if (by chance) you measure a correlation in your sample that is zero (or small enough that you can't prove the population value to be other than zero) when in fact the population value is substantially higher—or lower? In other words, what if you fail to "pick up" what's in reality a significant relationship in your sampling and testing procedures? You've missed what could have been an important statistical observation. This is the type of situation represented by the idea of Type II error.

Minimizing Either Error

It might seem as though the best research would set extremely high confidence levels as the criteria that **statistical tests** must meet, but this is not the case. If you set a confidence level of 99.99%, you'd almost rule out the possibility of Type I error, but Type II error would probably be unacceptably high; important conclusions that might otherwise have been drawn could be overlooked.

Type II error is harder than Type I error to control or assess. Perhaps some day other researchers will serendipitously rediscover the relationship you've accidentally overlooked. But there are steps you could have taken way back in the beginning of your research design to minimize the possibility of Type II error (overlooking an important result because you don't seem to have achieved statistical significance). Measuring accurately, controlling experiments carefully, following the principles of randomization scrupulously, using adequate sample sizes, and choosing an appropriate confidence level (not always 99%, especially for early research into a new problem!) all help to assure you'll find what you're looking for if it is represented in the measurements you make.

This same logic applies to all types of hypothesis tests, not just the example of testing whether a correlation is not zero. Some statistics texts give guidelines for estimating Type II error, although in general it is not as well understood or as widely considered as Type I error. Suffice it to say that just because an individual experiment doesn't support your hypothesis *you never have absolute proof that your hypothesis was wrong!*

HYPOTHESIS TESTING

Before looking more closely at particular tests, a short excursion into the logic of hypothesis testing is in order. In the correlation example, you tested the assertion that the true correlation in the population was zero. This follows a logic that is standard for hypothesis-testing studies.

Null Hypothesis

What you really do when you set up a hypothesis to be tested is to construct a **null hypothesis** that is *true if the hypothesis is not*. It is actually the null hypothesis that is tested. Statistical tests allow you to decide whether the available evidence will let you make the conservative assumption that your null hypothesis is true, or if your data force you to abandon this assumption. In other words, the logic is set up to prevent your jumping to new conclusions without strong evidence! Only if

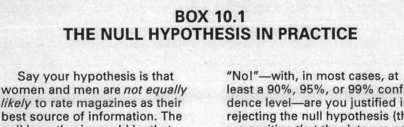

BOX 10.1
THE NULL HYPOTHESIS IN PRACTICE

Say your hypothesis is that women and men are *not equally likely* to rate magazines as their best source of information. The null hypothesis would be that women and men *are equally likely* to rate magazines as their best source. You test the null hypothesis, asking if the data are consistent with that idea. Only if the data jump up at you and yell "No!"—with, in most cases, at least a 90%, 95%, or 99% confidence level—are you justified in rejecting the null hypothesis (the proposition that the data are consistent with an explanation *other than* your hypothesis) and instead accept the hypothesis (in this case, the assertion that men and women rate magazines differently).

the evidence you've gathered is inconsistent with the null hypothesis, based on a given confidence level (that is, an acceptable probability of Type I error), are you in a position to advance your hypothesis as the alternative explanation.

Directional and Nondirectional Hypotheses

A **directional hypothesis** incorporates an assertion about the direction of an inequality, that is, it suggests which of two values should be higher. In the example in Box 10.1, you could hypothesize that women would be *more* likely than men to rank magazines as their number one source. The null hypothesis changes here, too; it should state in this case that men are *at least* as likely as women to rank magazines number one.

A statement that two values are simply different is called a *nondirectional hypothesis.*

A directional hypothesis is tested by what's called a **one-tailed test,** whereas a nondirectional one uses a **two-tailed test.** This seemingly small distinction can be quite important, as you'll see later, for some types of statistical tests, although the chi-square test (discussed shortly) is not generally one of them—it is used for nondirectional hypotheses about frequency distributions.

Parametric and Nonparametric Tests

Statistical tests for examining hypotheses are generally divided into **parametric** and **nonparametric** tests. The distinction has to do with the assumptions that are made about the data.

Parametric tests are used with categorical data. The correlation test presented in Chapter 9 is one example of a parametric test. Nonparametric tests are used with continuous data. Pearson's *r* is based on interval or ratio data, although there are other correlation coefficients that are nonparametric.

Nonparametric tests are very important in media research because many variables of interest—especially those derived from content analysis, which typically classifies media content into nominal categories—are not measured on continuous scales.

THE UBIQUITOUS CHI-SQUARE

Of the dozens of nonparametric tests (see, e.g., Siegal, 1956), by far the one most commonly used in mass communications research is the **chi-square test,** which determines whether two or more frequency distributions are proportionately alike or different. You're going to study it in some detail (and, yes, do some of the algebra and all the arithmetic, both of which are quite bearable!) because the logic is exactly the same as for more complex hypothesis-testing procedures. Understanding this one test in some detail is both extremely useful in and of itself and a good foundation for understanding other types of statistical tests. You won't have to justify the calculations algebraically, however; consult an advanced methods text if you are interested—or suspicious!

Distributions

Each distribution tested usually represents empirical data collected from two or more different groups (samples). For example, you might want to compare the frequencies with which women rate either magazines, newspapers, or television as their best information source to the frequencies for men.

However, a single empirical distribution can also be tested against some assumed theoretical distribution. For example, the actual preferences of voters for one political party or another might be compared to the distribution that would result if there was no particular preference—a 50-50 distribution assuming that just two parties (e.g., the U.S. Republican and Democratic parties) are involved. The null hypothesis for a test of this type is always that the distributions are the same; directionality is not an issue.

An In-Depth Analysis

Consider data that compare intended college major for high school students and college freshmen (Table 10.1).

It looks from Table 10.1 as though there are some differences between the preferences of the two groups, which might suggest shifts that occur after high school graduates enter college. Of course, the table might also represent differences in the populations or just in the samples involved; there's no way to tell this reliably just by looking at the data. But you would certainly like to be able to judge whether the two distributions are different in important ways.

One way that helps considerably in understanding the data, especially as the number of high school students in the study does not appear to be the same as the number of college students, is to calculate the number in each group and then the proportions (or percentages) for the two frequency distributions, as shown in Table 10.2.

Table 10.2 is easier to interpret. It now looks as though more college students intend to major in "other social science" (21% vs. 13%) and lots fewer in humanities (26% vs. 34%), for example, in comparison to the high school students. (Note that the percentages for the high school students don't exactly add to 100 because of rounding. Also, note that although the same number of high school and

TABLE 10.1

	Student	
Intended Major	*High School*	*College*
Mass communication	20	20
Other social science	11	22
Humanities	29	22
Biology/geology/natural science	10	20
Physics/chemistry/mathematics	16	21

college students chose mass communication the proportion of the total is different in each case.) But is this really a "big" (statistically significant) difference, or just a "little" (random) fluctuation?

Chi-square tests use the same rules of thumb that you've learned for making descriptive inferences about populations based on sample data. If there's a 95% (or 99%, or 90%) probability that the two distributions are different due to something other than random chance, then you have evidence considered sufficient to reject the null hypothesis of no difference between the two distributions and conclude that something potentially interesting is going on!

Contingency Tables

A table like those in the previous section is sometimes referred to as a "cross-tab" table, shorthand for cross tabulation, meaning the results are tabulated across two variables. A better name is **contingency table** because the table gives values of one variable *contingent on* the value of another. (If more variables are involved, multiple tables are usually constructed.)

The space that each value occupies on the table is referred to as a **cell;** the cells are arranged in rows and columns. There will be as many columns as there are values of one variables and as many rows as there are values of the others. For example, if Tables 10.1 and 10.2 included a third group of students, say, from elementary school, there'd be three columns in each table.

Using the Null Hypothesis

Chi-square calculations involve comparing the observed frequencies with the ones you'd expect *on the basis of your null hypothesis.* If there were no important

TABLE 10.2

	Student			
	High School		College	
Intended Major	*Number*	*%*	*Number*	*%*
Mass communication	20	23	20	19
Other social science	11	13	22	21
Humanities	29	34	22	21
Biology/natural science	10	12	20	19
Physics/chemistry/mathematics	16	19	21	20
Total	86	101	105	100

differences between high school students and college students in terms of their intended majors, you'd expect *each* of these distributions to be about the same as the *total* distribution for *all* students. To see this more clearly, calculate the total distribution of intended majors for all students (in numbers and percentages) shown in Table 10.3.

If there were no differences between the two groups (high school vs. college students), because 21% of all students combined chose mass communication as their intended major, you'd expect about 21% of the high school students *and* 21% of the college students to make this choice. Note that 45% of the students in the study are in high school (86 out of 191), and 55% are in college (105 out of 191). The expected value for the number of high school students intending to major in mass communications would be 45% times 21% times the number of people in the sample, which is 191. This is $.45 \times .21 \times 191$, or 18. Instead, the actual value observed is 20, reflecting a slightly higher proportion of high school students choosing mass communication in comparison to college students.

Expected Value

An expected value must be calculated for each of the cells in Table 10.3. There is a shorthand way to do this that may not make quite as much intuitive sense to you but that gives exactly the same answer. For each cell, take the total number in the whole row, multiply it by the total number in the whole column, and divide by the total number in the sample. Using the high school example cell, this would be $(40 \times 86)/191$, or (again) 18. It's useful to write the expected value (perhaps in a different color ink) beside each observed value.

TABLE 10.3

Intended Major	Student					
	High School		College		Combined	
	Number	%	Number	%	Number	%
Mass communication	20	23	20	19	40	21
Other social science	11	13	22	21	33	17
Humanities	29	34	22	21	51	27
Biology/natural science	10	12	20	19	30	16
Physics/chemistry/mathematics	16	19	21	20	37	19
Total	86	101	105	100	191	100

Calculation

The actual formula for the value of the chi-square statistic is based on comparing expected and observed values and looks like this:

$$\chi^2 = \Sigma \; \frac{(O - E)^2}{E}.$$

Here χ is the Greek letter *chi*. As before, Σ means summation (total of all cases) of whatever follows. O means observed value, and E means expected value; the difference between them is squared, always resulting—of course—in a positive value, which is then divided by the expected value. (Some texts use f_E and f_O, respectively, for observed and expected frequencies.)

In the student-major example, there are 10 cells, so the procedure is repeated 10 times and the results added together. For the first cell, with its expected value of 18 and its observed value of 20, this works out to $2^2/18$, or .22. Try it for the other 9 cells. If your arithmetic is correct, you should get a value for chi-square of 7.47.

Now, count the rows and columns. You also need (as for Student's *t*) to calculate a value for degrees of freedom. For this type of problem *df* is defined as one less than the number of rows (R) times one less than the number of columns (C), or $(R - 1) \times (C - 1)$. In the example, this is $(5 - 1) \times (2 - 1)$, or 4. As was true of degrees of freedom in other types of problems considered earlier, you may find it helpful to think of this number as the number of cells that are completely "free" to vary, hence the name. If you were making up data for an example, like the ones in this book, and you began with figures for the total for each row and each column, you could fill out four cells with any values that you liked (as long as they were not higher than the marginal totals for that particular row and column); the others would be constrained by the necessity to have everything add up right!

Chi-square is not a normally distributed statistic, and the shape of the distribution of possible values of chi-square depends on the degrees of freedom involved. However, as with *t,* statistics books and advanced methods texts provide tables of the distributions of chi-square for each possible number of degrees of freedom for reference purposes. The appendix to this book provides most of the chi-square values you are ever likely to need. A small portion of a chi-square table covers the situation in the student-major example:

df	*Acceptable Type I Probability*		
	.10	.05	.01
4	7.78	9.49	13.28

The chi-square value in the example, 7.47, is not quite high enough to allow you to conclude that there is a statistically significant difference in the choices made by high school and college students. You would have needed a chi-square value of 7.78 to assert, at a 90% confidence level, that there was a difference, or 9.49 to make this assertion at a 95% confidence level, or 13.28 to make this assertion at a 99% confidence level. Note that, in line with the discussion of Type II error earlier in this chapter, *this doesn't mean that there are no meaningful differences,* but you simply don't have enough evidence to assert that this is likely to be the case. Perhaps a larger study (or a differently designed one) would produce it. It's important, too, to recognize that even a statistically significant chi-square does not identify *which* differences within the two distributions are important; it only establishes that the two distributions *as a whole* are significantly different.

Cautions and Exceptions

Special cautions and exceptions apply to the use of chi-square tests.

Yates' Correction

A special correction called **Yates' correction** (calculated automatically by most statistical software) is required when the degrees of freedom for a chi-square test are equal to 1, that is, in a two row by two column (2×2, or "two by two") table.

This correction reduces the difference between the expected and obtained frequency by .5, regardless of the sign, before squaring.

Smallness of Frequencies

Also, chi-square tests are not reliable when the expected frequencies are quite small. Although statisticians vary in their recommendations, any time that *all* of the expected frequencies have values of 5 or more, there definitely should be no problem. Some researchers always combine or "collapse" categories before completing the analysis to assure that this condition is met; others point to statistical opinion that suggests that if no more than *one fifth* of the cells have expected frequencies below 5 there should be no problem, except in the special case of 2×2

BOX 10.2
LIMITS OF NONPARAMETRIC TESTS:
AN EXAMPLE

Say you've studied the sources that two newspapers use on important medical stories. On the basis of a chi-square comparison, you conclude that one newspaper used sources from medicine itself proportionately more often; the other tended to quote spokespeople from government, industry, or consumer groups more often. One paper is doing a better job representing the expert point of view, and one's doing a better job representing a broader range of viewpoints. (Of course, which goal is more important is a matter of opinion, not a researchable question.) It does not seem unreasonable to assert that you've uncovered an interesting pattern that probably applies to other situations as well. You just don't know anything about how to estimate the probability that studies of other, similar cases would reveal the same type of thing! What you really have is a type of case study, not a generalizable result, despite the appearance of at least one statistically significant comparison.

If, however, you measured column inches in each paper attributed to medical sources—a ratio-level measurement—you'd have more flexibility in the analysis. Provided the samples used were true random samples of each paper's medical coverage, a condition rarely met in content analysis research, you can use the parametric *t* test (described in the next section) to compare the two means, the results of which allow you to generalize to a population where the chi-square test does not.

tables where *all* cells must have expected frequencies of 5 or more. There is no clear consensus on this matter; it's certainly best to avoid *any* expected frequencies less than 5 whenever reasonably possible.

But there's a temptation to be addressed in meeting this criterion. There are no expected frequencies less than 5 in the example. But say you decided to reduce the data to fewer categories. Logically, you could combine "mass communication" with "other social science" and put the two science categories together. The result would not differ from that in the example tables. But if you left "mass communication" and "humanities" as separate categories and combined the remaining three science and social science categories together, for example, you'd achieve statistical significance at the 90% confidence level with the same data. (You can check this by working out the chi-square statistics in each case and comparing them to table values; remember that in either case the degrees of freedom are now reduced to 2.)

Is this legitimate, or is this a form of statistical "cheating"? The answer depends entirely on whether there's a logical justification for the combinations we choose. It's certainly a questionable practice to test out multiple combinations and then report only the ones that turn out to be statistically significant, although this can be an acceptable way to initially explore a data set.

Nongeneralizability

The final—and important—limit of chi-square and other nonparametric statistical tests is that, technically speaking, they do not allow you to generalize to a population from a sample. Researchers may not stress this enough in practice.

COMPARING TWO MEANS

The *t* **test** for comparison of two means is a very common, relatively simple, and quite useful statistical test. This is a parametric test for interval or ratio data only and is based on the same *t* statistic you encountered earlier. It's widely available in standard statistical packages; so you won't go through the calculations for it here, which are a bit more complex than those for a chi-square test. This useful statistic also describes the sampling distribution of the *differences* between two means.

Cautions in Using the *t* Test

There are a few quirks (as usual!) that you need to be aware of in making effective use of a *t* test.

The Two-Mean Limit

First, this test is valid only for comparing *two* means. If you have multiple means—say, for example, if you've calculated the separate scores for four different ethnic groups—you can't compare all the different possible combinations using repeated *t* tests. In fact, whenever you make multiple statistical tests on the same set of data, you are "cheating."

If you're working with a 95% confidence level, with a 1-in-20 chance of Type I error, if you run 20 different statistical tests on the same set of data, odds are, on average, that 1 of the 20 will turn up "proof" of a hypothesis just by chance, regardless of population values. This is not so bad in exploratory research, where

---

BOX 10.3
THE *t* TEST IN ACTION

Say you ask a student sample to rate on a 10-point scale the extent to which they believe the information they get from the mass media (1 = *never believe the information at all;* 10 = *always believe all of the information*). The mean answer score for the women in the sample is 4.6; for men, it's 5.2. How do you decide if this is just sampling error (a random result due to exactly which women and which men you have, by chance, included in your sample) or indicative of a real difference between men and women generally in terms of the extent to which they believe what the media tell them?

The *t* test comes to the rescue in situations of this type. It uses the same kind of logic as other hypothesis tests do. Your null hypothesis is that there is *no difference* between the two means, that for men and that for women. Sample results are compared to the theoretical sampling distribution of possible differences between two means to determine whether your null hypothesis should be rejected at whatever confidence level you've chosen. Note that the mean of this distribution will be zero if there's really no difference between the two populations!

The standard deviation of this *t* distribution is calculated on the basis of the variance in the two subsamples (men and women). Degrees of freedom for a *t* test are calculated as the sum of the number in each sample minus 2. The variance in the two populations is normally assumed to be equal. As you learned in your use of *t* to estimate population means, with large samples the *t* distribution is almost identical to a normal distribution; the shape of the distribution varies with *df* for smaller sample sizes.

you're trying to generate new hypotheses inductively that you expect to test later on new data, but it is not acceptable in true hypothesis-testing research.

Special modifications of the basic *t* test are available (and usually included in statistical packages) that enable comparing multiple means *simultaneously,* much like a chi-square test compares two or more whole frequency distributions. A positive result doesn't tell you which means are responsible but does indicate that there's too much variance among them for you to reasonably assume that it was produced by chance.

Independent-Only Means

The *t* test as described here applies only to two *independent* means; if two measures are related—for example, where the same subject is given two different tests or asked two different survey questions—the means are not considered independent, and other procedures must be used. The results of *t* tests are also sensitive to large differences in the sizes of the two subsamples.

Hypothesis Testing: Directional Versus Nondirectional

The hypothesis tested by a *t* test can be directional or nondirectional. Recalling the example in Box 10.3, you tested a nondirectional hypothesis. The hypothesis is that men and women are different; the null hypothesis is that they are the same. But there might be good theoretical justification for working with a directional hypothesis instead; you might have some logical reason (perhaps based on others' research) for proposing that women have a lower level of belief than men. The null hypothesis for this directional hypothesis would be that men have the same or a higher level of belief than women. *Using a directional hypothesis allows you to divide the Type I error exactly in half* because you are concerned only with the area under the sampling distribution curve at one end, not as divided into either of two ends.

One way of thinking about this is to realize that in a one-tailed test your null hypothesis is rejected more easily. You don't have to go out so many standard deviations to reach the 95% (or 90%, or 99%) mark. Note that statistical packages often report the confidence level reached by the *t* test data, which can in theory be anything from zero to 1.00. You're aiming, typically, for .95 or better.

If, in the example, a confidence level of .94 was achieved, you'd be disappointed! But if you use a directional hypothesis and a one-tailed test (only one "tail" of the normal curve is considered), your confidence level is .97 instead (you ignore half of the .06 Type I error in the .94 confidence level), meeting your 95% criterion!

The One-Tailed Caveat

A cautionary note: Although it's very appealing to *always* choose one-tailed tests, which make it easier to achieve statistical significance, this is definitely against the rules unless you have actually stated your hypothesis in directional terms in advance of calculating the means and running the test.

You must also have sound justification for choosing a directional hypothesis—not just a hunch. Some statisticians believe that the criteria for appropriate use of a one-tailed test are rarely, if ever, met.

Two types of circumstances might justify the use of directional hypotheses and one-tailed tests:

- You have research evidence (from your own pilot study or from other published studies) suggesting that a relationship is in a particular direction. For example, you might have data that suggest women are more (or, conversely, less) likely to be comfortable with a particular type of news presentation than are men.

- The logic of your research question implies that you are interested in identifying results only if they support a conclusion in a specific direction. Perhaps you want to test the hypothesis that a new teaching technique is more effective than an old one, for example, but because the new technique is more expensive you wouldn't want to use it unless it produced a measurable, statistically significant improvement—not just a difference—in the results. Here a directional hypothesis is called for on logical grounds, and a one-tailed test would likely be considered justified.

Remember, though, only in exploratory research is it appropriate to decide the form of a hypothesis to be tested *after* an initial examination of the data.

IMPORTANT TERMS AND CONCEPTS

Cell	**Null hypothesis**	**Type I error**
Chi-square test	**One-tailed test**	**Type II error**
Contingency table	**Parametric**	**Two-tailed test**
Directional hypothesis	**Statistical test**	**Yates' correction**
Nonparametric	***t* test**	

EXERCISES

1. As a class project, determine the gender and mass communication career preference of each member of your class by means of a survey. Run a chi-square test to determine whether the men and women in your class have different preferences. Use the chi-square table in the back of this book.

2. Does your local student paper or your regular local newspaper contain more front-page news having to do with your university? In a few paragraphs, sketch out how you would test this proposition. Will you use a one- or a two-tailed test? Why? Use column inches as your measure so you have ratio data for a *t* test. Can you figure out how to sample the coverage randomly? What compromises did you have to make, if any, in designing your comparison?

Sometimes, multivariate analysis can shed light on complex patterns that otherwise wouldn't be seen.

11

Explorations

In this chapter, you'll look at some of the more complex tools for data analysis that can help you describe and explore data sets in more detail. You'll use actual data from a survey of members of a university community about their information needs to illustrate some of these tools.

But first, a word about indexes and scales. Throughout this book, reference has been made to familiar scales, such as those that assess levels of agreement, without paying much attention to what a scale actually is or what it does. A scale is simply a measure that assesses some parameter, or characteristic, on at least an ordinal level. That *sounds* simple enough but involves complicated validity problems in practice. What is the relationship between the concept in which you are interested (for theoretical reasons) and the scale you use to assess it?

COMPLEX VARIABLES

Intelligence, which many educational psychologists have spent whole careers trying to define and measure, is not a **unidimensional** concept but a complex one, assessment of which actually requires several different scales. And each scale will involve not just one question but a whole series of questions. Dimensionality itself can be assessed by looking at relationships between individual scale scores and

161

establishing which ones are highly correlated with one another versus relatively independent.

Because as a student you've probably had a lot of experience with intelligence and achievement tests, this seems like fairly obvious reasoning. Yet communications researchers and others who work with less well-understood concepts face this type of problem all the time—sometimes without even realizing it.

Problems With Word Choice

If you're interested in studying the audience *credibility* of different information sources—for example, a scientific expert versus a government official, or television versus news, or a Hispanic versus an Anglo speaker—you could use a simple 5- or 10-point scale asking subjects to rate the *believability* of each of several sources. But are their self-assessments accurate? Perhaps not. A better approach might be to use an experimental design and present different groups of subjects with the same information from different sources and then ask them to rate the believability of the information itself without telling them the purpose of the experiment. The results might be quite different!

BOX 11.1
HOW DO YOU MEASURE INTELLIGENCE?

Say you want to measure the intelligence of a group of schoolchildren as part of a study to determine whether intelligence is related to the amount of information gained from viewing different styles of video presentation. You could ask children to assess their own intelligence on a scale ranging from 1 to 10, but of course this would really only be measuring the children's self-perceptions. You could ask their teacher to rate them on this type of scale, but teachers have prejudices, too—their assessments of individual students would be influenced by their likes and dislikes and their particular positive or negative experiences with particular children.

Intelligence is considered separate from achievement, although the two are obviously correlated, so tests of knowledge won't do the trick either. Instead, some kind of problem-solving test seems most appropriate—most closely related to the concept of intelligence. But intelligence is multifaceted; some children are better at solving verbal problems, others at mathematical problems, and still others at geometric or mechanical problems. So, how do you get the answers you need?

But there's one problem: Are "believability" and "credibility" the same thing? You'd be wise not to ask "To what extent is this information credible?" in an experiment of this type because the wording is abstract and the word "credible" is not as much a part of most people's everyday vocabulary as the word "belief." In other words, some subjects might not fully understand the word "credible"; others may define it differently from one another.

Instead, you might ask something like "How certain are you that this information is accurate?" But is belief in accuracy exactly the same thing as credibility, or has part of your original measurement intent been altered or distorted? Should you substitute a measure of whether subjects would actually *act on* the information provided, not whether they simply state that they *believe* it? Perhaps there's more than one dimension to "belief." Perhaps for some information, an opinion on its accuracy can be quickly changed if different information is presented, whereas other opinions may be more deeply held, and perhaps this depends partly on the type of source the information came from. And is a belief in *accuracy* really the issue in the first place? Should you, instead, ask respondents whether they "think the information is true"? Would this be assessing the same thing, or a different dimension of the same thing, or something else altogether? There are no easy answers to this type of operationalization problem.

Self-Perception Versus Reality

You need to be particularly alert to the fact that subjects' self-perceptions of such things as their own media use habits and preferences, let alone the *reasons* for these habits and preferences, may not represent reality. People may understate or overstate the amount of time they spend watching TV or their own susceptibility to advertising messages, for example. Sometimes, subjects are not even particularly self-conscious about such issues. Try asking some of your fellow students why they read the newspaper, or watch a particular television show, or play computer games. Most of the time the answer you'll get is something like "because I like it" or "because it's fun!" Although people's own explanations of their behavior should be taken seriously, when you ask them questions they've never thought about, their answers often don't seem to help your understanding much. Qualitative probing may be one way around this; substituting a measure other than self-reports is another.

In the latter case in particular, you need to begin with a clear concept of what it is that you want to measure. You also need to be careful about interpreting intercorrelated answers. If you ask subjects if information is *accurate* and if the same information is *truthful,* the answers are likely to be highly correlated. Have you made an interesting new discovery, or only reflected the fact that these words mean nearly the same thing to many people? If you believe they are truly different ideas, are they different dimensions of some broader concept (like, say, credibility), or are they entirely separate factors that people use when assessing information?

SCALE TYPES

In attempts to improve scaling results and to develop flexible approaches to measurement that can be applied to a broad variety of problems, numerous approaches have been developed. A few of the most common ones are described here to give you some idea of the range of options available.

Likert

The kind of 5- or 10-point scale discussed in earlier chapters is sometimes called a **Likert scale** because the technique was invented by a researcher with that name. Likert's technique involved generating many times more of these scale questions than a researcher actually intended to use for a study and then looking at the correlations among the answers to determine which ones actually seemed to be measuring different things and which ones the same things.

Scales that look like this but that you've just made up for purposes of your study, without going through the process that Likert suggested, shouldn't really be called Likert scales but Likert-*like* scales. It's easier, and less misleading, to just call them 5- or 10-point scales, as this book does. (Seven-point scales are also in common use.)

Applying the Likert Technique

These scales often measure **attitude,** that is, a general positive or negative orientation toward classes of items (whether objects or ideas or people) not considered unique to particular contexts. But Likert-like scales can also measure such things as credibility or believability, preferences, needs, satisfaction, and so on.

Likert's original technique can be useful in communication research. For each unidimensional item to be scaled, this approach involves comparing the scores on individual items to the total score for that respondent. Items whose answers aren't highly correlated to the overall score are considered to be measuring something else and are eliminated.

In Likert scaling, and in other research involving the presentation of long lists of questions or statements and requesting scaled answers, it's important to put the questions in an order unlikely to generate a series of similar answers from an individual respondent. Otherwise the respondent might fall into a pattern of answering "agree, agree, agree" or "disagree, disagree, disagree" without carefully considering the individual questions.

The solution may be systematically alternating positive with negative attitudinal items, or questions representing conservative versus liberal political positions, and so on, depending on the particular problem. (You'll recall this was mentioned briefly in an earlier chapter.) Otherwise, questions of this type are often presented in a random order. Because the possible influence of question order on respondents' answers can entirely be eliminated, however (remember this discussion in designing survey questions?), the ideal approach might be to present the questions in several different orders to different groups of respondents and test for differences in the answers, but this might not be considered necessary in a particular case.

Bipolar

A **bipolar scale** is often used in communication research. This scale (traditionally 7-point) might be thought of as an elaboration on the idea of the agree/disagree scale, but uses descriptive as well as evaluative answer choices. *Any* two adjectives that are opposite in meaning can be used at the two ends of the scale, such as competent-incompetent, smart-stupid, pleasant-unpleasant, and so on. Assessing dimensionality is a consideration, just as for Likert scales.

This type of scale was developed by early communication researcher Charles Osgood, who believed that the meaning of any term could be usefully described using only three of these scales, good-bad, strong-weak, and active-passive. Osgood and his colleagues thought of themselves as measuring meaning (semantics) with these scales. Today, researchers are quite unlikely to assert that there are only three simple dimensions important to meaning (a point of view that would be seen as excessively reductionistic).

Osgood-type scales are sometimes called "semantic differential" scales, his original term for them, instead of bipolar scales. These scales can be quite useful for characterizing people's reactions to public figures, advertised products, television programming, and other situations in which people's reactions are likely to be complex and multidimensional.

Applying the Bipolar Technique

Sometimes, bipolar scales are used to assess a **stereotype;** here the word has a special technical sense. It does not refer to a negative attitude toward a group of people but to a strong general opinion (whether positive or negative) that is relatively independent of the circumstances of the judgment. A political candidate is said to be "stereotyped" in this sense if he or she is rated equally highly on many different bipolar scales that assess somewhat different concepts.

In this situation, it appears as though (for whatever reason) people have a certain "mind-set" through which information received about the candidate is filtered; regardless of actual performance, personality, or qualifications, the candidate is seen in a positive (or negative) light. While in office, President Ronald Reagan seemed equally popular no matter what his actions were; he was probably stereotyped in the minds of many voters as an all-around "good person."

Guttman

Another well-known type of scaling is the **Guttman scale.** One goal of scaling is to be able to rank or group people in a reliable way according to some characteristic—be it a political characteristic such as conservatism, a personality characteristic such as extroversion, or an attitudinal characteristic such as support for a strong defense. A Guttman scale consists of a series of questions the answers to which reliably classify respondents in this way.

Applying the Guttman Technique

Say you have a Guttman scale consisting of five items. The idea is that all (or nearly all) of the respondents who answer the first one "no" will answer all of the others in the negative; all (or nearly all) of the respondents who answered the first one "yes" but the second one "no" will answer the third, fourth, and fifth "no"; all (or nearly all) of the respondents who said "yes" to the first two but "no" to the third will also answer "no" to the last two; and so on. The use of Guttman scaling results in ordinal data.

INDEXES

Social science researchers often rely on indexes rather than scales. The term **index** usually refers to an *indirect* measure of the variable in question. A simple example might be using the rapidity with which a class being offered fills up with registered students at the beginning of the term as an index of its popularity. You haven't surveyed anyone with questions about whether they like the class or not; you've just assumed that the faster the class fills, the more people like it. In reality, it might fill up faster because of the time slot in which it's being offered or for some other reason, but perhaps—for a particular research purpose—this is good enough.

Unobtrusive measures are often indexes. All index measurements are imperfect, but they can still be very useful. The important thing to remember is that indexes are used when direct measurement is difficult or impractical, and they are always inaccurate to some degree. The controversies over the significance of commercial indexes such as Nielson or Arbitron ratings reflect this.

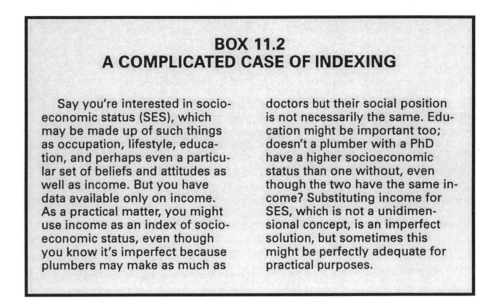

BOX 11.2
A COMPLICATED CASE OF INDEXING

Say you're interested in socio-economic status (SES), which may be made up of such things as occupation, lifestyle, education, and perhaps even a particular set of beliefs and attitudes as well as income. But you have data available only on income. As a practical matter, you might use income as an index of socioeconomic status, even though you know it's imperfect because plumbers may make as much as doctors but their social position is not necessarily the same. Education might be important too; doesn't a plumber with a PhD have a higher socioeconomic status than one without, even though the two have the same income? Substituting income for SES, which is not a unidimensional concept, is an imperfect solution, but sometimes this might be perfectly adequate for practical purposes.

BOX 11.3
INDEXES USED IN
MASS COMMUNICATION RESEARCH

What kind of indexes might be used in mass communication research? You might use something like box office receipts as an index of the popularity of a movie, for example, rather than conducting a survey of fans. You might use number of households with televisions tuned to a particular show at a particular time as an index of the show's real audience—or of the number of people who have listened to a particular advertisement. Or you might use the number of times a particular issue makes the headlines of the *New York Times* as an index of its position on the public agenda.

THE RIGHT TOOL FOR THE RIGHT JOB

Researchers can become so carried away with the technical details of measurement that they lose track of what they are actually studying, or of its real-world significance. That's why Chapter 1 presented the concept of "reification"—treating as real things that are not; this is a danger in using sophisticated scaling techniques. The bottom line should be whether a particular measure is the most useful for a particular research problem. That means the most reliable and valid, as well as the handiest one! This principle is why this segment of the book is called a "toolbox." No one would use a pneumatic drill when a simple screwdriver will do, although there will be times when doing a professional job absolutely requires a more complicated piece of equipment.

The ultimate test of any tool—whether statistical or mechanical—is its usefulness in solving particular problems. Exploring measurement issues can be a lot of fun for some people (honestly!), but it is never an end in itself.

EXPLORING COMPLEX DATA: THE TEXAS A&M STUDY

Now that you understand a bit more about scales and indexes, you're ready to turn to the data mentioned earlier in this book to see how more complex *analytical* (as opposed to measurement) tools can help you understand what's going on.

In fall 1994, students, faculty, administrators, and staff members at Texas A&M, a major research university of 40,000 students, were surveyed by mail to assess what their information needs were and how well these were, or were not, being met. The number of respondents in this relatively small class project was 138. The survey included a question about overall satisfaction (a 10-point scale) as well as ratings of individual media (the student paper, the local paper, campus newsletters, flyers and memos, electronic mail, and so on). Respondents were also asked to indicate, on 10-point scales, the relative importance to them of certain types of information and certain uses to which information might be put. If you've taken a media theory or media effects course, you will realize that this was in part a "uses and gratifications" study—a study of the uses to which information is put and the personal needs it fulfills. Demographic data were also collected from the respondents.

General Statistics

First, there are some statistics from this study that you already know how to interpert! The mean level of satisfaction overall was 7.15. Although you lack comparative data from other universities to base a judgment on, it seems reason-

TABLE 11.1

Use or Purpose Category	Correlation With Overall Satisfaction (Pearson's r)
Performance	.05
Planning	−.02
Opportunities	−.12
Benefits	.12
Community	.26*
Self-improvement	.05
"Just knowing what's going on"	.27*

*Statistically significant at the .001 level (99.9% confidence level).

able to conclude that this is a positive result—that the respondents were fairly well satisfied with existing information systems. The means for the individual media rated ranged from 4.76 for the university's central electronic information system to 6.71 for the daily student newspaper. On this campus there's also a weekly newspaper published for faculty and staff; it rated almost exactly as high as the student paper at 6.69. It should be no surprise that students rated the student paper higher (7.54) than did faculty (5.19) or staff (6.48). The faculty-staff paper was rated highest by staff (6.83); faculty and students rated it about the same (6.54 and 6.57, respectively; the "faculty" category includes administrators).

These descriptive data helped the research team (an undergraduate mass media research methods class) develop a recommendation that concentrated on improving the electronic system.

The "Just Knowing" Variable

The survey asked seven questions requesting ratings of the importance of particular uses or purposes to which university information might be put: improving job or school performance, planning a daily schedule, finding out about opportunities, understanding benefits, feeling a part of the community, general self-improvement, and "just knowing what's going on." Of these, understanding benefits and "just knowing" were rated the highest in importance (8.05 and 8.03, respectively, on a 10-point scale). Correlation coefficients between each of these scales and overall satisfaction are shown in Table 11.1.

In other words, the more important people thought that feeling a part of the community and "just knowing what's going on" were, the more likely they were to be satisfied with existing information systems. One explanation is that the existing information system is doing a good job meeting these two important needs. In fact, data from a question asking respondents to indicate their best-met needs revealed that "just knowing what's going on" was the answer given most often, followed by "feeling a part of the community."

This "just knowing" variable needs a closer look. It seems a bit surprising that this would rate as high in importance as things like information about sick leave and health insurance! At this point, you have no hypotheses—just a hunch and some curiosity. (Reasonable hunches are perfectly acceptable substitutes for hypotheses *only* in exploratory research!) So what else can the data tell you?

The Effect of Gender

A *t* test will tell you whether gender might possibly be related to the "just knowing" variable; this seems a reasonable thing to try, as other research has suggested that women may find some things about the social environment to be of more importance than men do. The mean overall importance rating of "just knowing" for the 58 men in the study was 7.74, whereas for the 80 women it was 8.24. This is not a huge difference; a statistical test was necessary to help judge its importance. A two-tailed *t* test of the (null) hypothesis that the two means are alike achieved a level of statistical significance of .145, that is, a confidence level of .855. This does not reach the confidence level of .90 often used in exploratory research, so the hypothesis of no difference should be accepted. You cannot conclude that men and women rate the importance of "just knowing" differently if you use a two-tailed test.

However, you do have some justification, based on previous research, for thinking that women might rate this variable *higher* than men, not just differently. So it's reasonable to test instead the directional null hypothesis that men's ratings of the importance of "just knowing" is the *same or higher.* Here you're performing a one-tailed test, and you're justified in dividing the significance level in half, to .073. This produces a confidence level of .927, meeting the 90% criterion for exploratory research. You reject the null hypothesis that men's ratings in the population as a whole are the same or higher than women's and accept instead the alternative hypothesis that women do indeed rate the importance of "just knowing" higher.

But you don't really know whether the differences between men and women really have anything to do with gender or might have more to do with other factors that are in turn related to gender. For example, there are more male than female faculty and administrators and more female than male staff members, as shown in Table 11.2. The chi-square statistic on this contingency table, which has 2 degrees of freedom, is 25.0. This is much higher than what's needed to achieve a 99% confidence level (a chi-square value of 9.21), although one of the six cells has an expected value of less than 5. So, are the differences between men and women in the importance ratings they assign to "just knowing" best attributed to gender

TABLE 11.2

	Faculty	Staff	Administrators
Men	13	10	8
Women	4	41	2
Total	17	51	10

itself, or might they really reflect differences among the different occupational groups included in the sample?

Analysis of Variance

A technique called **one-way ANOVA,** short for **analysis of variance** (which some statisticians point out is closely related to the *t* test), allows you to ask and answer questions about the relationship between a single categorical independent variable and a continuous dependent variable. Your hunch is that the perceived importance of "just knowing" may depend on gender.

Analysis of variance relies on the distribution of something called the *F* statistic, just as *t* tests rely on the distribution of *t* and chi-square tests rely on the distribution of χ^2. Part of the ANOVA result for your problem is this:

	F	Significance
Main effect (of gender)	2.150	.145

Note that the significance level for *F* is exactly the same as the significance level you obtained with the *t* test. Gender and the importance of "just knowing" seem to be clearly related. But the real advantage of **ANOVA** is that it can describe the effects of *multiple* independent categorical variables simultaneously as well as take into account any interaction between them. Because the distribution by gender within the different professional categories (faculty, staff, administrator, undergraduate student, graduate student) is not the same, according to the chi-square test above, how do you know if it's really gender, or professional group, or some combination of the two that best predicts the perceived importance of "just knowing"? Part of a **two-way ANOVA** that will help you sort this out is shown in Table 11.3.

TABLE 11.3

	F	*Significance*
Main effects	2.546	.031
Gender	.396	.530
Profession	2.612	.039
Two-way interaction between		
gender and profession	1.385	.243
Explained	2.030	.041

This table tells you that professional group predicts part of the variation in the dependent variable (the importance of "just knowing") and that this result is statistically significant (confidence level of 96% from the third line of the table). Gender seems to be much less important; its relationship to "just knowing" is not independently statistically significant, although note that significance for the two variables *taken together* as predictors of "just knowing" is still slightly higher than for professional group alone (confidence level of 97% from line one).

Interaction Effect

Finally, ANOVA treats the interaction between the two variables as an independent predictor of the dependent variable. The **interaction effect** is important in many mass media-related problems. This term refers to the fact that the relationship between an independent variable and a dependent variable may be different, depending on the value of each.

In the example, the relationship between the importance of "just knowing" and professional group may be different for men than for women—or, conversely, you may think of the relationship between gender and "just knowing" as being different in different professional groups. For instance, perhaps "just knowing" is more important among male faculty than female faculty but more important among female than male staff members—or the other way around! Like nonlinear relationships, such effects are easy to overlook in data analysis. One set of effects may "mask" the other in aggregate data. Although the interaction effect above did not achieve statistical significance, it has a substantial enough significance level to deserve a closer look.

Analysis of variance can handle more than two independent variables. Note that with three independent variables, however, there are three possible main effects, three possible two-way interaction effects (from these pairs of variables: 1 and 2, 2 and 3, 1 and 3), and a possible three-way interaction. With four independent variables, there are six possible two-way interactions alone! It gets hard to interpret the results in a meaningful way, so it's important to use previous data, theory, and sometimes the results of exploratory analysis to "narrow down" the list of potentially important independent variables.

Variable Relationships

ANOVA techniques yield much more information about variable relationships than what's been briefly reported here. But note that although the term "effect" is typically used to describe these relationships, ANOVA really analyzes the extent to which variables covary, that is, the extent to which a dependent variable can be predicted on the basis of one or more independent variables. Causation is still something the researcher can only infer, not something "proven" by a set of ANOVA data.

Remember also that it's best to have equal cell sizes for most analysis of variance problems. In the example, the cell sizes are not equal. There are more women than men in the sample and more staff than faculty and more faculty than administrators. This can alter the validity of the results and needs to be corrected for, typically by using an appropriate statistical software package as the calculations can be complex.

IDENTIFYING FACTORS

You now have evidence that professional group is an important predictor of the degree of importance assigned to "just knowing what's going on" and that gender may also be related but to a much lesser extent. You also know that there's a positive correlation between the perceived importance of "just knowing" and the degree of satisfaction seen in the existing information system. It turns out that staff members rate "just knowing" higher in importance than do faculty (8.04 vs. 7.04, respectively, on a 10-point scale), which may be a partial explanation of why staff members are more satisfied overall, although there's not a big difference in satisfaction between the two groups. Further, students rate "just knowing" the highest (at 8.47), yet are slightly less satisfied than the other groups overall.

Factor Analysis

In light of the discussion earlier in this chapter about scaling, however, what are these questions actually measuring? Are the questions about "feeling a part of the community" and "just knowing what's going on" measuring the same thing, or different things? (Ideally, you would have sorted this out with pilot and pretests

TABLE 11.4

Factor Matrix	Factor 1	Factor 2
Performance	.81377	.07838
Planning	.73000	.04904
Opportunities	.68012	.17673
Benefits	.49572	.27822
Community	.16800	.88257
Self-improvement	.50092	.61493
"Just knowing what's going on"	.04292	.86025

prior to conducting the survey, but because the time available to conduct this small study was quite limited, this was not done in advance.)

A technique called **factor analysis,** which looks at the intercorrelations among a set of variables, can help you decide. Factor analysis tries to determine whether a complex set of data can be represented by a smaller number of underlying abstract "factors." The particular type of factor analysis you'll use is a standard one called *principal components analysis.* Considerable preanalysis of the data is required to perform a valid factor analysis. Table 11.4 shows what one important outcome of a factor analysis in SPSS® performed on the data from this study would look like.

The procedure has identified two factors for your data set. The statistics in Table 11.4 (called "factor loadings") represent the degree of relationship between each of the variables and the hypothetical underlying "factors" that the analysis has identified. (In other words, they are much like correlation coefficients between each variable and each of the two "factors.")

Factor 1 is most closely associated with performance, planning, and opportunities; Factor 2 is most closely associated with feeling a part of the university community, "just knowing what's going on," and (to a lesser extent) self-improvement, although this latter item seems to be related to both factors to some degree.

Naming Factors

It's customary to use descriptive names for each factor, based on what they appear to represent, *although these are always somewhat intuitive and subjective!* You might call Factor 1 the "instrumental" factor, as the variables closely associated with it all seem to have something to do with getting things done and moving ahead. You might call Factor 2 the "emotive" factor, as the variables most closely associated with it seem to have to do with feeling like an insider rather than an outsider in the university community. Note that some variables, like self-improvement in this example, can be closely related to *more than one* factor.

Recommendation

What would you recommend to the university on the basis of this evidence? Any recommendation would have to be extremely tentative, but perhaps university information providers at this institution need to be more sensitive to the fact that information that makes people feel a knowledgable part of the community, however valuable, may meet some people's needs but not others. Some of the "instrumental" needs are among those that were rated least well met by the existing system. The factor analysis helps give you a basis for reasoning from this complicated set of data to a concrete suggestion for either action or further investigation.

OTHER MULTIVARIATE TECHNIQUES

Multiple Regression

We've really only scratched the surface of **multivariate analysis** techniques. Another common way to "model" or describe complex relationships among many variables is provided by **multiple regression** analysis. Remember that a correlation

---

BOX 11.4
EXPLORATION WITH FACTOR-ANALYTIC RESULTS

You might want to find out whether there's a difference among faculty, admistrators, staff, and students in terms of which factor was most important overall, for example. You would surely want to calculate the correlation between Factor 2 and overall satisfaction, since rating both "feeling a part of the community" and "just knowing" as important are associated with higher satisfaction.

You can also use factor analysis to develop an index of a particular factor (or set of factors). The "emotive" factor is most closely and uniquely associated with the "knowing" variable; answers to that question may be a fairly good indicator of the importance of Factor 2 to that particular respondent. The association between Factor 2 and the perceived importance of feeling a part of the community is even a bit higher, but that variable has more of a relationship with Factor 1—the "instrumental" factor—as well. (In practice, you probably wouldn't want to choose just one question as an index; factor analysis is often used for far more complex data sets than what you've looked at here.)

coefficient can be interpreted as the slope of a line graphing the relationship between two variables that are linearly related. If the correlation's positive, the line slants up to the right; if it's negative, it slants down.

You'll probably recall from high school algebra that the slope of a straight line is defined by an equation in this form: $y = ax + b$, where x is the variable on the horizontal axis, y is the variable on the vertical axis, and b is a constant (actually the point at which the line intersects the vertical axis, because if x is zero, then y takes the value of b).

The procedure for calculating a Pearson's r correlation coefficient is based on the idea of finding the straight line that best represents the relationship. This is defined as the line that minimizes the *squared* distances between actual data points and the line itself. This is sometimes called linear least squares regression and is used to suggest how one variable can be predicted from another. But you can also create equations that predict one or more dependent variables from *multiple* continuous independent variables, using multiple regression.

In the university information study, another way of looking at the data would have been to ask how well the importance ratings of different purposes predict the overall degree of satisfaction. Using a technique called stepwise regression (a common form of regression analysis) and the statistical package SPSS®, you discover that an equation involving the "just knowing" variable and the "opportunities" variable best predicts overall satisfaction. In one case, the relationship is positive, in the other negative; in other words, multiplying the "just knowing" importance variable by a positive number and the "opportunities" importance variable by a negative number, plus adding a constant, gives the best prediction of satisfaction. This makes a lot of sense based on the analysis you've done of this data set so far.

Stepwise regression asks at each stage of equation construction which additional variables it would be best to add. While the importance of "community" is more closely related to satisfaction than is "opportunities," both "community" and "just knowing" are components of the same underlying "emotive" factor. So adding "community" to an equation that already includes "just knowing" (this is the "stepwise" part of stepwise regression!) doesn't add as much additional information. It stands to reason that adding a variable from the *other* factor would do more to improve your prediction! "Opportunity" ratings are closely related to the "instrumental" factor.

Discriminant Analysis

A technique called **discriminant analysis** is used to figure out which variables among a complex set best divides (or "discriminates") one group from another. For example, you might want to know which stands on issues most reliably predict, or discriminate, between Republicans and Democrats in the United States.

Cluster Analysis

Another technique called **cluster analysis** is used to classify *cases* rather than variables. For example, audience or market segments that share similar tastes and preferences might be identified using cluster analysis. Unlike discriminant analysis, cluster analysis does not begin with a predetermined set of categories (such as political party affiliation) but determines the categories based on the data. Unlike factor analysis, it doesn't calculate hypothetical underlying factors and their relationship to the variables measured but instead looks directly at the correlations among the variables themselves.

Path Analysis

Path analysis is a technique used to construct what are considered reasonable causative models based on correlations in data sets such as large surveys. Although a good theoretical understanding of the data relationships is still critical, path analysis can help you decide (on the basis of correlation strengths) which variables are more likely to be causative. For example, path analysis might be used to help decide whether it's better to think of occupational choice and income as results of level of education or of level of education as the result of occupational choice and income!

Time-Series Analysis

Time-series analysis is popular in communication studies for solving "chicken and egg" questions where the sequence of events in time is a factor. For example, does the political agenda help set the media agenda, or is it the media agenda that primarily sets the political agenda? Knowing which comes first, the chicken or the egg, can help! That's what time-series analysis is essentially designed to do.

IMPORTANT TERMS AND CONCEPTS

ANOVA (analysis of
   variance)
Attitude
Bipolar scale
Cluster analysis
Discriminant analysis
Factor analysis

Guttman scale
Index
Interaction effect
Likert scale
Multiple regression
Multivariate analysis
One-way ANOVA

Path analysis
Stereotype
Time-series
   analysis
Two-way ANOVA
Unidimensional

EXERCISES

1. Which of the types of multivariate analysis (factor analysis, multiple regression, analysis of variance, path analysis, discriminant analysis, cluster analysis, time series analysis) you studied in this chapter are likely to be most appropriate to each of the following problems? Justify your choice briefly in each case.

   - Defining the attitudes that underlie "environmentalism"
   - Deciding what makes someone describe themself as an "environmentalist"
   - Describing different subgroups within the environmental movement
   - Predicting degree of interest in environmental issues on the basis of degree of interest in other political issues
   - Determining the most likely causes of someone's *becoming* an environmentalist
   - Deciding whether the importance assigned to environmental issues is best predicted on the basis of education, political affiliation, or some interaction between the two
   - Describing how the national agenda of environmental issues is set

2. What complex problem involving multiple variables interests you? Perhaps you'd like to know why people choose to buy some advertised product brands and not others, determine the most likely demographic factors to predict people's positions on an important social issue, or characterize the market for suburban newspapers that compete with their nearby big-city cousins.

   State your research problem clearly. What do you *think* the important variables are likely to be? Why? Decide what would have to be measured. What types of scales or indexes would you use? What type of multivariate statistical analysis do you think would be most appropriate to your problem? Why?

PART IV

COOKBOOK
Analyzing Qualitative Data

Finding patterns in qualitative data can be like listening to music; similar themes are found in different forms.

12

Qualitative Research Revisited

ood qualitative research is every bit as difficult as good quantitative research, although it's not as easy to explain or to learn. Experience is the best teacher. A central advantage of qualitative research strategies is their flexibility. Although there are general guidelines that can be offered, qualitative research always involves the exercise of good judgment, which is why this part of the book is called a "cookbook."

One important criticism of qualitative work is that it's too easy to select and report only the examples that fit the researcher's preconceptions; this is sometimes called **thesis hunting.** Of course, some qualitative researchers might respond that the preconceptions behind quantitative research results are simply better disguised. But the real response to this criticism is that good qualitative work proceeds with an open mind, takes all data available into account as systematically as possible, is guided by a carefully chosen research question rather than the impulses of the researcher, and makes a contribution to the development of theory (even when it is directed primarily toward answering a practical question). In other words, qualitative work is as rigorous as quantitative work. Doing qualitative research is not the same as writing an opinion piece!

THEORY TESTING

How is a theory "tested" by qualitative methods? Theory's usefulness is evaluated in terms of its ability to help you understand the phenomena you observe. If, in situation after situation, a particular explanation is a "good fit" for the data—if it is helpful in allowing you to improve your understanding of what's going on—then that piece of theory is upheld.

The integrity of this process in the case of qualitative research depends on the researcher's alertness to information that does *not* fit a particular explanation, rather than formal tests of hypotheses. A conflict theorist, for example, may be interested in the media's role in maintaining the power of those already in control but may also note that the mass media do not always support status quo positions. Careful observation here may show that the media can instead be used to advocate for change and express opposition. Can the theory be altered to accommodate these observations? Or is a new theory required? Qualitative research is rooted in empirical investigation no less than quantitative research.

Middle-Range Theories

Qualitative studies and quantitative studies alike also need to be guided by theory. Sociologist Robert Merton (1968) once called for the development of *middle-range theories* that could guide meaningful empirical inquiry, theories that would connect grand, sweeping characterizations of the forces at work in society with problems that are of a manageable size for conducting empirical studies. His work had an important influence on modern sociology.

A parallel form of thinking is needed in mass communication studies. Although useful middle-range theories do exist in mass communication research, such as agenda-setting theory, uses and gratifications theory, theories about selective influence, about stereotyping, about violence effects, and so on, they often don't seem well unified by "grand theories" about the interaction between media and society. There have been attempts in this direction (e.g., DeFleur & Ball-Rokeach's, 1989, idea of "dependency theory"). But middle-range theories may be better developed for quantitative research purposes because mass communication research was heavily quantitative in its early years.

Using Theory

Good qualitative research is very theoretical, but the link between grand theory and a stategy for gathering empirical evidence on a specific research question may not be as clear. Theory (as well as methods) is often borrowed from the other social sciences. This is not necessarily a bad thing. Although some mass communications researchers are insistent that the field be recognized as independent of the other social sciences, one of the big problems in media research has been a tendency to look at the media independently of the social institutions with which they are closely interrelated, as though their effects could be isolated for study.

The traditions of qualitative research as developed in cultural anthropology and other fields, as you've learned, encourage a more holistic approach, but this certainly complicates your task as a beginning researcher.

Whereas experimental researchers are more likely to be interested in psychological theories that concentrate on the individual, qualitative researchers are more likely to be interested in the media's broader relationship to society and to other social institutions. Following this line of thinking, the media in part are studied in part as institutions with defined roles in maintaining social order. Whether this is seen as a significant foundation of social harmony in a democracy or as an instrument through which an elite maintains its power depends on one's theoretical perspective—functionalist or conflict theorist. Either way, researchers know that media representations are the products of social institutions that exist in a particular culture and that media images both reflect and influence that culture's understanding of issues and people. So the research questions you ask must be informed by at least a general theoretical understanding of the media's role in society.

CHOOSING A RESEARCH QUESTION

Case Studies

How, then, should you ask a research question in preparation for doing qualitative work? The case study approach discussed earlier is one common way of developing a research question for a qualitative study.

Agenda Building/Setting

In one type of case study, you choose a particular event (or series of events) and study it using a variety of qualitative methods, often including interviews, content analysis, and participant observation. (These methods can be combined in a single study, or one method can form the basis of an entire research project.) How did the sequence of events unfold, and what was the media's role in this sequence? *Agenda-building* studies, which take a broader, more qualitative approach than the traditional *agenda-setting* study (see, e.g., Lang & Lang, 1983) are of this type. How did Watergate, for instance, evolve into a social crisis?

Institutions

Another type of case study centers on particular institutions rather than sequences of events. How does a particular organization—say, a modern corporation with extensive public relations activities, or an activist group concerned with drawing public attention to a particular issue that it thinks is important, or a software firm, or one of the more traditional mass media organizations such as a newspaper or a television station—actually function, and how does it interact with the broader society? What are the differences in worldview between members of the organization and outsiders, and how are these important in understanding how that institution works? Although some of these questions may sound abstract, this type of case study provides information that can be extremely useful to those in professional journalistic work, including public relations activities.

Social Settings

Yet another approach to qualitative research is to study a particular **social setting** in which the media play an important role, or, more specifically, to look at how a particular form of media plays a role in that social setting. For example, what role does television really play in today's families? What role do talk shows play in the lives of at-home moms? Why are sports bars so popular for watching televised sporting events? How do college students use computers? Or what does it mean to be a science fiction fan? Of course, the dividing line here isn't an absolute one; a study of science fiction fans would likely include data on fan clubs and publishers as social institutions! So, research questions about social settings and about the roles within them of particular forms of media can also form the basis of qualitative research.

Quasi-Experiments

Qualitative research can also be quasi-experimental; rather than concentrating on a particular sequence of events or social setting, you're interested in such social psychological questions as how individuals process information and form opinions, but you seek richer data and more of an exploratory approach than quantitative methods can provide. For example, depth interviews and focus group research (along with content analysis and quantitative attitude assessment) have been used to investigate how people interpret news about science (Priest, 1994).

The dividing line between quasi-experiments and regular experiments is a fine one. The research questions asked in a quasi-experimental study are similar (although more open-ended) to those asked in more strictly controlled experimental studies. They may even involve formal hypotheses; framing hypotheses can be a useful way to clarify issues and organize the discussion of results, even where all the data to be gathered are qualitative. Qualitative data can be summarized in quantitative form, as you'll see later.

Public Image Studies

Media content studies that are based on qualitative analysis often begin with a question about the public image of a particular group, issue, or object in the mass media (or in one particular medium). How do American movies typically portray technology? How do the news media portray women politicians (as opposed to men)? How are minorities portrayed on entertainment television? Although such questions can be asked and answered based on quantitative content analysis, the subtle aspects of media images that may be of most interest are more amenable to qualitative treatment. These studies often involve comparisons between groups or of how the same group is portrayed in different media or at different periods of time; using comparative data makes the conclusions more meaningful and less subject to the "thesis hunting" critique. Techniques borrowed from the study of rhetoric and literature are often useful here (along with those from social science) as means to examine the structure of a text or image.

Methodology and Data Results

Qualitative research studies of the media begin, then, with a research question that guides the analysis. Most of the methods you've learned about (participant observation, depth interviews, focus groups, and qualitative content analysis) begin with data in the form of words. Sometimes, the data are in written form (participant observation notes or print media stories). Sometimes, they are in visual form rather than verbal (videotapes of television programming or movies); studies of these materials usually rely on extensive written notes, however. Sometimes, they need to be transcribed from audiotapes (taped interviews or focus group discussions).

Mixed Methods

Particular studies can combine qualitative and quantitative methods. Qualitative analysis can be used to supplement a quantitative content study by presenting those aspects that aren't captured by the numbers, for example. A case study may use quantitative data on content and on public opinion and a qualitative reconstruction of the sequence of events. Also, qualitative research should begin, just as quantitative research does, with a search for other published studies that can help guide the analysis.

DATA MANAGEMENT

Tape Transcription

How do you turn a pile of tapes or a notebook into a research report? Being well-organized helps! Working with transcripts of interview or focus group data rather than the tapes themselves, for example, makes it easier to be systematic. However, transcribing tapes of natural conversations is more difficult than it may appear. You'll discover some interesting things in the process. Even well-educated people don't normally speak in clear, grammatically correct sentences; this makes **transcription** more difficult. The transcriber must listen very carefully to avoid on-the-spot editing of partial or incorrect speech and "filling in the blanks" where the recording isn't perfect. Regardless of the quality of the tape, there will be times when two people are speaking at once or when someone's speech is trailing off at the end of an unfinished thought are difficult to interpret.

Purpose of the Transcript

Think about the purpose of the transcript. It's important to capture all of the main ideas in the words of the research participants. After all, the goal of qualitative research is to gain insight into someone else's perspective, not to impose your own, so it's important to be careful not to put words in the mouths of the speakers even in a small way. It's not important whether a particular speaker said "uh" or "and" in between two thoughts—an incredible amount of time can be eaten up agonizing over such alternatives or trying to decipher speech that remains unintelligible even after being replayed several times.

Organization

Transcripts

Organizing qualitative information is important. Labeling the tapes and transcripts with information about when the interview or focus group took place and any other identifying information is important—so is numbering the pages! Journalists who tape-record interviews may only be interested in getting important quotes word-for-word. Transcript data for qualitative research, on the other hand, should be as complete as possible. (Focus group transcripts, by the way, should include remarks made by the group leader or researcher in case there's later an issue of how the questions were asked, how the problems were presented, or the nature of the "probes" used to stimulate discussion.) Just remember that your transcript is unlikely to be perfect. Natural conversation contains far more gaps, omissions, misstatements, and errors than you may have ever realized.

Participant Observation Notes

Participant observation data (and interview notes) should likewise be labeled and dated. It's also a good practice to make some notes about the setting of your project. You may wish to return to the same data years later, and you might be surprised at how many details can be forgotten in the meantime! Describing the setting is also good practice for writing the research report, as your audience will be complete strangers to the context of your project until you explain it.

IDENTIFYING THEMES AND PATTERNS

Whether you are working with participant observation notes, transcriptions of interview or focus group data, or actual mass media stories or programs, identifying recurrent themes and patterns is often the next goal. What do people consistently talk about in a given social setting? What aspects of issues are consistently presented in the media? What concerns are common across several different

BOX 12.1
THE PROCESS OF TRANSCRIBING

Even experienced secretaries who transcribe dictated letters or memos, in which someone has made an effort to speak in complete sentences that can be easily understood and that follow written-language conventions, sometimes have trouble transcribing research tapes of natural conversation! It's not necessary (or, in most cases, possible) to get *all* of the words precisely right. It *is* necessary (and possible!) to accurately record the exact words used in, say, 90% or more of a taped interview or discussion so that the transcript is substantially a true representation of the original even when it is not word-for-word.

Some dictaphone machines have foot pedals that allow you to keep typing with both hands while advancing the tape. Some even have a speed control, so that speech can be played back at just slightly slower than normal speed. But perfectly adequate transcripts can be made using any regular tape recorder.

A good microphone is important for focus group work. Make sure that it is centrally located to pick up speakers seated anywhere in the room and check the recorder's operation (and its batteries, if needed) beforehand.

interviewees? You cannot list *all* the themes; there are many possible sets of themes that could legitimately be extracted from the same original set of data. Let your research question be your guide:

- If you are trying to understand how advertising agencies are structured as social institutions, be especially alert to discussion of professional roles, appropriate business strategies, work task assignments, and other relevant aspects.
- If you are trying to identify important aspects of the public image of doctors, be alert to the subtle ways some aspects might be consistently highlighted in very different contexts.
- If you are trying to find out what role docudramas play in conveying information about real-world issues, listen for statements that relate fiction to fact.
- If you're more interested in the role that media play in everyday social life, concentrate on the type of interaction you saw among those you observed, as well as direct statements about the media.

BOX 12.2
TAKING GOOD NOTES

There's no convenient formula for taking good participant observation notes, but it's probably better to be inclusive rather than exclusive. Observations that don't make sense to you at first or don't seem significant can turn out to be important later. Also, a review of how you gained insight from the beginning to the end of a project—how your notes and observations changed over time—might be helpful in gleaning aspects of the "insider" perspective that you may have adopted without thinking about it.

You might try keeping direct observations on one side of a two-column page and your own comments, reactions, questions, and analysis on the other. You could use another color of ink for insights that occur to you later in the course of your analysis, as you work toward drafting a descriptive text, or to identify examples that you think might be especially useful.

Your own thoughts, feelings, and reactions (recorded during the observation period itself) are important data. You want to be systematic and open-minded but not necessarily "objective" in the positivist sense. You need to get "inside" the research setting in your own mind to develop an interpretive perspective from someone else's point of view—and then to be able to communicate its key elements.

Whatever your research question, be especially alert to specialized terminology and labels. The reasons for this should be apparent from earlier chapters; the specialized use of language is an important clue to others' worldviews.

Each of Box 12.3's qualitative studies of the same social setting would use different methods and ask and answer different types of questions. One would identify themes or recurrent patterns in the office workers' use of soap operas and

---

BOX 12.3
STUDYING EFFECTS OF "SOAPS":
TWO EXAMPLES

What is the role of the "soaps" (those daytime dramatic television serials) in the lives of office workers? A participant observation study done in an office setting might reveal that soap operas play a critical role in the lives of these workers. In such a study, you would pay special attention to the time of day when soap operas were viewed (break time!), by whom (all the *women* in the office?), and how they were discussed (often as though the characters were members of these workers' own families). You would also pay special attention to the opportunities for social interaction that watching the soap operas provides for these workers. In some office settings, everyone participates in soap opera viewing, helping one another "catch up" when episodes must be missed.

The shows seem to provide an important opportunity for staff members to solidify their friendships (even for those whose day-to-work is done independently) and make their lives seem more interesting or meaningful (they may really seem to *care* what happens to the characters). They may also help office workers establish a group social identity that is separate from the office hierarchy, which doesn't seem to matter when everyone is a soap "fan" together.

Another study of the same setting, based on a slightly different research question, would produce different conclusions. Why are *soap operas* used for these social purposes, as opposed to, say, talk shows or mystery series? This study would probably combine content analysis with interview data to try and get a sense of what's appealing about this particular type of show. Do the plots make viewers feel better about their own lives by including so many characters with serious problems? Do they encourage viewers to come to grips with real-world controversial social issues by presenting such issues as adultery, abortion, and homosexuality in an entertainment format? Or do they seem more likely to fulfill a purely escapist function?

the structure of their interactions and discussion with one another. The other would be more concerned with themes in the programs themselves and in interviewees' comments about them.

The nature of the research question should guide the identification of themes. For example, a case study of the emergence of the perception that drug abuse is a major problem in a particular city might be concerned with themes in the media coverage itself and patterns that emerge in interviewees' self-reported actions and reactions, as well as patterns in the historical record. Did the police department, city manager's office, district attorney, and mental health authorities take action before—or after—media accounts describing drug abuse as a local problem appeared? What was the sequence of events?

Grounded Theory

Identifying themes and patterns is partly a matter of judgment; there's no magic formula for it. But in cases where a systematically collected qualitative data set (whether of media content or of interview or focus group transcripts) is available, a technique called **grounded theory** analysis (from Glaser & Strauss, 1967) is extremely helpful. This technique (sometimes called the constant comparative method, a term you may recall from the discussion of the anthropological research

---

BOX 12.4
USING GROUNDED THEORY ANALYSIS:
AN EXAMPLE

Say you begin the analysis of a focus group discussion of the reported dangers of electromagnetic fields by noting that several participants first made comments about how they'd changed their own habits and about how they were afraid for their children. Later comments might fall into one of these two categories, or they might require the addition of a new one. If someone mentions fearing for other relatives, not just children, does this require a new category or should the "fears for children" category be expanded to "fears for family"? That's a judgment call.

Generally speaking, it's better to start out making the categories more narrow than broad because they can always be combined. Deciding where a theme or topic ends and a new one begins is often a problem and deserves to be addressed carefully.

tradition in Chapter 2) makes qualitative analysis a bit more systematic than it otherwise might be.

You begin by assigning the initial data (whether discussion or description) to a few tentative categories, then continually add new data, asking at each stage whether the new data reasonably seem to fit the old categories or whether a new category—or sometimes a revision of an earlier one—needs to be constructed.

Grounded theory analysis, if implemented with care, is both very taxing and extremely systematic. At each stage of looking at new data, you must ask if the categories being used "fit" or if the new information is really different enough to call for the creation of a new category. Then when a new category is created, a review of the material that's already been classified is usually called for to see if instances that occurred earlier might possibly have been overlooked.

The goal is to use consistent categories but to allow them to emerge from the data rather than imposing your preconceived ideas that may misrepresent what's really going on. This allows you to be true to the worldview of those being studied and at the same time to be consistent through the analysis of an entire set of data. The results of grounded theory analysis can also be summarized numerically. Even though the frequency tabulations that result shouldn't be considered "measurements" in the sense that scales and indexes are, they are still very useful for communicating the regularity with which certain themes reemerge in a data set in comparison to others.

ANALYSIS OF VISUAL DATA

Analyzing visual data is potentially many times more complex than analyzing written words. Visual presentations contain rich symbolism, suggest subtle reactions and interactions, and present other complicated patterns in ways that you do not always know how to summarize in a meaningful way. For this reason, qualitative analysis of visual material is highly appropriate; you don't know how to assign numerical values to most of the interesting things about visual content. It is therefore doubly important that the analysis of visual information be guided by a theoretical perspective and a specific research question; otherwise, the number of potential observations that could be made is practically infinite.

Method of Analysis

There's no single, well-accepted, widely tested, systematic social scientific approach to the study of visual content, although there are many rich traditions in the humanities that can be and are drawn on here.

Participant Observer Viewpoint

One way to approach the qualitative analysis of visual data is by adopting a participant observer stance. Earlier, you learned about the term "close reading," a descriptive term for an ethnographic approach to studying media content. "Reading" doesn't have to refer only to a written text, however. The idea is simply to experience a visual presentation in the same way that a participant observer might experience a particular social setting. Be alert to your own reactions. How did the material make you feel? What did it remind you of? Why does the material appear to be compelling?

A study of the appeals of mystery movies, even if done by someone who was not themself a movie buff, might be approached this way. How does the "text" (the visual presentation) seem to "invite" or encourage reader involvement and particular interpretations? Mysteries often end by revealing that the apparent solution is not the real one. This could be an important observation if it helps you understand the cultural appeal of the mystery movie. How consistent is this pattern, and how does it seem to structure the audience's involvement with the film?

Statements

Another approach is to look systematically for instances of types of statements or suggestions relevant to one particular aspect of a visual presentation. For example, you might be interested in the public image of scientists as portrayed in science fiction shows and so would be especially alert to statements made about scientists and to implications about scientist characters and their motivations. Or you might be interested in the images of professional women in contemporary TV sitcoms such as *Murphy Brown* or *Designing Women*. What aspects of these characters' lives might be interpreted as making statements about the role of the professional woman in modern society? Is it significant that these characters are almost all single, for example?

Settings

Perhaps you're more interested in how work settings (as in the *Cheers* series or in hospital or "cops and robbers" shows) are portrayed. Taylor (1989) collected qualitative data that suggest that work settings are consistently presented as being family-like, a finding that has important implications about the character of modern life.

Technical Aspects

Yet another approach is to consider the technical aspects of the visual presentation itself and how they help convey certain moods or suggest certain audience interpretations. What does a "slow fade" or a certain kind of camera angle suggest to the viewer? How are visuals used on the evening news? Do these draw attention to certain aspects of a story? What are the characteristics of the standard shot of a national newscaster on location at a catastrophic event? Are there technical aspects of the way, say, sports events or news about war are presented? Are these the same, or different? To the extent they might be the same, you might be justified in asking why. Does this tell you something about your culture, or is it an accident of technology and media tradition?

Where videotapes are used as a resources for this type of analysis, several viewings are advisable. Check your notes from the first time around against your observations the second time. Are they accurate? Are important verbal and visual data recorded exactly as they appear? Do you have any new or different impressions the second time? Use the advantages of modern videocassette recorders to play, replay, and replay again segments that seem especially important. Watching visual material for research purposes can, quite frankly, be exhausting; it's very different from watching as an audience member for purposes of being entertained or informed. Odds are you'll never be able to watch the same type of material in quite the same way again!

IMPORTANT TERMS AND CONCEPTS

Grounded theory
Social setting
Thesis hunting
Transcription

EXERCISES

1. Use a "close reading" of a television show you don't normally watch as your data for analysis. Videotape at least two episodes, preferably three, and watch each at least twice. (You might need to choose a show that appears more than once a week, depending on the time your instructor allows for this exercise.) What themes emerge that transcend a single episode? What emerges in the second viewing that did not emerge in the first?

2. Interview three friends about their newspaper reading habits. What papers do they read, when, and why? What do they seem to get out of this experience besides information—a sense of belonging to a community, a well-defined break from other activities, something to share with family or roommates? Use grounded theory analysis to determine if there are any common themes that emerge in the three interviews.

Representing a qualitative data set descriptively is as much art as science.

13

Writing Descriptive Summaries

ualitative data must be presented in a way that appropriately represents what has been discovered. Here, your skill as a writer is very important, for whereas quantitative studies can rely on numbers, tables, and statistical tests to give as accurate as possible an account of what was discovered, qualitative studies use description to communicate research results. Only your verbal descriptions are available to the reader as an explanation of the conclusions drawn. So, putting together a descriptive account is almost inseparable, in qualitative work, from the actual analysis of data.

In a sense, the descriptive account of a qualitative research project is a persuasive project. You have identified important themes and patterns in a complex series of observations. You have invested work and care to be sure your conclusions are justified. Now you must persuade your potential readers that these themes and patterns were actually present in the data and not figments of your imagination!

At the same time, you must write in a way that is true to the point of view of those you are studying as well as to your own observations (the data). You must organize the material so that the reader will "see" the same answer to your original research question that you've seen. You want to give as much detail as possible, but at the same time you cannot literally report everything you observed or your reader will be overwhelmed. (What's involved in writing a research paper is discussed in Chapter 15.)

THE "INSIDER" VIEW

You had to get "inside" your own data during the analysis and learn to look at the world from someone else's perspective—whether that of members of a social group you studied, of an institution that played a key role in your case, or perhaps the creators and consumers of a particular kind of media product.

Now your job is to communicate this "insider" view to your readers. You are really speaking for those you studied, in a sense—giving their point of view a voice. (If you are studying media material, you might think of yourself as speaking for those who created it as well as those who read or view it.) What does the world look like from this other vantage point? What's important, and what less so? Are there important distinctions made between, say, groups of people, or positions on issues, or types of activities that are different from the ones you yourself make? Are these distinctions represented in specialized terms? What's their significance?

In the case of media products, ask yourself what certain representations might be intended to communicate, and how they might be interpreted by their most likely audiences. Are there multiple possible interpretations suggested? Sharing these with your reader might be an important communication strategy for you.

Context

In Chapter 2, you learned that ethnographic descriptions are often organized according to different aspects of everyday life: family organization, political structure, technology and work, and so on. Describing whole cultures at this level of detail requires an entire book, however. Your research question is likely more limited, but you must still give your reader some sense of all of the important aspects of the social setting or case you've chosen (see Box 13.1).

Background Information

Perhaps you've completed a qualitative case study of a key event. Here you need to give your reader the background and history necessary to make sense of it. Even if you're studying a national issue rather than a local one, you can't assume that your readers have followed the general developments with as much attentiveness as you have.

Write for a reader you envision has been on a long vacation or is from another country! Don't assume that your readers have enough background knowledge of the case. Describe important events that preceded the actual period that you studied and give a chronology leading up to your study period.

Background information provides the context for your later discussion of the results of your content analysis, just as details of the social setting provide a context for understanding the day-to-day activities you observed there or for interpreting the sequence of events reported in a case study.

Media Data

What if your study involves qualitative analysis of media data itself rather than a social setting or case? The same principle applies. Assume that your readers are reasonably smart people but have never read the newspaper or watched the programming you're about to describe. Tell them that the *New York Times* is an elite daily newspaper or that *Sesame Street* is a children's educational show on U.S. public television, even if these things seem obvious. Who are the publishers or producers? Who is the intended audience?

For something very well known, a short paragraph or so of background material may do. But don't skimp in describing the details of the media material itself! Is there a stock format for the programming with which you're concerned? Who are the key characters or personalities?

If you're working with print material, describe it. Your reader will need to understand if the magazine you're studying is written for conservative housewives or "career girls," and the best way to convey this is descriptively. What's a typical

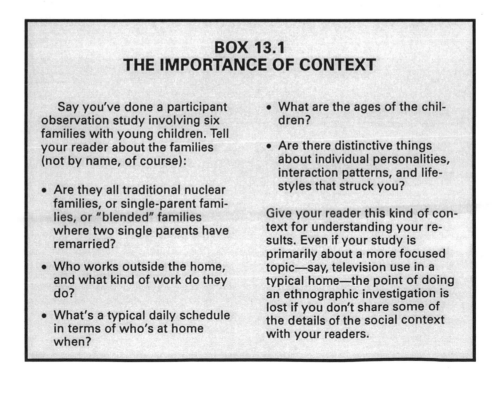

BOX 13.1
THE IMPORTANCE OF CONTEXT

Say you've done a participant observation study involving six families with young children. Tell your reader about the families (not by name, of course):

- Are they all traditional nuclear families, or single-parent families, or "blended" families where two single parents have remarried?

- Who works outside the home, and what kind of work do they do?

- What's a typical daily schedule in terms of who's at home when?

- What are the ages of the children?

- Are there distinctive things about individual personalities, interaction patterns, and lifestyles that struck you?

Give your reader this kind of context for understanding your results. Even if your study is primarily about a more focused topic—say, television use in a typical home—the point of doing an ethnographic investigation is lost if you don't share some of the details of the social context with your readers.

cover like, or a typical table of contents? What kinds of advertising are carried? You may want to include a few brief examples of the writing style.

Statement of Research Question

Although description is generally the heart of a qualitative study, it's important to include a clear statement of the research question. Consider using statements in the form of hypotheses to clarify your thinking (including its link to theory) and communicate this more clearly, even though you're not using a formal hypothesis-testing research model. You will also include a review or discussion of the academic literature (others' work that has helped shape your own), as is done when reporting a quantitative study (more details of the conventions for reporting the results of research—those that apply to both qualitative and quantitative work—are presented in Chapter 15).

Taking an Alien's Perspective

Unlike quantitative researchers, you can't rely on numbers, tables, or statistical tests. You must use your own best judgment about what is going on and which parts of it might be important. Never overlook the things that appear to be obvious; learn to look at them more carefully—like an alien from outer space (recalling Chapter 1). Things that seem to be taken for granted in a particular case or social setting may well be important clues.

**BOX 13.2
FILLING IN BACKGROUND BLANKS**

Say you've studied the emergence of a local environmental controversy. Tell your readers about the community, the key players in the controversy, and something of the known science that's involved. (In the case of environmental or other technical controversy, research institutions such as universities become key players.) You'll need to describe the local media, local activist and industry groups, perhaps something of the structure of the local city government. Are there strong personalities in positions of leadership? Particular mass media or individual reporters that have taken the lead in developing this story?

CHOOSING REPRESENTATIVE EXAMPLES

Having introduced your research site to your readers, your next task is to convey to them the themes or patterns that you've determined best characterize your observations. Here the important thing is to provide detailed examples that will demonstrate to your readers that the patterns you've extracted are good interpretive abstractions from what you've actually observed.

Adequate Description

Say you're describing a series of focus groups conducted to help you understand how your respondents reacted to news of the Gulf War. You've noticed a repetitive pattern of relating this news to what they know of earlier wars and other national crises. This could be an important key to understanding how public opinion is formed in these cases; historical analogy could be an important strategy that news audiences use to make sense of current events. What parts of the analogy seem to be most important? As much as possible, let your reader share with you the sense of discovery of this theme. Give enough descriptive examples from specific group discussions that your reader will be convinced of the appropriateness of your conclusions. (Here's where the advantages of having transcribed your recorded discussions are most obvious!)

Quality Versus Quantity of Examples

You don't need *dozens* of examples of a particular theme, but you do need two or three good ones.

Transcriptions

It's customary when reporting transcribed conversations or discussion to reproduce the original speech as closely as possible, including mistakes, hesitations, and things like "ah" and "um." (The *sic* designation used when quoting someone else's errors is not necessary; you can assume your reader understands that conversational speech is not grammatically perfect.) Ellipses (. . .) can be used to indicate pauses; unclear portions of the tape should be shown with bracketed question marks, something like this:

Uh, it reminded me of . . . like hearing about Kennedy's assassination, er [?] something like that, I guess.

In this example, the speaker is actually talking about his or her own experience of an event and comparing it to another, similar experience ("like hearing about") rather than commenting on the event itself. If respondents in your study consistently focus on their own responses in this way, then this might be another important conclusion of the study, which you would want to illustrate with additional examples.

Alternatively, perhaps the use of this perspective was confined to this one comment only, or it might be attributable to how the discussion was led. Review the transcript to double-check the way the focus group leader managed the interaction. Perhaps you are more concerned with presenting other information you gleaned and don't want to divert your readers' attention. That's OK too! You can't (and wouldn't want to) include everything.

Participant Observation Notes

In reporting participant observation results from your study of the role of soap opera watching in the lives of office workers (Box 12.3 in Chapter 12), one striking observation might be the extent to which the workers talk about soap opera characters as though they were members of their own families. Again, snatches of conversation can help demonstrate this:

A: What happened to Joe? I thought he'd come back.
B: Ah . . . he turned back up, he was in Chicago with his old girlfriend, but it didn't last.
A: Well I'm glad of that!

Here, speaker A is expressing a personal emotion about this turn in the plot, just as though Joe was someone she knew and cared about as a real person. Someone could walk into the middle of this conversation and never know that the talk was about a fictional television show! Other examples of this kind would help the researcher *show* the reader how this works.

Media Content

Descriptions of media content (whether part of a case study or done for the purpose of understanding the content itself) serve the same purpose in qualitative research. Rather than trying to put your readers in the position of being participants in a social setting, however, you're trying to uncover the structure of the media presentation of the material. So, in a sense, readers are being put in the position of reading or watching the same content but with your awareness of how details of the presentation might be affecting their responses:

> The film opens with the camera panning across the empty desert until a shimmering lake, surrounded by a strip of green and dominated by two metal towers, comes into view. The contrast between the desert "wasteland" and the artificial oasis leaves an unmistakable imprint.

Or

> The typical homocide story in this paper is in some way bizarre or grotesque; run-of-the-mill murders don't make the grade. Characteristic stories found in this content analysis described a homeless man burned to death, the apparent hate-crime beating death of a gay man, and a seven-year-old victim of child abuse.

You can organize a qualitative content analysis by the themes you discovered were consistently present in your material, by how different programs or publications treat the same topic or group of people, or in any other logical way that represents a coherent response to the demands of your research question.

Grounded Theory Approach

If you've used a grounded theory approach, you'll have numbers to work with. Be careful not to treat these too much like measurements. They are only descriptive categorizations that you've assigned to qualitative data and then counted for your own convenience (and that of your readers)! Parametric statistical tests will not be appropriate, although nonparametric chi-square comparisons might be very useful in some cases.

Summarizing qualitative data in quantitative form is a shorthand technique for reducing complex information to something you can communicate easily. The danger is, of course, that you will lose the advantages of qualitative research (richness of detail, depth of insight) without gaining the advantages of a quantitative approach (accuracy of measurement). Combine charts or tables giving frequency data with a descriptive summary for presentation of more purely qualitative results.

If you now have the impression that writing up qualitative results is more art than "science," you're correct—qualitative research is an interpretive activity. The challenge is to remain true to observations made in the spirit of the traditions of social science *and* that are true to the worldview you are trying to understand. Communicating those observations in readable and understandable language is an important goal.

RELATING DATA TO CONCLUSIONS

At this point, return to your original research question and the theoretical understanding you have of your research problem. Are the themes and patterns that you expected to find actually there? Or did your results surprise you? What have you learned that you did not anticipate? It is through asking and answering these questions that qualitative research contributes to theory building.

Many research problems appropriate for qualitative study call for a descriptive answer from a particular point of view. For example, what is the worldview of today's corporate executive like? How do talk shows portray social issues? How did the safety of nuclear power plants in the state of Washington creep into the news following Chernobyl? Usually, though, there is also a theoretical purpose to such studies.

Do your data suggest a confirmation, a revision, or a rejection of theory? Here the thinking is much like the hypothesis-testing type of quantitative research:

■ If you began an agenda-building case study with a theory that states that agendas are built up through complex interaction among many social institutions, including the media, are your findings consistent with this? Or did you find that some one institution (perhaps a media institution, perhaps not) seemed to take the lead to a greater extent than you anticipated?

BOX 13.3
INTERPRETATION VERSUS OPINION:
A CAUTIONARY NOTE

Your job is to represent your honest interpretation of what you found. Especially in interpretive research, you don't want to get editorial opinions about what *should* have happened in a particular case, or how we *should* represent particular groups or ideas, or how a certain kind of organization *should* function mixed up with your presentation of the data and conclusions. Statements like these are not inappropriate *as part of the discussion*.

Increasingly, researchers recognize an ethical obligation to do research that bears on real-world problems, and academic journal editors in mass communication often prefer to see manuscripts that offer policy recommendations that are research based. Just don't mix these up with your ethnographic material— what you write as an "outsider" trying to capture an "insider" point of view.

- If you began a study of an international news-gathering organization with theory that suggested why this organization might produce particularly ethnocentric news, was this actually the case? Or not?
- If you began researching children's use of video games thinking that they are more likely to reinforce aggressiveness than cooperative play, is this what you found?

GENERALIZING QUALITATIVE RESULTS

Can qualitative data, however carefully analyzed or presented, ever provide definitive answers to questions about the media and society? Studies of particular cases, social settings, and types of media content are not generalizable in the sense that experimental or survey results are intended to be generalizable to a larger population. They have a different objective: gaining meaningful insights into particular social phenomena. These insights *in the abstract* are often quite generalizable. The answers that are situation specific are not intended to be.

Earlier in this book you learned that sampling is not the same kind of issue for qualitative researchers as it is for quantitative researchers because qualitative research seeks insights into a worldview that is assumed to be shared by the members of a culture or subculture (or insights into a particular form of media imagery that is believed to be characteristic in important ways of media images more generally).

Specific details of an individual organization, a small group of families, a particular case, or a single broadcast series or publication are not (and need not be) generalizable in all respects, but what you learn about specific situations can generate at least tentative conclusions that have broader significance.

You might learn, for example, that under some circumstances television can pull families together (or apart), that some institutions are characterized by such a strong "insider" worldview that effective public relations is difficult for them, that media can construct images of ethnic minorities that are powerful reinforcers of cultural stereotypes (or that break them), that new media organizations are in some ways the same (and in some ways different) from older ones. These important insights are generalizable in a different sense than the results of statistical tests are.

Inductive Analysis

Qualitative research contributes to the goal of building a body of accumulated knowledge not by formal hypothesis-testing but by more free-ranging exploration of actual social practices. The structures of social organizations, the deeper meanings of media products, the patterns of political events are extremely important—and extremely difficult (if not impossible) to reduce to measurable variables.

Qualitative research—which, as you've learned, is primarily inductive rather than deductive—also helps generate new theory that can be tested either quantitatively or through additional qualitative studies.

Keep this in mind in considering how your data have answered your research question! If you set out with a clearly framed research question, considered relevant theory, gathered data carefully, and analyzed and presented them systematically, you will have made an important contribution. Avoid overgeneralizing, of course, or "reading too much in," especially if your data set is limited. But even small studies can demonstrate significant theoretical propositions.

Applying the Ethnographic Stance

The ethnographic stance is especially important when dealing with problems in cross-cultural or international communication; it helps you avoid looking at the world only from your own culture's point of view, whether or not ethnographic methods are actually used in a particular study. Because feminist scholarship also proceeds from a point of view, an explicitly woman-centered one, it also requires this ability to "shift gears" and to look at the world through more than one subcultural lens.

Even when working entirely within your own culture and a subculture that is not much different from your own, however, you can learn much about yourself as well as others by having some practice in adopting someone else's point of view.

EXERCISES

1. Some of the exercises earlier in this book asked you to do interviews or engage in participant observation or analyze media material through a "close reading" of its content. Use your notes from one of these earlier exercises to construct a careful descriptive account of the themes and patterns you found.

2. Now go back over the same data again, using a "grounded theory" approach to generate categories and a frequency distribution describing their occurrence. Are there important differences in the two analyses? Did grounded theory find patterns that your first interpretation did not? How about the other way around? Which do you think is a more appropriate summary of the data set? Why?

PART V

BRANCHING OUT
The Wider World of Research

Future researchers will have plenty of uncharted territory to explore.

14

Research Horizons

To return to the discussion of philosophy of science presented in Chapter 1, the "sociology of knowledge" approach asks you to look carefully at the social origins of scientific information, including social scientific information. This has resulted in a serious rethinking of the assumption that science is in an absolute sense "unbiased" or "objective" and raises new methodological and ethical questions about the whole enterprise. After all, science (including social science) developed throughout the 19th century as an activity of upper-class white men. What is its significance today for everyone else?

Today's media research is headed in a number of new and important directions, some of which are influenced by a "sociology of knowledge" perspective. In this chapter, you'll learn about feminist and international-intercultural perspectives on communication research and look at the challenges and different research opportunities posed by new media technologies. You'll also revisit the question of the limits of social science for settling policy debates and learn more about the ethical dimensions of what you do, about communicating research results to others, and about other opportunities for presenting your results publically.

THE FEMINIST CONTRIBUTION

In recent decades, feminist scholars have sometimes argued that much of modern science has been done from a subtly **masculinist** (or male-biased) point of view (see, e.g., Keller, 1985). This does not in any way imply a rejection of the fruits of scientific knowledge where these are seen to improve the quality of life, but it does entail a recognition that social values and political forces have shaped the *kind* of science that we have today.

Feminist scholars try to rectify this by approaching research from a point of view that is not intended to be "objective" in the old, unexamined sense but is, instead, deliberately and explicitly accomplished "from a woman's point of view."

Feminist researchers in social science are often (although by no means always) conflict theorists, as their work is directed in large part toward understanding how the power of men has been maintained, historically, in society (for an excellent discussion of the variations in perspectives on feminist analysis, see Steeves, 1988).

Feminist Scholarship and Feminism

Feminist scholarship and research is to some extent distinct from feminism as a political movement, but there is a clear connection. Feminism as a political movement argues for the rights of women. Feminist scholarship and research looks at the means through which these rights have historically been denied and tries to understand the social dynamics involved.

In mass media studies, the limited images of women that have been presented in many media, both entertainment media and news, and the historical limitations on women achieving their full potential in mass communication careers are both seen as parts of this problem. Although there's still a long way to go, increasing attention in mass media research to gender issues—from gay and lesbian as well as feminist perspectives—is a present-day reality.

Concept of Empowerment

Feminist scholars also look at the activities of women who have been successful as evidence of the levels of competence and effectiveness that women can achieve and in the hopes of improving our understanding of the conditions under which barriers to women's success can be overcome. Furthermore, feminists often argue that their work is not directed at achieving understanding for its own sake. The purpose of understanding how women have historically been denied power and the ways that they have successfully resisted this denial is to help work toward women's further **empowerment** in the future.

These scholars point out that the problems chosen for research often reflect male priorities and that even the choice of methods is symbolic of traditional male ways of thinking. In science generally, much research effort is directed toward controlling or dominating nature. Some feminist critics of science believe this is a masculinist goal—that women are more likely to find working *with* nature rather than *against* it preferable (although other feminists are reluctant to make this kind of generalization about "women's values").

Subject-Object Distinction

In social science, research that divides the world into researchers and those who are the objects of the research is similarly seen by some feminists as yet another attempt to dominate and to maintain an artificial separation between some (more powerful) people and other (less powerful) ones. So at least some feminist scholars reject the **subject-object distinction** inherent in experimental work, which they may find dehumanizing, altogether, and a few object to quantitative social science on similar grounds.

Does feminist mass communication research actually require different methods? Not necessarily, but a majority of feminist researchers (again, certainly not all) prefer qualitative methods for themselves—if not on philosophical grounds, then on practical ones. Feminist researchers are very often interested in how the world looks *from a point of view* (that of women). As you've seen, qualitative research is better suited to accomplishing this goal. Feminist researchers are also particularly sensitive to the power differential that exists between the researcher and the object of that research. Several books on the adaptation of social science methods to the problems of interest from a feminist perspective are beginning to appear (e.g., see Carter & Spitzack, 1989).

Participatory Research

What gives researchers the right to publish results and build careers on the basis of data they have taken from a particular group of people without giving anything in return? And what gives the researcher the right to decide what is and is not an important research question in the first place?

The idea of **participatory research**—research in which those being studied have a voice in the direction the research takes—is one response to these questions. Participatory research is not something done *only* by feminist scholars, but feminists are among those who first raised these questions and for whom this approach is especially appealing.

This approach to research tries to give research participants more control over their own lives—to empower them rather than to take knowledge away from them without giving anything in return. Those who might otherwise have been seen merely as the "objects" of the research may be invited to define research problems and priorities and to participate as members of the research team.

Variety of Perspectives

A valuable hallmark of feminist scholarship has historically been its acceptance of a variety of perspectives—despite occasional disagreements about the "acceptable" methods for doing feminist scholarship. So feminist scholars have taken leadership roles in requesting that mass communication research journals take research done using qualitative methods as seriously as quantitative work. And the feminist critique of science has raised questions about the "objectivity" and direction of scientific research—including mass communication research—that are important for all researchers, not just those especially interested in questions of gender.

You can benefit by understanding the underlying critique of mainstream research that feminist scholars offer:

- That traditional research approaches reflect cultural biases in subtle ways
- That quantitative research can overlook many of the most important aspects of human social life

---

BOX 14.1
COMMUNITY-BASED RESEARCH

The idea of participatory (or community-based) research is currently generating considerable interest for research of all types. For mass communication research, a community-based approach might mean asking a community what it thought its key problems or questions might be and then inviting its participation in developing solutions. Is the community more concerned about the effects of television on children, or about getting out HIV/AIDS information to those who need it? How is the community represented in existing local media, and what would it take to get a community newspaper off the ground? How could local women most effectively publicize a support group? The questions that community members might ask may not be the ones that would be thought important from an academic point of view!

▓ That some forms of research can be self-serving on the researcher's part at the expense of the participants' interests

▓ That research participants should have the right to a say in the general direction that research takes

INTERNATIONAL AND INTERCULTURAL MASS COMMUNICATION

The reminder from feminist scholarship that your own cultural and gender biases influence the way you think about research problems is also extremely important in international and intercultural communication studies.

International communication refers both to communication between and among separate countries and to the study of the ways that mass media systems differ from one country to the next (sometimes called comparative media systems).

Intercultural communication refers to communication between different cultural groups, including communication by and about ethnic minorities within multiethnic societies and communication between cultures that takes place across political boundaries.

Ethnocentric Assumptions

Both areas of study require special attention to how ethnocentric assumptions can interfere with effective communication and, as feminist scholars have argued, perpetuate limiting stereotypes and the traditional power of some groups at the expense of others. International and intercultural communication studies also remind you that U.S. media systems, the legal and political systems in which they operate, and your expectations about their roles are unique to your own culture, not shared around the world (see Hachten, 1987, for more information on how these systems vary).

If you are a mass communication student in a country with a strong "free press" tradition, you may be surprised at what you might learn. Not only is yours not considered the ideal system everywhere in the world, but some of your colleagues in other countries do not consider systems like the U.S. press "free" at all because of heavy dependence on information from government sources and on revenue from advertising. At the same time, situations around the world in which the press is still heavily controlled by government coercion or out-and-out censorship become apparent.

Looking at cultural variation in the roles and day-to-day function of media around the world also helps you challenge your own culture-bound assumptions about how media systems "should" work (for examples of international communication studies, see Martin & Hiebert, 1990).

Research Study Challenges

Doing international studies does pose special methodological challenges. It's not easy getting access to foreign broadcasts and publications to do content analysis, for example. In the developing world, the meaningfulness of survey data is open to question; samples may not be as representative and respondents may be less familiar with survey procedures. Also, the practical problems posed by the cost and difficulty of international travel, language and cultural barriers, and obtaining permission for research in a foreign country are all too easy to underestimate.

The end result is that some international studies—even very carefully planned and significant ones—are less complete and less methodologically perfect than they would be if the same study had been carried out in the researcher's own country. Compromises are sometimes essential. Also, researchers whose home countries are in the less developed world—and who may therefore be in the best position to do culturally sensitive work—may lack the financial and other resources for research afforded those in the developed world.

Cultural Variation Awareness

Although international communication studies use the same methods as other mass communication studies, they must be especially sensitive to cultural variation

---

BOX 14.2
GLOBAL APPLICATION OF RESEARCH METHODS

Any of the methods discussed in this book can and have been used in the field of international communication studies. For example, content analysis has been used in studies of how the Western (European and North American) press covers the less developed Third World. Participant observation has been used in case studies of how media organizations in other nations operate. Survey data have helped in exploring the relationship between public opinion and media coverage in different parts of the world and how actual media habits are the same or different in different cultures. Some of these studies provide important tests of theory: If agenda-setting processes work in the United States or Great Britain, then they should work across Europe, for example.

in the interpretation of questions and in expectations about how the media function. To take just one example, the role of the print press in a developing country with a low literacy rate is simply not the same as its role in an industrialized Western democracy. This will complicate any attempt at comparing the two societies in terms of media content or structure.

Cultural variation is not confined to the difference between the industrialized and the developing worlds, however. The relationship between the mass media and government in Great Britain and the United States is remarkably different, even though the two nations share a language and a large proportion of their respective cultural and legal histories. For example, government plays a much bigger role in British broadcasting (as it does throughout much of Europe) than it does in the United States. And major newspapers are much more closely associated with particular political perspectives in Great Britain (and elsewhere in Europe) than in the U.S., even though the First Amendment to the U.S. Constitution was originally written to protect a partisan (rather than an "objective") press system.

Effect of Imported Media

Another issue in international/intercultural communication is the effect on a culture of imported media products. When village farmers in India watch *I Love Lucy* or *Little House on the Prairie,* how does this influence their worldviews and their perceptions of themselves? On the one hand, it is so difficult to evaluate the effects of media even within a single culture that the problems of studying this type of effect across cultures seem overwhelming; on the other hand, the appeal of this "natural laboratory" for understanding media effects is enormous! But this is not a good type of problem for the hypothesis-testing model used in much media effects research in the United States. Rather, case studies based on techniques like participant observation are much more likely to yield meaningful insights.

Ethnic Diversity

Pluralistic societies are increasingly ethnically diverse, and communications systems must allow for this. Practical business objectives like being able to advertise new products effectively to diverse audiences, as well as social ideals such as the promotion of democratic dialogue that is inclusive rather than exclusive, depend on this.

How do the mass media in the predominantly Anglo culture of the United States represent African Americans or Spanish speakers or Asians or Native Americans in entertainment programming? Are their perspectives well-represented on the news? Are advertising messages reaching these groups, or are they offensive? Are there minority as well as majority writers, editors, producers, and announcers? And just what images of minority groups *should* the media be expected to provide? One African American in the United States might think *Sanford and Son*'s portrayal of a ghetto junk dealer is an honest and positive portrait of a minority businessman who has succeeded within the boundaries of his own circumstances; another might think the same image is insulting and embarrassing.

Studying these images without making implicit judgments about what they ought to look like is difficult. But the importance of understanding how media images contribute to your acceptance or rejection of minority subcultures can hardly be overstated.

NEW MEDIA TECHNOLOGY

It's become customary in books about media research to have an ending chapter about what to do with **new media** technologies! Instead, this book has used examples of new media such as computer-based information systems, video games, and electronic mail throughout.

In many cases, the same theories and methods used to understand traditional media can be used to understand these new forms. If violence on television is a problem, violence in video games may be a problem in the very same way. If newspapers set social issues agendas, then electronic news systems may do exactly the same. This kind of thinking tests our understanding of how media work against new situations and so contribute to the accumulation of social scientific knowledge. It's still worthwhile to pause for a moment, however, and consider how the new media are different and how they present new and as yet unsolved research problems.

New Versus Traditional Media

The new media—which mean everything from cable TV systems and high-definition television to computer-based videotex, hypertext, and multimedia systems to cellular telephones and videophones to music on compact discs—are distinctive in that they are more personalized and less "massified" than traditional media (Rogers, 1986). Some of the old assumptions about the "mass" media are therefore challenged by these new media, although traditional print media like magazines are also said to be becoming more narrowly targeted and even newspapers are perhaps more clearly divided into specialty sections (business, features, "hard" news) read only by particular segments of the population.

Some of the new media are primarily tools for interpersonal rather than one-to-many communications—for example, electronic mail, a means of communicating between individuals. Yet even this distinction is breaking down; electronic mail is easily converted to mass "mailing" purposes, and information sent electronically to a single recipient can be copied and sent with ease to many others until thousands or more are reached.

Methodological Approach

Do new media need to be studied by new methods? At first, it seemed as though the new media required not only new methods but new theories! Certainly new issues are raised, particularly in the policy arena. However, mass communication researchers have recently been reevaluating their original notion of "mass" media in the sense of messages sent uniformly to entire populations.

Audiences have always had more control over what they pay attention to and how they interpret it than this idea might suggest—and they have always had some degree of choice. It now appears less as though the new media require new methods

---

BOX 14.3
RESEARCH CHALLENGES OF THE NEW MEDIA

There *are* new problems with the new media. Perhaps most important among these is the question of whether these new technologies make access to information easier or increase the gap between the educated elite with access to tremendous amounts of information and those at the other end of the spectrum. What's really changed here is less the methods used than the whole underlying concept of mass-mediated communication.

The new media often pose new social, ethical, legal, and policy questions that sometimes stretch the limits of *all* social science, not just those of particular methods. Legislation currently being considered in the U.S. Congress will create the regulatory environment that will shape the new electronic media in the 21st century—the so-called National Information Infrastructure of which today's university-based Internet information system will be only a primitive ancestor. This prospect raises entirely new research challenges that strain the limits of existing methods as researchers try to project their knowledge of current relationships into an uncertain future.

as that the degree of active audience control over what information is actually received and what it is taken to mean is much higher than was assumed.

The design and evaluation of electronic information systems can be based on experimental and focus group work, just as the design and evaluation of advertising messages for traditional media have used these methods. New media organizations can be studied by participant observation just as traditional media were studied in this way.

MEDIA POLICY AND THE LIMITS OF SOCIAL SCIENCE

Some extremely important problems, as this book has mentioned, are just not researchable by the methods of social science. McLuhan's (1989) "global village" is a reality. All but a few remote corners of the globe are connected by telephone, television reaches almost everywhere (and in some areas may be spreading faster than the literacy rate for print messages), media products have global-scale impacts that know no cultural, political, or geographical barriers.

Questions to Consider

Is something possibly being lost in the process, with the world threatening to become a kind of international cultural oatmeal rather than a nicely diverse stew? Is the growing complexity of electronic information systems in this era of talk about "information highways" going to create a whole new social divide between the information "haves" and "have nots"? Are press and broadcast systems run as business enterprises going to do the best job of representing the full spectrum of interested public voices, or is increased government involvement necessary? Should extreme violence on television be banned? What are the real effects on democracies of political advertising—good or bad?

These are just a few examples of the types of media-related problems now facing researchers that cannot be resolved by social science research. Social science cannot predict the future or specify what types of media systems are the best "fit" for particular social, cultural, or political systems. The value of social science lies in its ability to help you understand the present. However, the best policy decisions for the future will be those that are the most thoroughly grounded in an understanding of present conditions, and the best social science research is that which has not lost touch with important social policy issues. Despite the limitations, public media policy needs to be informed by the best social science there is. It's just that even the best social science is not going to resolve debates about social values and political choices.

ETHICS AND THE CONDUCT OF RESEARCH

Throughout this book, you've been made aware of ethical issues involving the people who participate in your research as subjects, respondents, or informants. This is the aspect of ethics that you must be aware of during the actual conduct of an experiment and the aspect that normally requires formal college and university approval ahead of time. But it's only one of many aspects of the **code of ethics** you must apply when conducting social scientific research.

Publishing scientific results is an ethical obligation of scientists (including social scientists); it's part of their job, their contribution to the accumulation and advancement of knowledge, and—as most of the money for research comes from tax dollars—a means of making scientific information publically available. It's also the way their work is evaluated at contract renewal or promotion time—that's what's behind the old "publish or perish" cliché about university life!

Fraudulent Data

As science has become more competitive, news reports of scientists who alter their data to fit their theories have become more common. Obviously, this is both unfortunate and unethical. Traditionally, only positive (statistically significant) results have been considered important enough to result in research publications and recognition for academic researchers, even though some argue that negative results are often just as useful and should also be published—if only to steer other researchers away from unproductive "dead ends." However, this is still uncommon, and those who fail to prove their hypotheses in some of the more competitive scientific fields are under considerable pressure. Jobs, promotions, and research grants are at stake. Although cases of outright fraud are likely to be extremely rare, there's no way of being certain.

Power of the Peer Review

Other situations are not so clear-cut in terms of right or wrong. The *New England Journal of Medicine* has traditionally refused to publish research papers reporting results that have already been released to the mass media. Although this seems to go against the scientific tradition of open dissemination and sharing of information, releasing results of scientific research that have not been peer reviewed may be considered misleading, especially for information (like the results of medical studies) that might affect people's important personal decisions.

Peer review is a highly respected system for judging the quality of research. However, it's not perfect. Editors have a lot of discretion as to which reviewers to choose for a particular manscript; some are tougher judges than others. And both editors and reviewers may have strong preferences regarding types of problems or methods chosen. Nevertheless, it's the best system we have; no one has invented

---

BOX 14.4
ETHICAL DILEMMAS
FACING STUDENT RESEARCHERS

These are ethical dilemmas that affect student researchers directly in addition to the human subjects issues stressed throughout this book. Although these dilemmas are more likely to occur for graduate students, they can apply at any level and should also be understood by those who might *write about* research professionally.

These issues involve who does the research work, who gets credit for it, and who has access to the information the research produces. Should students help with a professor's own research project for a grade or for extra credit, when the research will be published under the professor's name alone? Probably not. At least a footnote acknowledging these students by name should be included. Also, students who help in exchange for a grade should be learning something about research, not just acting as "slave labor" to accomplish simple, repetitive tasks. (That's what *paid* labor is for!)

What if a professor and an advanced student do a project together? If the student helps design the project, not just gather or summarize data according to directions someone else provided, the student ought to be listed as a coauthor of the report. If the student is the *leader* throughout the project, from the preliminary idea through the data gathering and analysis to the actual report writing, then the student deserves to be listed as the first author. (Order of authorship is important in the world of academic publishing; the first author is generally considered the leader of the research team. Sometimes, team members who work as coequals switch off in the spirit of fairness, so one article is by Smith and Baker and the next by Baker and Smith.)

In any case, all authors of a published research report are responsible for its contents. Any coauthor who does not agree (at least in principle) with the report's conclusions or who thinks that there might be any question of honesty involving the data can ask not to be listed as coauthor, and this request should be honored.

an alternative that is more fair (for more discussion of the ethics of scientific publishing, see LaFollette, 1992).

Concerns about publicizing results that have not been peer reviewed are not so great in mass communication research because, although publishing results is very important, big research grants are usually not at stake and members of the general public are not so likely to make personal decisions on the basis of your research (as they might, for example, on the basis of reports about new medical findings).

Data Ownership

Similar issues affect media researchers more directly. If a part of the mass media industry wished to fund a major study of the effects of their industry on children, who would "own" the data—that is, who would have the **intellectual property rights** to the results? Would industry executives be more likely to give the contract for the project to a researcher they felt would be sympathetic, perhaps one whose past research had concentrated on positive effects rather than negative ones? Would the researcher have the right to publish in any form he or she wanted, to draw whatever conclusions seemed most reasonable, and to share the raw data with others? Would there be pressure on the researcher not to release the results without industry executives' approval? Worse yet, would there be pressure on the researcher to release only data that did not put the industry in an unfavorable light, or to draw only positive conclusions?

Although these issues have not been especially visible ones in media research, the body of research associated most closely with the argument that the mass media have little effect on people was originally funded by the television industry. And issues involving unreasonable industry control over scientific results are very active ones in science generally. Mass communication researchers who don't think that these types of ethical conflicts are important in our field may be naive. Researchers have a clear ethical obligation to report findings honestly and to state their conclusions with appropriate qualifications, whether these findings put the industry in a positive light or a negative one. If funding sources expect to have some special rights to a researcher's results, this should be spelled out in the contract—and the researcher would do well to think twice before signing!

Availability of Data

Who owns the data in the case of unsponsored projects (those without outside funding) or **sponsored projects** where there's no special contractual limit? Everyone who is interested in a research project (let alone those who participated in it) should have access to the data and the right to reanalyze and say something new about them. The original research team ought to have "first rights" to publication, although unpublished data may be released to someone else at the researcher's discretion with the understanding (as always) that appropriate credit will be given if the results appear in print.

All of these traditions are more along the lines of "gentlemen's agreements" than enforced rules. The American Association of Public Opinion Research, the American Psychological Association, and many other groups composed of professional social science researchers have codes of ethics to cover such situations. The Association for Education in Journalism and Mass Communication has considered drafting such a code specifically for mass communication research.

Journalists and others who write about research can be confronted with all these issues and more:

- Who should be given credit for research work?
- At what point in a research project is it appropriate to report results?
- Should only "breakthroughs" make the news?
- How should competing scientific ideas be presented?
- How much attention should be paid to the influence of funding sources on a researcher's choice of problems—or, more critically, on the conclusions drawn?
- What's the appropriate, responsible balance between healthy skepticism and reckless disregard of facts?

Similarly, those working in public relations, public information, or advertising in highly technical areas can find themselves in an ethical minefield. The lines between scientific truth and speculation or between reporting scientific conclusions and promoting a point of view are not always clearly drawn.

For mass communication research questions, public controversies over the best way to manage and regulate new media technologies and the social influence of media images of ethnic groups, of men and women, and of appropriate behavior (e.g., violence or single parenthood) are often emotionally charged. Science and technology of other types are at the root of the majority of modern social issues—whether medical knowledge, knowledge of environmental science, genetic information, data on the risks and benefits of energy-generating options (coal, nuclear power, solar heating), or knowledge of the sociology of crime and punishment. All of these issues put research—and research ethics—on the front page!

IMPORTANT TERMS AND CONCEPTS

Code of ethics
Empowerment
Feminist
Intellectual property rights
Intercultural communication
International communication

Masculinist
New media
Participatory research
Sponsored projects
Subject-object distinction

Writing a research report is a traditional task, although modern technology helps.

Writing the Research Report

esearch conferences and research publications are the heart of the research community in mass communications, as for other scientific and social scientific disciplines. It's in these forums that new ideas are heard, good work is rewarded, policies and priorities are set, and problems and trends are discussed.

CONFERENCE PRESENTATIONS

A presentation at a research conference often represents the first public hearing that a researcher's work gets.

Poster Sessions

Increasingly, some larger research conferences are turning to what's called a **poster session** (a tradition borrowed from the "hard" or natural sciences) rather than the formal speech as a format for presenting results. Instead of being allotted a short 10 or 15 minutes to address an audience about their research, some of those whose papers have been accepted for inclusion in the conference program are invited to display posters summarizing their work. Interested conference participants can "drop by" informally to find out about the research at a time that's convenient within a prespecified block of a few hours. One of the reasons why this option is more and more popular is because of the increased opportunities for interpersonal interaction it provides.

Oral and Written Reports

The formal oral presentation and the written report that underlies it are still the typical means through which a researcher first tells others the results of recent work. This is no less true for mass media researchers than it is for physicists or biologists! Whether or not you are ever called on to write one, understanding how research reports are constructed—and why—is an important way to understand more about research. It's in the written research report that the connections to others' research, the link to theory, and the reasoning behind specific methodological decisions—as well as the actual results!—are communicated.

Thoroughness

When beginning research students write research reports they often have difficulty with its conventions, especially if they have been well trained in the art of journalistic writing. A research report is like a term paper: Every decision and its justification and implications should be documented, and every source consulted must be cited and referenced with care.

Often, scientists (including social scientists) are highly critical of mass media coverage of science because mass communication researchers *cannot* state all of the qualifications and discussion that scientists consider completely essential—and are used to seeing in research articles. This doesn't mean that research reports

BOX 15.1
ORIGIN OF THE RESEARCH ARTICLE

Research articles had their historical origin in letters written by amateur researchers (naturalists, astronomers, explorers, and so on) to the earliest scientific societies in the 17th century. From the beginning, these were communications designed for an audience familiar with the research process and highly concerned with all of the methodological details and theoretical implications the work entailed. Readers often wanted enough detail to try to replicate the experiment themselves, so research reports could not be just abbreviated accounts.

must be wordy (they aren't), but it does mean they need to be comprehensive and carefully put together.

Acceptance or Rejection

Today, the report of a study may begin life as an unpublished photocopied paper written for discussion, be accepted for presentation at a professional conference, and then be revised for submission to a research publication. Often, the result will be rejection; good journals may have acceptance rates of 10% or less of manuscripts submitted! But at each of these stages, feedback and criticism (either formal or informal) can help the author revise the paper appropriately for eventual publication.

Conference programs, like the contents of scholarly journals, are often decided by blind review, so conference organizers and journal editors almost always provide authors with anonymous written comments from reviewers. Good, detailed, constructively critical reviews are invaluable, even when rejection is recommended.

BOX 15.2
THE VALUE OF CONFERENCES

There are both regional and national research conferences and journals. Regional meetings and publications will be somewhat less competitive because they represent a smaller geographic area, so if you think your research is good enough to be heard or read, they are the place to begin! Some conferences require those who submit papers to be graduate students and faculty, although there are regional conferences that encourage or even concentrate on undergraduate work.

The big annual meetings of mass communication organizations for college educators, like the Association for Education in Journalism and Mass Communication, the International Communication Association, the American Association for Public Opinion Research, and the Speech Communication Assocation, provide hundreds of researchers with forums in which to present their research work.

If one of these organizations is meeting near you and you are especially interested in research, talk to your instructor about attending, even if you're an undergraduate. If you're a graduate student, just go! Not only will you learn more about the research process and current trends and discoveries, you might get some good material for a journalistic piece about new research results.

Unfortunately, some good papers are never presented or published because there's no appropriate forum. Others have problems that can't be overcome; perhaps no one can be persuaded that the research question is important or that the approach taken is capable of answering it. Still, in many cases, persistent scholarly authors will eventually be rewarded with success.

CONSTRUCTING RESEARCH REPORTS

Believe it or not, writing the research report itself is a fairly straightforward task if you've followed the rest of this book reasonably closely and if you are prepared to "switch gears" and adopt a slightly different writing style from the one you may be most used to!

Research articles can be tedious and boring to read, but please remember, this is *absolutely not necessary.* However, they are complete and thorough and are written for a very specialized audience: other researchers—your fellow students, your instructor, and other people who study, teach, or do research about mass communication. You can assume that they're reasonably well acquainted with what social science research is and why research on the mass media is important. But you must also assume that they're critical judges of the decisions you've made in developing a research problem, choosing a method, and using it to reach justified conclusions. Your job is to explain how these decisions were reached—including your first one, the choice of a research problem—and anticipate their objections.

The Art of Persuasion

Your task is to "tell the story" of your research project—how it evolved, what other projects influenced it, and what you found out. In a sense, a research report is a persuasive project; you must persuade your readers that your problem is important and your results sound. Although there is some variation in scholarly journals as to the exact format that might be used (and your instructor's preferences may also vary), the basic task is the same.

Steps to Follow

Introduction

Begin by explaining your general research problem in broad terms. Why is it important? How does your specific research question relate to it? Give your reader as good an idea as possible of what kind of a study you did to answer this question.

Literature Review

After the introduction, discuss the research literature that you looked at in preparing to investigate your problem. Devote a few sentences or more to each study that you used to gain insight into yours. Literature reviews can be organized chronologically (from earliest to most recent), by theoretical or methodological approach, or in any other way that will help your reader make a logical connection between your study and those that have gone before.

Hypotheses and Methodology

If your project was based on testing specific hypotheses, state them clearly—in a list rather than a paragraph. Then describe and justify your methods—both your choice of a general methodological approach and your specific decisions—about variables, measurements, and the kinds of statistical analysis you used in a quantitative study or about the setting, the case, or the choice of media material for a qualitative one. Make it clear exactly what data you collected, including any gaps or limits, and exactly what was done with them.

All methods have advantages and limitations; suggest these with respect to your specific research problem. If your sampling was not quite representative, if your method didn't work as you expected, or if your understanding of the problem turned out to be less than perfect, say so. This adds to (rather than detracts from) your credibility, as sharp readers will see your study's defects anyway—perhaps more clearly than you yourself!

Results

Next, describe your results in detail. Include tables and charts as needed to communicate numbers or provide descriptions for qualitative work. You should give your reader enough information to reach the same conclusions as you did based on the same data.

Conclusion

Finally, write a conclusion. What are the most important things you learned? What is their significance? Do they suggest the need for changes in government policy, public education, or media organizations' operations? Do they tell us something significant about ourselves as a culture, or about human society in general?

You can take an editorial approach as long as your general direction is thoroughly justified by the data you've collected and presented. This is often the place where the implications for either social policy or professional practice are set forth and the most important needs for additional, future research are suggested.

The Art of Defense

Be as clear and direct in your presentation as possible—don't ramble or repeat—but be sure to include all the detail necessary to answer your readers' questions. Remember, your report is written for people who know a great deal about research methods and who are likely to consider it their job to be critical! So defend yourself. Give a sound reason for your choice of method. Some reasons are practical: Perhaps a certain publication collection was available to you, or you had an opportunity to observe a particular media organization during an internship. This kind of reason is fine, so long as the opportunity was used to find out something interesting or important! Be honest about imperfections in design or execution of your project—*all* research has them.

SCHOLARLY PUBLICATION STYLE

The format of research articles varies depending on the journal publishing them. Three refereed (blind peer-reviewed) journals you should look at for models (because they represent leading journals with three very different styles) are

---

BOX 15.3
COMMERCIAL RESEARCH REPORTS

Research reports of market or other "in house" research designed for a commercial purpose, rather than scholarly publication, may not be intended to be generally available and are written for a slightly different audience. Managers and marketing specialists are not always sophisticated about research methods and may be more concerned with the results, so discussions of methodology should be limited and emphasis placed on implications for business decision making.

If sample size is too limited or the sample too unrepresentative to be the basis of general conclusions, the reader needs to know this. It's likely though that a technical description of sampling procedures will be of much less interest.

Journalism Quarterly (JQ), Journal of Communication (JOC), and *Critical Studies in Mass Communication (CSMC).*

JQ once published a large proportion of quantitative studies, and although its content is now more mixed, it still tends to prefer a style in which the traditional components of a research article reporting on an experiment (described in the preceding step-by-step section) are clearly presented.

JOC often publishes articles using a wider range of styles, reflecting a somewhat wider range of types of material in which this publication is interested.

CSMC has historically published a higher proportion of qualitative work and—appropriately—often uses a more narrative style.

These journals show you how research articles should be structured and can help you see how the basic research report configuration can best be modified to fit your own material.

Citation Style

Citing references appropriately is a critical component of scholarly writing because the building of new research results on top of old, resulting in the development of cumulative knowledge, is such an important characteristic of the scientific enterprise. Citation style varies from journal to journal. Some use a footnote style that is probably similar to one you have used in high school or college English classes. More typical, however, is some variation on "American Psychological Association" style, the style in which the author and year of publication are contained in parentheses as they have been throughout this book. This is an efficient and effective approach for most research work; year of publication provides important context for your readers.

The Purpose of an Abstract

The research article (published or unpublished) is often accompanied by an **abstract,** a concise, one-paragraph summary of the problem, the method, and the results. Abstracts published in sources like *Communication Abstracts* (for the interdisciplinary mass communication literature) and *Dissertation Abstracts* (for doctoral dissertations in any discipline) are excellent tools when doing library research because they give far more information than titles and authors alone. Consulting these can save you time that might otherwise be wasted tracking down articles that turn out to be less relevant than they appeared. Some journals also ask authors to suggest keywords that can be used for indexing the article in an index to that particular publication (if one exists) or in library indexes.

A CONCLUDING NOTE

Above all, study the *best*—not the worst —scholarly writing! Research discussions do not need to be obtuse, although many of them are written for those already familiar with methodological issues and procedures. They do not need to be dry, and they don't necessarily address problems that no one but you thinks are important! You considered your problem interesting enough to spend time, energy, and thought exploring. Now your job is to convince others and to tell the world what you found out.

IMPORTANT TERMS AND CONCEPTS

Abstract
Poster session

Appendix

TABLE A1 Random Numbers

0430	2613	7878	5595	8076	3068	4113	7962	4989	3987
6095	8618	7024	5831	8995	0902	3972	4894	2153	5764
6720	4690	2123	7101	1166	0087	3042	4745	4690	3173
8948	4609	9126	2814	8383	2951	1958	8212	4131	5313
3268	0189	9175	0473	4295	2993	7027	4153	3864	7542
5473	1540	5681	3933	7826	3823	9933	3101	6742	2364
2951	2169	3096	8663	8147	5255	1756	0650	8493	7024
1031	4981	9118	7969	2688	8229	2863	5320	6124	9920
6010	3219	2640	2737	6055	7298	7628	8430	8159	8506
7534	1369	9935	4358	1490	3193	2906	8893	6850	0891
1529	4760	9897	8352	9742	3222	4402	5286	7490	8293
8640	4369	2154	0167	8358	4086	2082	4454	8300	6078
4802	5490	5571	5666	2838	6789	4990	4780	8211	9244
5575	7527	5181	5048	6590	2984	3675	3713	9279	2444
8567	8238	4885	2201	9949	6557	9036	0762	5741	0075
3274	7170	8828	3802	8740	0349	3301	0854	6672	7755
7241	5444	3332	9411	0974	9305	1968	6590	2879	8846
9775	0637	0620	3371	1320	2326	5367	2505	7106	8327
5967	8343	1255	6275	8485	2979	4725	8253	1482	7908
7751	6866	9343	2573	9731	6516	8446	2564	4320	5098
5351	8360	4701	0334	6325	6623	5137	9967	3771	2139
9489	7125	7285	6006	9644	8078	4301	8991	7505	7908

SOURCE: The statistical tables in this appendix are adapted from material in Donald B. Owen, *Handbook of Statistical Tables,* copyright © 1962 by Addison-Wesley Publishing Company, Inc. Reprinted courtesy of the publisher.

TABLE A1 (Continued)

4123	5242	6491	7400	5045	7933	0171	4898	3955	2712
6300	7627	8988	6159	9272	7495	1516	3011	4975	1997
8692	3259	4187	0708	1821	5341	9440	0223	3858	0821
3971	0814	5119	6038	1296	2652	0170	3593	1459	0425
1458	9604	6418	7922	3438	3212	8105	6187	9651	2711
1532	5944	6461	2186	6531	9642	7027	4512	1871	1547
4358	4732	2836	7479	7775	9372	5429	3719	3704	0959
4771	3705	1207	6469	3964	3735	6951	6726	1822	6737
8320	3056	6632	6155	3391	6854	2468	7444	0255	3133
0780	1789	7331	2176	2761	8899	6595	9499	3543	5813
4070	5232	3454	6773	8100	2066	1208	3083	6906	8123
5346	1848	1476	0788	5314	8818	2993	6710	8478	8989
9998	3687	9759	6679	2548	1029	3827	7357	1508	7640
3645	8649	3296	0892	7380	0197	4126	0455	6421	0426
2557	6761	7808	5045	9141	5541	4223	6136	9505	4995
1087	9755	4751	5061	2832	4231	1508	7534	0844	5725
6355	5538	2461	5869	0447	6704	1861	2725	8901	8212
8426	6186	9022	1265	8066	7173	8981	0181	0794	0397
3513	0498	9207	7115	3367	8342	0415	4787	7058	6874
8415	9346	4334	2976	3382	5732	4626	8733	5606	0797
5604	4248	5282	1402	4514	2419	9922	0440	3763	4844
3293	0554	1972	9984	1488	1936	0002	4826	8885	4399
0482	6386	7228	6668	5710	7267	1942	7027	4138	9070
4496	8432	0507	5735	8649	3503	4284	4731	2598	8563
9909	4716	7697	8245	5921	3583	7679	4077	1490	4665
8029	7193	5378	7464	5161	8795	4537	2816	8367	6919
8435	7008	0739	8069	8406	0862	1831	1584	5723	8733
4520	9775	0803	8260	7956	4495	6670	6761	6847	4544
1306	1189	5731	3968	5606	5084	8947	3897	1636	7810
0422	2431	0649	8085	5053	4722	6598	5044	9040	5121
6597	2022	6168	5060	8656	6733	6364	7649	1871	4328
7965	6541	5645	6243	7658	6903	9911	5740	7824	8520
7695	6937	0406	8894	0441	8135	9797	7285	5905	9539
5160	7851	8464	6789	3898	4197	6511	0407	9329	2265
2961	0551	0539	8288	7478	7565	5581	5771	5442	8761
1428	4183	4312	5445	4854	9157	9158	5218	1464	3634
3666	5642	4539	1561	7849	7520	2547	0756	1206	2033
6543	6799	7454	9052	6689	1946	2574	9386	0304	7945
9975	6080	7423	3175	9377	6951	6519	8287	8994	5532
4866	0956	7545	7723	8085	4948	2228	9583	4415	7065
8239	7068	6694	5168	3117	1586	0237	6160	9585	1133
8722	9191	3386	3443	0434	4586	4150	1224	6204	0937
1330	9120	8785	8382	2929	7089	3109	6742	2468	7025
2296	2952	4764	9070	6356	9192	4012	0618	2219	1109
3582	7052	3132	4519	9250	2486	0830	8472	2160	7046
5872	9207	7222	6494	8973	3545	6967	8490	5264	9821
1134	6324	6201	3792	5651	0538	4676	2064	0584	7996
1403	4497	7390	8503	8239	4236	8022	2914	4368	4529
3393	7025	3381	3553	2128	1021	8353	6413	5161	8583
1137	7896	3602	0060	7850	7626	0854	6565	4260	6220

TABLE A2 Critical Values of Chi-Square

Degrees of Freedom	Level of Significance		
	.10	.05	.01
1	2.706	3.841	6.635
2	4.605	5.991	9.210
3	6.251	7.815	11.345
4	7.779	9.488	13.277
5	9.236	11.071	15.086
6	10.645	12.592	16.812
7	12.017	14.067	18.475
8	13.362	15.507	20.090
9	14.684	16.919	21.666
10	15.987	18.307	23.209
11	17.275	19.675	24.725
12	18.549	21.026	26.217
13	19.812	22.362	27.688
14	21.064	23.685	29.141
15	22.307	24.996	30.578
16	23.542	26.296	32.000
17	24.769	27.587	33.409
18	25.989	28.869	34.805
19	27.204	30.144	36.191
20	28.412	31.410	37.566
21	29.615	32.671	38.932
22	30.813	33.924	40.289
23	32.007	35.172	41.638
24	33.196	36.415	42.980
25	34.382	37.652	44.314
30	40.256	43.773	50.892
35	46.059	49.802	57.342
40	51.805	55.758	63.691
45	57.505	61.656	69.957
50	63.167	67.505	76.154

TABLE A2 (Continued)

Degrees of Freedom	Level of Significance		
55	68.796	73.311	82.292
60	74.397	79.082	88.379
65	79.973	84.821	94.422
70	85.527	90.531	100.425
75	91.061	96.217	106.393
80	96.578	101.879	112.329
85	102.079	107.522	118.236
90	107.565	113.145	124.116
95	113.038	118.752	129.973
100	118.498	124.342	135.807
110	129.385	135.480	147.414
120	140.233	146.567	158.950
130	151.045	157.610	170.423
140	161.827	168.613	181.840
150	172.581	179.581	193.208
200	226.021	233.994	249.445
300	331.789	341.395	359.906
400	436.649	447.632	468.724
500	540.930	553.127	576.493

References

Bandura, A. (1977). *Social learning theory.* Englewood Cliffs, NJ: Prentice Hall.

Becker, H. (1963). *Outsiders: Studies in the sociology of deviance.* London: Free Press of Glencoe.

Berger, P. L., & Luckmann, T. (1966). *The social construction of reality: A treatise in the sociology of knowledge.* Garden City, NY: Doubleday.

Blumer, H. (1933). *The movies and conduct.* New York: Macmillan.

Carter, K., & Spitzack, C. (1989). *Doing reseach on women's communication: Perspectives on theory and method.* Norwood, NJ: Ablex.

DeFleur, M., & Ball-Rokeach, S. (1989). *Theories of mass communication* (5th ed.). New York: Longman.

Fernea, E. W. (1969). *Guests of the sheik.* Garden City, NY: Doubleday.

Fiske, J. (1978). *Reading television.* London: Methuen.

Gans, H. (1979). *Deciding what's news: A study of CBS evening news, NBC nightly news,* Newsweek *and* Time. New York: Pantheon.

Geertz, C. (1973). *The interpretation of cultures: Selected essays.* New York: Basic Books.

Gerber, G., Gross, L., Morgan, M., & Signorielli, N. (1986). Living with television: The dynamics of the cultivation process. In J. Bryant & D. Zillman (Eds.), *Perspectives on media effects.* Hillsdale, NJ: Lawrence Erlbaum.

Gitlin, T. (1980). *The whole world is watching: Mass media in the making and unmaking of the New Left.* Berkeley: University of California Press.

Glaser, B. G., & Strauss, A. L. (1967). *The discovery of grounded theory: Strategies for qualitative research.* Chicago: Aldine.

Hachten, W. A. (1987). *The world news prism: Changing media, clashing ideologies.* Ames: Iowa State University Press.

Keller, E. F. (1985). *Reflections on gender and science.* New Haven, CT: Yale University Press.

Kuhn, T. S. (1970). *The structure of scientific revolutions* (2nd ed.). Chicago: University of Chicago Press.

LaFollette, M. C. (1992). *Stealing into print: Fraud, plagiarism, and misconduct in scientific publishing.* Berkeley: University of California Press.

Lang, G. E., & Lang, K. (1983). *The battle for public opinion: The president, the press, and the polls during Watergate.* New York: Columbia University Press.

Lowery, S. A., & DeFleur, M. L. (1988). *Milestones in mass communication research: Media effects* (2nd ed.). New York: Longman.

Martin, L. J., & Hiebert, R. E. (1990). *Current issues in international communication.* New York: Longman.

McLuhan, M. (1989). *The global village: Transformations in world life and media in the 21st century.* New York: Oxford University Press.

Mead, M. (1935). *Sex and temperament in three primitive societies.* New York: William Morrow.

Merton, R. (1968). *Social theory and social structure.* New York: Free Press.

Minium, E. W. (1970). *Statistical reasoning in psychology and education.* New York: John Wiley.

Noelle-Neumann, E. (1984). *The spiral of silence: Public opinion, our social skin.* Chicago: University of Chicago Press.

Potter, W. J. (1994). Cultivation theory: A methodological critique. *Journalism Monographs,* No. 147.

Priest, S. H. (1994). Structuring public debate on biotechnology: Media frames and public response. *Science Communication, 16*(2), 166-179.

Radway, J. (1984). *Reading the romance: Women, patriarchy, and popular literature.* Chapel Hill: University of North Carolina Press.

Rice, R. (1984). *The new media: Communication, research, and technology.* Beverly Hills, CA: Sage.

Rogers, E. M. (1986). *Communication technology: The new media in society.* New York: Free Press.

Siegal, S. (1956). *Nonparametric methods for the behavioral sciences.* New York: McGraw-Hill.

Steeves, H. L. (1988). What distinguishes feminist scholarship in communication studies? *Women's Studies in Communication, 11,* 12-17.

Taylor, E. (1989). *Prime-time families: Television culture in postwar America.* Berkeley: University of California Press.

Tuchman, G. (1978). *Making news: A study in the construction of reality.* New York: Free Press.

Webb, E. J. (1966). *Unobtrusive measures: Nonreactive research in the social sciences.* Chicago: Rand McNally.

White, D. M. (1950). The "gate keeper": A case study in the selection of news. *Journalism Quarterly, 27,* 383-390.

Glossary

Abstract

Concise written summary of a research article. Often appearing at the beginning of full-length articles published in academic journals, abstracts are also used in conference programs and research literature indexes.

Academic journal

Publication that contains primarily research articles. Almost all well-respected academic journals are blind peer reviewed; that is, articles are accepted or rejected based on the opinions of researcher-reviewers who don't know who wrote them.

Acculturation

Process of becoming adapted to a new culture, partially by adopting its value system. Immigrants become acculturated to the culture of their new nation.

ANOVA

Methodological shorthand for *analysis of variance*. ANOVA distinguishes among independent variables in terms of the strength of their contributions to the variance in a dependent variable.

Applied

Research done primarily to answer a question of immediate practical significance. Good applied research uses theory; its main purpose, however, is solving immediate problems rather than understanding theoretical issues. (See **Basic** research)

Attitude

Persistent, evaluative response to an object, person, or idea. Attitudes are considered difficult to change; they can be positive or negative.

Basic

Research done primarily to answer a theoretical question. Good basic research addresses important questions; its main purpose, however, is understanding theoretical issues rather than solving immediate problems. (See **Applied** research)

Behaviorist

Researcher (or research project) characterized by an emphasis on readily observable behaviors rather than internal thoughts and feelings.

Bell curve

Well-known so-called normal distribution. Many naturally occurring variables, such as height or weight, follow this curve; some artificially created variables, such as intelligence, are made to approximate the same shape.

Bipolar scale

Question that asks respondents to choose a numbered point on a line connecting two opposite poles, labeled with adjective pairs. The point chosen corresponds to the respondent's thoughts or feelings about an object, person, or idea.

Blind review

Process through which articles describing research projects are evaluated by reviewers who do not know who wrote the paper. The goal is a review unaffected by personal friendships or the reputations of either authors or their institutions.

Case study

Research design that focuses on one or more specific institutions or events (cases). Case studies are carried out with the intention of shedding light on general processes, but the results are not generalizable in the statistical sense.

Categorical

Data that can be arranged in categories, like color, shape, or name. However, the categories cannot be arranged in a logical rank order, as would be the case for ordinal data.

Cell

For a frequency distribution involving two or more variables, a category defined by particular values of each of those variables. The total number of cells is the product of the possible values of the total number of variables.

Census

Complete count of a population. Where a survey is based on a partial count, or sample, a census tries to include all members.

Chi-square test

Test for whether two frequency distributions are alike or different. The data for a chi-square test can be nominal or ordinal rather than a higher level of measurement.

Cluster analysis

Statistical technique for separating cases into clusters based on shared characteristics.

Code of ethics

Set of rules specifying appropriate behavior. Many professions (including medical doctors, attorneys, and researchers in a variety of fields) have their own codes of ethics.

Coding

Assigning numerical codes to raw data for purposes of analysis. Values for nominal variables can be assigned numbers so that computers can be used to process the data, even though the particular values assigned are arbitrary.

Coefficient of determination

Amount of variability (or variance) in one variable that can be predicted based on knowledge of the values of another varible. The coefficient of determination is the square of the correlation coefficient.

Cognitive

Having to do with internal thought processes. In comparison to other branches of psychology, cognitive psychology is less concerned with emotions and observable behaviors and more concerned with thinking, including information processing.

Collective behavior

Behavior that is characteristic of groups, such as crowd behavior, rumor transmission, or public opinion formation. Collective behavior cannot be reduced to the actions of individuals considered in isolation.

Confidence interval

Range of possible values that we believe a variable might reasonably be expected to have in the population, based on results from measuring that value in a sample.

Confidence level

Probability to be achieved that the results observed did not occur by chance. The researcher chooses an acceptable level in advance; it is usually 95% or 99%; 90% is acceptable for exploratory research on new problems.

Conflict theorist

Social scientist who emphasizes the existence of conflict and competition in society, as opposed to one who emphasizes stability and harmony.

Confounding variable

Variable that has not been included among those measured in an experiment, or otherwise controlled, but has an influence on the dependent variables. Confounding variables make the interpretation of results difficult or misleading.

Constant comparative method

Method for developing categories from the data in a qualitative study rather than defining them in advance based on the researcher's preconceptions. As new data are analyzed, the categories are continuously reviewed.

Content analysis

Collection and analysis of data about media content. No single method or technique for content analysis exists; it can be quantitative or qualitative, theoretical or applied.

Contingency table

Table (or series of tables) giving frequency distributions for two (or more) variables simultaneously, such as age and gender. Each category defined by particular values of the variables (such as middle-aged women) is called a *cell*.

Continuous

Data that result from measurements on a continuous scale, as opposed to categorical data. Interval and ratio level measurements yield continuous data.

Control group

In an experimental design, a group of subjects to whom no treatment is applied. Control group measurements tell the researcher what the values of dependent variables might have been if no experimental manipulation of an independent variable had taken place.

Controlled experiment

Experimental design that uses a control group or other means, such as statistical controls or the physical control of laboratory conditions, to isolate the effects of the independent variables more accurately.

Correlation coefficient

Measure of the amount of change or variation in one variable that is associated with change in another. If two variables are highly correlated, extreme values of one will commonly be associated with extreme values of the other.

Cultural relativism

Recognition that moral and ethical standards vary across cultures. A cultural relativist recognizes that behavior considered deviant or wrong in one culture may be acceptable or even demanded in another.

Cultural studies

Branch of communication scholarship that looks at the mass media as products of a particular cultural tradition with a certain set of ideological beliefs. The cultural studies approach originated in Great Britain.

Culture

Shared knowledge held by members of a social group; the knowledge that is necessary to function appropriately and effectively as a group member, including beliefs, values, behavioral norms, and communication conventions.

Deductive

Making a specific conclusion based on general premises. Hypothesis-testing research tests propositions based on general theories and is therefore considered deductive.

Degrees of freedom (*df*)

Number of values of a variable that can be said to be free to vary, that is, that could take any possible value without changing important characteristics of the data set. *Df* are needed to read statistical tables appropriately.

Demographics

Basic, largely standard, descriptive variables used to describe human populations, such as gender, age, ethnicity, income, education, religion.

Dependent variable

This is a variable the value of which we expect will change when experimental treatments are applied; outcome variable that is affected by the factors we are trying to assess.

Depth interview

Interview designed to explore someone's point of view in detail. Unlike survey interviews that ask as many people as possible a short series of identical questions, depth interviews are flexible and lengthy; they usually involve fewer respondents.

Descriptive

Study designed to describe a particular sequence of events or social setting rather than to test theories of causation. Many descriptive studies are qualitative, but survey research is also primarily descriptive.

Descriptive statistic

Statistic intended to describe a set of numbers accurately and succinctly, such as the mean value of a variable. Inferences about causation are not normally possible on the basis of descriptive statistics.

Deviant

Person or action that is contrary to a society's rules for acceptable behavior. Activity considered criminal, unethical, immoral, or insane in a particular culture is deviant behavior.

Dichotomous categories

Any category that is one member of a set in which there are only two choices, such as gender or the answers to "yes or no" questions.

Directional hypothesis

Hypothesis that includes a statement about the direction of a relationship as well as its existence. For example, a hypothesis that says that older children understand advertising better than younger children is directional.

Discourse analysis

Method for looking at argumentation and dialogue in a systematic way. This idea is similar to that of *rhetorical analysis,* and some scholars use the terms interchangeably.

Discriminant analysis

Statistical technique for identifying the characteristics that most reliably divide one group from another. For example, discriminant analysis might be used to determine what opinions predict political party preference.

Empirical

Based on data obtained from direct, systematic observation rather than speculation or secondary information. Both qualitative and quantitative research can be empirical.

Empowerment

Giving more power to, or enhancing the power of, a group of people. Research that is designed to empower those being studied is sometimes called *participatory research.*

Ethnocentricity

Characteristic of looking at things from one's own cultural perspective. Some social science research and some news accounts are ethnocentric in that they do not take into account cultural variation in values or beliefs.

Ethnography

Rich, holistic description of all aspects of a culture; originally, this usually meant an anthropologist's description of a preliterate culture.

Ethnomethodology

Study of the ways in which the members of a particular culture make sense of their social environment. Ethnomethodology is a field rather than a method of study; ethnomethodologists commonly use qualitative techniques.

Experiment

Research project in which at least one variable is artificially manipulated or changed to test its effect on other variables.

Explanatory

Study designed to identify or to test theories about causation. Explanatory studies can be either qualitative or quantitative; however, experimental approaches involving precise measurements are most commonly said to be explanatory.

Exploratory research

Research designed to understand a new problem rather than to rigorously test hypotheses or produce a definitive description of a social setting. Exploratory research is inductive.

Factor analysis

Statistical technique for identifying a limited number of factors that might lie beneath a complex set of relationships.

Feminist

From a woman's point of view. Research and scholarship, as well as political activity, can be feminist in this sense; when used in this way the term implies a theoretical rather than a political position.

Field experiment

Carrying out an experiment under natural (or "field") conditions. For example, observing the introduction of a new type of technology in a media organization would be a kind of field experiment.

Focus group

Discussion group created for the purpose of research. Focus groups can be used to assess people's reactions to products, messages, or ideas.

Forced-choice question

Question with a limited number of answers from which respondents must choose. A "yes or no" question is a forced-choice question, as is a question that requires someone to choose their ethnicity from a list of alternatives provided.

Frequency distribution

Simple count of the number of times that each item in a set of categories appears— for example, the numbers of men and women in a particular experiment or the numbers of people receiving each of the possible grades on a test.

Functionalist

Social scientist who focuses on the way in which various social institutions contribute to the stability and harmony of the social system as opposed to examining sources of conflict.

Grounded theory

Theory derived systematically and inductively from qualitative data; more specifically, theory based on a method for deriving categories from a qualitative data set rather than using preexisting assumptions. (See **Constant comparative method**)

Guttman scale

Scale that classifies subjects consistently into ranked categories along a certain dimension based on their answers to a single, relatively simple series of questions.

High culture

Cultural products, such as entertainment, designed to be appreciated only by those of high socioeconomic class and educational level.

Holism

Study of cultures or societies as integrated wholes; the belief that studying particular characteristics of social groups as isolated fragments can be misleading.

Hypothesis

Statement logically derived from a theory. Experiments are designed to test carefully constructed hypotheses; if done correctly, their findings support, refine, or reject the theory.

Independent variable

A variable the value of which is altered, or manipulated, systematically in an experiment to observe whether changes in a dependent variable result.

Index

Numerical scale used, for convenience, to represent a variable that has not been measured directly. For example, grade point average might be used as an index of academic ability, but it is not a direct measure.

Inductive

Reasoning from the specific to the general; the development of theory based on observations rather than through testing hypotheses. Many descriptive studies are inductive.

Inferential statistics

Statistical techniques designed to allow the researcher to draw conclusions (that is, to test hypotheses or to estimate population values) based on limited information.

Informant

Someone who participates in an ethnographic study by providing data in response to the researcher's questions; a source of cultural information from an "insider's" perspective.

Instrument

Tool used for measurement. In social science, this term most commonly refers to a paper-and-pencil tool, such as a questionnaire.

Intellectual property rights

Ownership of information. In research, questions about who has the right to examine or analyze data are intellectual property right issues.

Interaction effect

Effect on a dependent variable resulting from the interaction of two or more independent variables.

Intercoder reliability

Measure of the extent to which two or more coders agree on the classification of material into categories for research purposes. In media research, these measures are most commonly used in content analysis.

Intercultural communication

Communication between cultures or subcultures; the study of the problems that arise in communication among people of different cultural or ethnic backgrounds.

International communication

Communication across national boundaries; the study of the problems that arise in communication of this type and of the variations in media systems and philosophies that exist among contemporary human societies.

Interpretive

Research, usually qualitative, in which the reactions and interpretations of the researcher are seen as an integral part of the methodological approach rather than as a source of distortion.

Intervening variable

Variable believed to mediate, change, or control the influence of an independent variable (IV) on a dependent one (DV). For example, perhaps income of parents (IV) influences educational achievement, which in term influences income (DV).

Interview schedule

List of questions for use in a semistructured depth interview. Unlike survey questions that are to be asked in the same order in the same way of each respondent, an interview schedule (or interview guide) is flexible.

Labeling theory

Theory that says that how people and their behavior are labeled, or categorized, creates social expectations that influence future actions. For example, those labeled deviant will begin to act according to others' expectations.

Level of measurement

Usually divided into nominal, ordinal, interval, and ratio, this term refers to the degree to which a particular measurement has certain properties that some types of statistical tests require.

Likert scale

Series of questions answered on a numerical, usually 5- or 7-point, "agree-disagree" scale. Likert scale items must be chosen according to a specified procedure; however, the term is often misused to refer to all questions in this form.

Linear

Relationship between two variables that can be described by a straight line when the vertical axis of the graph represents one of the variables and the horizontal axis represents the other.

Low culture

Cultural products, such as entertainment, for which the intended audience is primarily those of limited educational level and lower socioeconomic status.

Margin of error

Range of likely population values. If 60% of people sampled agree with a statement and the margin of error is 2%, the population value is believed to be between 58% and 62% agreement.

Marginalization

Putting off to the margins; making less important, less powerful, or less visible. Minority ethnic groups and women are marginalized in many societies.

Masculinist

Done or said from a male point of view; promoting male values; sexist. This term is usually used to indicate the opposite of feminist or the absence of feminism.

Mean

Average value in a set of numbers derived by summing all scores and dividing by the number of scores. The mean is the most common measure of central tendency.

Measure of central tendency

Standard approximation of the most typical, common, central values in a frequency distribution from which most scores do not vary by extreme amounts. The mean, median, midpoint, and mode are all measures of central tendency.

Measure of dispersion

Standard approximation of the extent to which scores in a distribution deviate or vary from the typical, common, central values. Variance and standard deviation are well-known measures of dispersion.

Median

Score in a frequency distribution above which half the other scores fall and below which the other half fall. If there is an even number of scores, the midpoint is halfway between the two scores in the middle.

Method

Principles underlying the choice of particular research techniques. Often used interchangeably with the term methodology, this term refers to the researcher's more general approach.

Midpoint

Point halfway between the highest score and the lowest score in a frequency distribution; the mean of the highest and lowest scores.

Mode

Most common score in a frequency distribution. For example, the modal age among college freshmen is probably 18, although the mean age is probably much higher.

Model

Abstract, simplified representation of a complex system or process. Where multiple variables are known to interact, statistical techniques can be used to model the most important relationships.

Multifactorial

Involving numerous independent variables or treatments ("factors"). Multifactorial experimental designs can be extremely complex.

Multiple regression

Technique for developing an equation that best represents the relationship between continuous independent and dependent variables.

Multistage sampling

Sampling at several different levels, points, or stages. For example, sampling all counties in the United States and then sampling the populations of the counties selected would be two-stage sampling.

Multivariate analysis

Any statistical technique, such as multiple regression or multivariate analysis of variance, designed to study relationships among numerous variables simultaneously.

Negative correlation

Relationship between two variables in which an increase in one is associated with a decrease in the other. For example, number of hours spent watching television might be associated with children's decreased school performance.

New media

New technologies and technological systems used for mass communication, such as fiber optic cables, computers, satellites, videoconferencing facilities, or electronic mail systems.

Nominal

Data based on classifying cases into meaningful categories that cannot be ranked or ordered in a logical way from lowest to highest. Eye color is an example of nominal data, as is ethnicity.

Nonlinear

Relationship between two variables that is best represented graphically by anything other than a straight line. (See **Linear relationship**)

Nonparametric

Refers to a large group of statistical techniques that make minimal assumptions about the data to which they are applied and that can be used with nominal data, data for which the shape of the distribution is unknown, and other special cases.

Nonverbal communication

Communication that takes place without words; "body language." This can include facial expressions, gestures, and even posture; some nonverbal communication is probably unconscious.

Normal distribution

Distribution that many naturally occurring variables follow. (See **Bell curve**) Some researchers routinely check their data distributions for "normalcy" before deciding which statistical tests to apply.

Norms

Rules or guidelines for behavior accepted in a given culture. Many sociologists believe that norms are a key characteristic of every society; the mass media help establish these behavioral expectations.

Null hypothesis

Exact complement or opposite of the hypothesis. Statistical tests test null hypotheses rather than hypotheses themselves; only if the data clearly force rejection of the null hypothesis are they said to support the hypothesis.

One-tailed test

Statistical test based on the assumption that the hypothesis is directional. Where there is good justification for this assumption, it is easier to meet the criteria for rejection of the null hypothesis.

One-way ANOVA

Analysis of the relationship between the variance in a single independent variable and that in a dependent variable.

Open-ended question

Interview or survey question where a list of possible answers is not provided and the respondent self-determines what answer to give; the opposite of a forced-choice question.

Operationalization

Finding a way to measure or assess a variable; turning an abstract concept into a variable on which concrete empirical data can actually be collected.

Ordinal

Data involving categories that can be assigned to a logical rank order without assumptions about the distance between one category and the next. For example, answers to Likert-type scale questions are ordinal.

Parameter

True population value; the theoretical value that a census would produce and that inferences from sample data are intended to approximate.

Parametric

Type of statistical test that makes specific assumptions about the variables and parameters being approximated. Use of parametric tests is normally restricted to interval and ratio data.

Participant observation

Qualitative research technique associated with ethnography. In participant observation, the researcher tries to become a member of the culture being studied, and his or her own reactions become part of the analysis.

Participatory

Research that takes into account the objectives of the people being studied; a reaction against the tradition of researchers pursuing their own goals without asking about their effects on those who are the objects of study.

Path analysis

Technique based on correlation data that try to establish which among a set of interrelated variables are most reasonably thought of as causes and which as effects.

Pearson's *r*

Common correlation coefficient used with interval or ratio data. Like those for most other correlation coefficients, values for this statistic range from positive 1 to negative 1, with zero indicating no relationship between two variables.

Peer review

System through which articles intended for publication in academic journals, papers intended for presentation at academic conferences, and grant applications are reviewed by specialists with appropriate expertise.

Pilot study

Small-scale study designed to generate ideas, refine techniques, and test methods prior to initiating a larger-scale project.

Positive correlation

Relationship between two variables in which an increase in one is associated with an increase in the other. For example, number of hours spent studying might be associated with children's better school performance.

Positivist

Proponent of stance asserting that the goal of social science is precise empirical measurement of phenomena of interest and that this goal is attainable.

Poster session

Special session at an academic meeting in which researchers put up poster presentations describing their research. The use of poster sessions allows more researchers to describe their work and to interact with others.

Posttest

Test or other measurement administered after the treatment in an experiment. Post-testing reflects the effects of the treatment, conditions that were already present, plus any changes that might have occurred incidentally during the experiment.

Preliterate

Culture that does not have a written language. Anthropologists once referred to such cultures as "primitive"; more recently, recognition of the technological complexity of preliterate societies has made that term obsolete.

Pretest

Test or other measurement administered before the treatment in an experiment. Pre-testing reflects the effects of conditions that existed prior to the experiment.

Pretest-posttest design

Experimental design in which the measurement of the dependent variable takes place both before and after the administration of the treatment (manipulation of the independent variable).

Probability sampling

Form of random sampling used to select participants in an experiment or survey. In probability sampling, every member of the population has an equal chance of being included in the sample.

Psychoanalytic

Concerned with analyzing unconscious processes. Now primarily a branch of psychotherapy, the psychoanalytic approach has contributed much to our general knowledge of human psychology.

Qualitative

Any method for doing social science research that uses general observations, depth or semistructured interviews, and verbal descriptions in place of numerical measures.

Quantitative

Any method for doing social science research that uses numerical counts or measures and statistical analysis in place of verbal material.

Quasi-experiment

Social science research that follows the general principles of experimental research but does not take place under completely controlled conditions. An example is a field experiment.

Quota sampling

Sampling technique based on filling quotas for age, ethnicity, gender, and so on. While not as satisfactory as probability sampling, this technique is often more practical, especially for market research.

Range

Difference between the lowest and highest scores or values obtained for a particular variable. In a distribution with a lowest score of 10 and a highest score of 80, the range is 70.

Raw

Data that have not been processed or modified. This term often refers to frequency distribution data that have not yet been summarized in any other way.

Reductionism

Approach to research that emphasizes the study of component parts instead of the whole; usually meant critically. Quantitative techniques are reductionist in comparison to qualitative ones.

Reification

Treating imaginary or illusory things as though they were real; usually meant critically. For example, some opinion research might erroneously assume that attitudes exist as concrete objects rather than researchers' abstractions.

Reliability

Whether repeating the same measurement or experiment will yield the same or similar results. For quantitative research to be meaningful, reliability must be reasonably high.

Representative sample

Sample that contains close to the same proportions of various demographic groups as the population. This can be achieved through probability sampling, quota sampling, or some other means.

Research method

Basic approach to obtaining empirical data, whether quantitative or qualitative. Surveys, experiments, participant observation, and focus group work are all examples of research methods. (See also **Method** and **Technique**)

Researchable problem

Problem that can be solved or at least illuminated by the application of social science research methods. Many media-related policy issues are actually matters of judgment rather than researchable problems.

Respondent

Someone who participates in a survey by answering questions; the term for a study participant most commonly used in sociology.

Response

Behavior that occurs as a result of a particular stimulus. In behaviorist psychology, the researcher is concerned with observable behavioral responses, not internal emotional or cognitive states.

Response bias

Tendency to give the researcher what he or she wants; a bias toward the answers believed to be seen as "correct," socially appropriate, and so on.

Sampling distribution of means

Distribution of all possible means that might have been obtained if successive samples of the same size had been drawn. Even where data are not normally distributed, this distribution is usually normal.

Sampling frame

Source of the sample; the list of population members from which the sample is chosen. For example, all people listed in a telephone book, or all registered voters, or all families with children enrolled in a particular school might be chosen as the sampling frame.

Social construction

Generation of a shared reality through communication and other social interaction. Sometimes called *constructivism,* this term refers to a theoretical position that emphasizes how social life influences our perceptions.

Social institutions

Organizations in society that endure despite the departure of individuals. School systems, large corporations, and religious organizations are examples of institutions as are families, sororities, social clubs, and media organizations.

Social psychology

Branch of either sociology or psychology that is concerned with the psychology of human social groups, including the ways in which group membership affects individual thought and action.

Social role

Prescribed way for someone in a given social relationship to act. Father, secretary, teacher, and girlfriend are all examples of social roles; norms for individuals acting in these roles are different from the general norms of the society.

Social setting

Particular social situation used as the object of a research study; these are usually social institutions, whether a large organization, an individual family living together, or a media institution.

Socialization

Process through which a child becomes a member of the society in which he or she is raised. Socialization involves the internalization of social values; the mass media contribute to this process.

Solomon four-group design

Experiment using four groups: a control group receiving no testing, a control group receiving a posttest only, a treatment group receiving a posttest only, and a treatment group receiving both a pretest and a posttest.

Sponsored project

Project that receives funding from governmental, academic, industry, or private sources. Both human subjects procedures and intellectual property right issues can become more complex for sponsored projects.

Standard deviation

Square root of the variance of a distribution; a linear measure of dispersion. For known distribution shapes, the number of scores falling within a certain number of standard deviations from the mean is also known.

Standard error

Likely range within which a population value that has been estimated on the basis of a sample value will fall, given a certain confidence level.

Statistical analysis

Application of statistical techniques or methods to a particular data set. Statistical analysis can be descriptive, exploratory, or hypothesis testing.

Statistical test

Technique for determining whether a set of data do or do not support a particular hypothesis. Based on a particular confidence level, a statistical test asks whether observed results might have occurred by chance.

Statistical significance

Confidence level achieved by a particular statistical test. Normally, an acceptable confidence level is chosen in advance; test results then either do or do not achieve statistical significance at the chosen level.

Stereotype

Rigid set of attitudes or expectations. Although this term commonly refers to negative expectations about a group of people, such as an ethnic group, it can also refer to expectations about a single individual or a thing and can be positive.

Stimulus

Event occurring in the environment that causes a response. In behaviorist psychology, study is limited to observable stimuli and the behavioral responses they produce.

Subculture

Specialized culture that exists within a larger, more complex one. The existence of ethnic subcultures, professional subcultures, and so on is characteristic of modern pluralistic societies and complicates communication.

Subject-object distinction

Division between the social scientist as researcher and the people he or she is studying. The significance of this distinction is a matter of some debate among philosophers of social science.

Subject

Participant in an experiment. Use of this term is consistent with an experimental approach in which the researcher strives to achieve maximum objectivity and to control conditions to the greatest extent possible.

Survey

Series of questions asked of a relatively large number of people believed to be representative of an even larger population. Surveys may be in person, by telephone, or by mail; a variety of sampling techniques are used to choose the respondents.

Symbolic interactionism

Branch of sociology that is concerned with the roots of both self-identity and social meaning in the symbolic communication and other interaction that occurs between two or more individuals.

Systematic random sampling

Sampling in which the first element is chosen randomly, a specific number of elements are then skipped over before the second element is chosen, and so on; used where the sampling frame is a list, such as a telephone book.

t test

Statistical test for comparing two means. Although special tests are available for other situations, a simple *t* test should only be used to make a single comparison.

Technique

Procedure that is part of or that contributes to a method. The term is more specific than method or methodology. For example, most statistical procedures are more accurately described as techniques rather than methods.

Theory

Explanatory idea that helps to account for empirical data. Although the types of theories used in qualitative versus quantitative work and the ways in which these theories are tested differ, explanation is always the goal.

Thesis hunting

Tendency to choose only those pieces of data that support a theoretical idea and ignore the rest. Most commonly a criticism of qualitative research, thesis hunting can also be a failing of quantitative researchers.

Time-series analysis

Set of techniques for attempting to determine the relative order of items in a complex sequence. For example, content analysis might ask whether a particular theme was more common before or after certain historical events.

Transcription

Word-for-word typescript recording conversational data from interviews, focus groups, or other verbal communications. Transcription is one way to create a qualitative data set that is conveniently available for systematic analysis.

Treatment group

In an experiment, the people on whom an influence is being measured. The "treatment" can result from the experimenter's manipulation of any independent variable, such as exposure to different types or sources of information.

Triangulation

Using substantially different methods to study the same problem, such as a combination of qualitative and quantitative approaches. Achieving parallel results with different methods vastly increases the researcher's confidence in those results.

Two-tailed test

Statistical test that tests a nondirectional hypothesis, such as a hypothesis of difference. In a two-tailed test, extreme values in either direction will result in rejection of the null hypothesis.

Two-way ANOVA

Analysis of the independent and interactive effects of two independent variables on a single dependent variable.

Type I error

Rejection of a null hypothesis that is actually true; the acceptance of a hypothesis that should not have been accepted. The probability of Type I error is set by the researcher; it is the complement of the confidence level.

Type II error

Acceptance of a null hypothesis that is actually false; the rejection of a hypothesis that should have been accepted. The probability of Type II error is related to the statistical power of the test used and the confidence level.

Unidimensional

A characteristic, such as an attitude or personality variable, that is best represented as a single factor, as opposed to one that is actually a composite of two or more interrelated factors.

Unobtrusive observation

Observation in which those being observed are not aware of the researcher's presence. Unobtrusive observation in public places is generally considered legal but always poses ethical questions.

Validity

Whether the researcher is measuring or observing what he or she thinks is being measured or observed. Misleading survey questions, initial observations of a poorly understood culture, or experiments based on erroneous reasoning all lack validity.

Value system

What is thought to be important or valuable in a particular culture; what is considered worth pursuing and preserving; what gives life its meaning.

Variable

Characteristic that can be measured or assessed empirically; an abstract quality that can take on any one of two or more values in a given instance.

Variance

Amount of variation in a set of data; a standard measure of dispersion that is the square of the standard deviation. Variance is related to the distribution of the area under a frequency curve. (See **Standard deviation**)

Yates' correction

Adjustment necessary for a chi-square calculation when there is only one degree of freedom, that is, when a two-row by two-column table is being analyzed.

Index

NOTE: **Boldface type** indicates references to glossary entries. References to material in boxes are indicated by (box) following the page number.

About the Author

Susanna Hornig Priest is Associate Professor of Journalism at Texas A&M University at College Station. She holds a doctorate in communication from the University of Washington, a master of arts in sociology from the University of Nevada, Las Vegas, and a bachelor of arts in anthropology from the University of California, Berkeley. Her work is centered on science in American culture as expressed in the mass media; she is also interested in feminist scholarship, new media technology, and international communication issues. She is a member of the elected Standing Committee on Research of the Association for Education in Journalism and Mass Communication. She has been a regular paper reviewer for a number of AEJMC divisions and for the International Communication Association for many years and has also reviewed manuscripts for a variety of refereed journals. Her own research, which is both qualitative and quantitative, has been published in *Critical Studies in Mass Communication, Howard Journal of Communication, Journal of Communication, Journal of Broadcasting and Electronic Media, Journalism Quarterly, Mass Communication Review, Science Communication, Science, Technology & Human Values,* and *Southwestern Mass Communication Journal.*